# Theology, Ethics and Transcendence in Sports

# Routledge Research in Sport, Culture and Society

**1. Sport, Masculinities and the Body**
Ian Wellard

**2. India and the Olympics**
Boria Majumdar and Nalin Mehta

**3. Social Capital and Sport Governance in Europe**
Edited by Margaret Groeneveld, Barrie Houlihan and Fabien Ohl

**4. Theology, Ethics and Transcendence in Sports**
Edited by Jim Parry, Mark Nesti and Nick Watson

# Theology, Ethics and Transcendence in Sports

Edited by Jim Parry, Mark Nesti and Nick Watson

First published 2011
by Routledge
270 Madison Avenue, New York, NY 10016

Simultaneously published in the UK
by Routledge
2 Park Square, Milton Park, Abingdon, Oxon OX14 4RN

*Routledge is an imprint of the Taylor & Francis Group, an informa business*



Typeset in Sabon by IBT Global.
Printed and bound in the United States of America on acid-free paper by IBT Global.



*Library of Congress Cataloging-in-Publication Data*

Theology, ethics, and transcendence in sports / edited by Jim Parry, Mark Nesti, and Nick Watson.
p. cm. — (Routledge research in sport, culture, and society ; 4)
Includes index.
1. Sports—Religious aspects. 2. Athletes—Religious life. 3. Sports—Psychological aspects. I. Parry, S. J. (S. Jim) II. Nesti, Mark, 1959– III. Watson, Nick, 1960–
GV706.42.T47 2010
796.01—dc22
2010017401

ISBN13: 978-0-415-87851-7 (hbk)
ISBN13: 978-0-203-84075-7 (ebk)

**From Jim:** *To LGI, 26.08.2008*

**From Nick:** *To Kate: 'A wife of noble character who can find? She is worth far more than rubies' (Proverbs 31:10)*

**From Mark:** *For Catherine, Vincent and Beth*

# Contents

# Foreword

*Professor Robert J. Higgs*

Bragging is generally offensive on field or off, but here I am not that concerned about reaction. In the interest of manners, though, I will ask to be pardoned for that offense in order to render praise where praise is due, in this case to *Theology, Ethics and Transcendence in Sports*, to the editors and to the contributors.

In August of 2008 I am glad to say that I served as a reader for this text and was much impressed by what I saw even it its embryonic form. Here is a bit of what I wrote at the time.

This kind of book is desperately needed in the modern world. Sport is not the cause of our social and cultural problems, but I would be hard put to suggest another area of our lives that better reflects the symptoms owing to their connection with what Thorstein Veblen in *Theory of the Leisure Class* (1899) calls the "occupations" of predatory cultures, government, religion, warfare and sports. . . . Here is a sincere and honest endeavor to shed light on the crucial issues of modern sport, especially from a theological and ethical perspective.

Very effectively the book engages the issues of winning, prayer, the relation between science and technology, sin and evil, ethical and spiritual concerns, sectarianism and resulting antagonism, to name only a few of the themes. A familiar credo in sports and politics and even traditional religion is "winning is the only thing," but the spirit in this book echoes the admonition in Proverbs 4:7, "With all thy getting get wisdom and with wisdom get understanding." Sport is about "standing"; genuine scholarship, on the other hand, is about "understanding."

"Winning is the only thing" is warped, but that may not be the most distorted axiom, which might well be the following, generally regarded in a spirit of humor which is necessary for us to retain: "Sport is not a religion—it is more important than that," attributed to Paul "Bear" Bryant and others.

Not surprisingly, *Theology, Ethics and Transcendence in Sports* is even more impressive in final form than previously.

The text moves on several fronts, the physical, intellectual, spiritual and ethical but not necessarily the doctrinal although that may be part of the consideration too in certain essays. I was taken, for example, by the superb piece by Ian Lawrence on Marvin Andrews, who in his fidelity reminds me of that of Thomas Paine, a theist of another persuasion, who articulated a key point about faith in the *Age of Reason*: "Infidelity does not consist in believing, or in disbelieving; it consists in professing to believe what one does not believe." The other essays, identified by Watson in his excellent and comprehensive "Introduction," are also timely, provocative and evocative, covering a wide range of themes common to sport and spirituality.

Without exception, the essays are enlightening that, to borrow a phrase from Emily Dickinson, "dwell in possibility" but always with a keen appreciation of limits of realism and human experience. Name the issue and more than likely several perspectives can be found as in Shirl Hoffman's "Prayers out of Bounds," one of the most balanced, insightful and comprehensive treatments on the subject I have seen; Scott Kretchmer looks at sport amid "Dichotomies and Dualisms in Religion" and in a section called "the Ambiguous Genealogy of Games"; Jim Parry and Irena Martinková examine "Zen and Sports" to find ways of abandoning concepts of duality by means of "direct experiencing," a topic that also informs Patrick Kelly's discussion of the Buddhist "one-pointedness of mind" and "merging of action and awareness" in "Flow, Sport and the Spiritual Life."

Ivo Jirásek looks into the labyrinth of all possibilities in aspects of spirituality in the idea of the journey, especially in distinctions between tourism and pilgrimage, a recurring theme in the writings of American transcendentalists Emerson and Thoreau, who regarded his daily walks around Walden as going to "the holy land." Susan Saint Sing builds a strong case for spirituality in an impressive survey of the best that has been thought and said in arts, philosophy and sciences over the ages about the phenomenon of play and creativity, including that of God.

All the contributors are well aware that what we call dichotomies or polarities are concepts existing along a continuum in a state of relation to one another and other qualities, much, as Aristotle said, every virtue sits between two vices, courage, for instance, between cowardice and foolhardiness. Tracy Trothern especially emphasizes this connection in a captivating and relevant paper called "Better than Normal? Constructing Genetically Modified Athletes and a Relational Theological Ethic." Already futurist Ray Kurzweil speaks confidently of "Spiritual Machines," the title of one of his books.

Not only are new symbiotic possibilities introduced in the text but also eternal mysteries such as sin and evil. There is a widespread belief that both are no longer around but that seems hardly the case as the daily news reminds us, as did Karl Menninger a few years back in *Whatever Happened to Sin?* and Ernest Becker in *The Denial of Death* and in *The Structure of Evil.* Not only does *Theology, Ethics and Transcendence* open up an integrated approach to sport and traditional disciplines, but it takes a fresh look at old topics in imaginative frameworks as in Mark Hamilton's wonderful essay on Augustine's notion of evil as the absence of good, also famously the response of Emerson, himself an advocate of sport.

*Theology, Ethics and Transcendence in Sports* raises pressing questions, old and new, as does *Sport and Spirituality: An Introduction* (2007), several of the same editors and scholars involved in both projects. Ideally, what is needed is a paradigm shift in the study or sport, a multidisciplinary approach on a topic regarded by some as "the little brother of war" (at least Lacrosse), more important than religion, even a key to victory in politics, and as Simon Kuper in an article on July 25, 2009, the most popular topic in the world, number one in *standing*:

> If we would know ourselves, as counsel on the ancient Temple at Delphi advises, the study of sports in all its connections to the rest of art and life would seem to be an ideal quest for *understanding* of self and the world.

# Introduction

*Nick Watson*

This volume comprises papers delivered at the *Inaugural International Conference on Sport and Spirituality* (IICSS), August 28–31, 2007, that was hosted by the *Centre for the Study of Sport and Spirituality* (CSSS, 2003–2009), York St. John University (see Collins, 2007). Although there have been two valuable past conferences in North America on sport and religion,[1] this meeting was the first to bring together such a diversity of academics and practitioners for a critical discussion about the spiritual and religious dimensions of sport. Over 70 delegates from 11 countries attended this event and these included ex-Olympic and amateur athletes, historians, theologians, clergy and a rabbi-sport psychologist, sport chaplains, Olympic scholars, philosophers, sociologists, sports coaches and physical education teachers and those involved in disability sport and sports ministry. One of the defining aspects of this conference was the 'coming together' of academics and practitioners (e.g., coaches, physical educators, sports chaplains and ministers etc.).[2] This is something which it is hoped will continue in this field and will be one aspect of the Second International Conference on Sport and Spirituality, that will be hosted by the Centre for Sport, Spirituality and Religion (CSSR) at the University of Gloucestershire, England, under the leadership of Professor Andrew Parker.

The broad scope of the inaugural conference, covering both religion and spirituality, was intentional due to the embryonic nature of this field and I am sure future conferences and symposia may have more specialist themes and criteria. At this point I will, however, resist getting bogged down in an etymological and conceptual 'minefield,' by trying to provide clear definitions and explanations of organized religion and the much broader concept of spirituality. The authors, I sense, who are writing from a range of faith traditions and none, implicitly address this point. This will allow the readers to wrestle with different conceptions of spirituality and religion in sport and thus come to their own conclusions. In introducing some of the chapter themes addressed in this text, I also hope to do two things. First, provide a rationale for the need for this work and contextualize it within wider cultural shifts and trends in the academy. Second, provide a *brief* overview of how the disciplines within sports studies—or what Dunning (2004: 6) has perhaps more accurately called the 'sport and society' field (not sport sociology)—have, or have not, addressed spirituality and religion. In doing this, I will also introduce the chapter themes that will be described in more detail in the part introductions written by Jim Parry and Mark Nesti.

The timing of the proposed text is concurrent with the shift toward spirituality both in popular culture and other academic disciplines, such as medical science and the natural sciences. Evidence of this is demonstrated by the burgeoning literature on the science-religion interface (e.g., Polkinghorne, 2005) and the relationship between religious and spiritual practice and physical and mental health. Many well-known American university departments, such as Harvard Medical School, have compulsory modules on spirituality and religion, and world-renowned journals such as the *Lancet* and the *British Medical Journal* are publishing work on the role of prayer and spirituality in health and rehabilitation (e.g., Bernardi et al., 2001). Professor Harold Koeing, the co-director of the Centre for Spirituality, Theology and Health at Duke University Medical Centre, USA, is arguably the leading authority in this area, having published over 300 scientific peer-review articles and nearly 40 books (e.g., Koeing 2001, 2008) that examine the potential role of religion and spirituality in healing and human wholeness—one of the roles of sport and physical exercise.

This upsurge of interest in the spiritual and religious dimensions of life within the academy is mirrored in Western society. Over the last few decades people have slowly become disillusioned with the hollow promises of materialism, commercialism, celebrity culture and the overly 'competitive' nature of modern life, as often personified in big-business professional sport. One only has to browse the shelves of any major bookstore to observe this trend, with an exponential increase in publications and sales of books on spirituality, religion and so-called self-help manuals (with promises of life transformation!). Writing, I would suggest, prophetically for the times in which we now live, Adrian Van Kaam, in his book *In Search of Spiritual Identity* (1975: 181), notes '. . . we are on the rebirth of the awareness of the human need of the transcendent.' This interest in existential meaning and an awareness of the spiritual I have myself found, through enriching discussion and debate with students when teaching courses on sport, spirituality and religion, in which students are challenged to consider concepts beyond (and as a complementary perspective to) the confines of traditional secular sports studies.

As modern sport is unavoidably intertwined with commercial and political agendas, this book will help to provide an important corrective to the often utilitarian and 'win at all costs' culture of modern professional sport, which cannot always be fully understood through secular ethical, psychological and sociological inquiry. Following the mapping of the human genome in 2000 and the subsequent possibilities of 'genetically modified athletes' (Miah 2004), Tracy Trothen's chapter, which is a theological analysis of genetic modification technologies in sport, is then an important and timely one. This book will also importantly emphasize the positive aspects of sport, through the examination of sport as a playful endeavor (Scott Kretchmar; Susan Saint Sing's chapters), sport as a means of understanding life's pilgrimage and the spiritual nature of bodily movement (Ivo Jirásek), and sport as a quest for human excellence in elite sport (Mark Nesti; Nick Watson). Although serious theological reflection on the sporting world is sparse in the disciplines of theology and religious studies[3] (see footnote for definitions), some of these avenues of empirical research and scholarship have been explored by theologians and religious studies scholars.

Notable theologians, such as Jürgen Moltmann (1972) and Wolfhart Pannenberg (1985: 323–339), have written about the spiritual possibilities of play, a primal human urge and foundational aspect of sports participation. Moltmann (1989), along with the well-known liberation theologian Leonardo Boff (1989), have also written short essays on the politics and religious dynamics of Olympia and the impact of communism on 20th-century sport, respectively. These essays were published, with others, in a special edition of the *International Journal of Theology* (1989, Vol. 5, No. 205) that was devoted to sport and later published as a book (Baum & Coleman, 1989). Theological reflection on athletic Pauline metaphors (e.g., Seesengood, 2005; Pfitzner, 1967, 2009; O'Gorman, 2010a: Ch. 1), the Isthmian games during the first century (e.g., Savage, 1996) and work examining the 19th-century Victorian Muscular Christian movement in England and America by church historians (McLeod, 2003; manuscript in preparation) and sociologists of religion (Ladd & Mathisen, 1999) are further examples of scholarship from outside the traditional sports studies arena. Indeed, the importance of sport in the modern world has not escaped the attention of the Vatican. Reflections on this topic can be found in the addresses of Pope Pius XII to Catholic sport associations and this interest flourished during the pontificate of Pope John Paul II (1986), an avid sportsman himself, who held two international sport gatherings in Rome's Olympic stadium, and viewed modern sport as a 'paradigm of mass psychology.' This long-held enthusiasm for sport by the Holy See led John Paul II to establish an office for 'Church and Sport' within the Pontifical Council for the Laity in 2004, led by Father Kevin Lixey (e.g., Costantini & Lixey, 2009; Liberia Editrice Vaticana, 2008).

Religious studies scholars are also beginning to publish books on the topic (e.g., Hutch, 2006) and articles (e.g., Grimshaw, 2000; Bain-Selbo, 2008b), and book reviews (e.g., Watson, 2009) are emerging in religious studies journals that address sport, religion and spirituality. Joseph Price himself, a religious studies scholar and the author of an important work on sport and religion (Price, 2001), is the series editor of a line of books on sports and religion (Mercer University Press), the most recent being Eric Bain-Selbo's (2008a) book on the religious aspects of American football in the southern United States. This growing awareness and acceptance that sport is an important topic of study within the theological and religious studies community is long overdue, considering that sport has arguably surpassed other previously dominant cultural expressions such as art and music.

I would argue that there are a number of reasons for the seeming reluctance of theologians to examine sport, and the first reason I will discuss is foundational. The historical baggage of dualistic philosophy (Plato and Descartes) in modern secular thinking and theology has led to the 'mind-body split,' and thus a false hierarchy, in which the mind (academics) is viewed as disproportionately more important than the body (sports and physical education). Twietmeyer (2008: 461) offers further critical insight on this idea:

> Philosophic ignorance is an important influence . . . because many people are ignorant of any possible philosophical alternatives [to positivism and natural science], they believe that Cartesian dualism and scientific materialism are the only ways to describe the human person . . . I am convinced that it is several of the intellectual habits of modernity that deserve the largest scrutiny, namely Cartesianism, utilitarianism, and scientific materialism. All three are deeply unfriendly to the intrinsic value of kinesiology and physical education. In addition, they all have similar consequences on the level of significance assigned to physical activity in human culture. The Cartesian dualist, seeing kinesiology as a discipline dedicated to the body, immediately subordinates the field to the intellectual pursuits of the mind.

Twietmeyer's critique certainly points to what I would argue is the 'dumb-jock' reputation that is tied to the sports world (see Martens, 1979) and the related suspicion (often unspoken) of the importance, academic rigor and worth of the discipline of sports studies in traditional academic subjects, such as theology. In this regard, the discipline of theology has also had a long-held suspicion—that is now slowly changing—of what one might term the 'high arts' (music and dance), even though, as Jeremy Begbie (2000: xii) highlights, the arts have 'been recognized as powerful theological interpreters' through history. I would suggest, then, that sport, perhaps due to its *perceived* 'unspiritual,' sinful and pagan nature and its 'dumb-jock' reputation, may well be classed as a 'low art' by some!

During the last decade there has been an exponential growth in the publication of academic books and journals and the formation of research centers addressing the *theology of popular culture*. A recent book on this topic, written by the director of the UK Network for Theology, Religion and Popular Culture, Gordon Lynch (2005), surprisingly, however, only makes passing reference to sport. This is certainly not a criticism of the author, or the quality of his book, but more a historical reflection of the limited regard that the discipline of theology has for sport as a valid subject for examination. Considering the mass popularity of sport, it is hoped that this book (mainly written by scholars from within sports studies) will begin to interest and engage theologians and religious studies scholars in more serious study of the complex and pervasive phenomenon of sports, as has slowly occurred in sports studies.

Due to an exponential increase in books and research articles that have addressed a range of topics across the world religions during the last ten years, the *International Journal of Religion and Sport* (Mercer University Press) has recently been launched, with the first edition published in 2009. Further, evidence of the growing interest in this area of research is shown in the peer-review journal *Stadion: International Journal of the History of Sport*, requesting papers for a special edition on sport and religion (2009/2010). In addition to the CSSR, a number of other research centers and organizations[4] from across the faith traditions have also evolved which seek to explore the spirituality and religion in sport and thus provide a vehicle for research and publications, as described next.

Following the publication of Michael Novak's seminal book *The Joy of Sports* (1994/1967) and works by other pioneers in the area, Shirl Hoffman (1992) and Robert (Jack) Higgs (1995), there has been a steady flow of single and coauthored books (e.g., Feeney, 1995; Higgs & Braswell, 2004; Hoffman, 2010; Krattenmaker, 2010; Price, 2001; Riesen, 2007), edited volumes (e.g., Prebish, 1993; Preece & Hess, 2009; Price, 2001; Magdalinski & Chandler, 2002; White & Deardorff, 2008) and journal articles that have broadly examined the sport-religion interface, mainly, but not exclusively, from a Judeo-Christian perspective. For a concise overview of the historical, sociological and theological relationship between sport and religion, which spans approximately 3,000 years, James Mathisen's (2005) chapter is arguably one of the best. Notable Jewish scholars, such as George Eisen (1998) and Jeffrey Gurock (2005), have provided specific analyses of the interface between Judaism and sport, which has been supported by the establishment of The Centre for Sport and Jewish Life, whose director is Rabbi Dr. Mitchell Smith.

Scholars from the closely related discipline of leisure studies have also examined the role of spirituality and religion in a range of sports, recreation and leisure contexts (e.g., Heintzman 2003a, 2003b). Much of this has been facilitated by the *Christian Society for Kinesiology and Leisure Studies*, which has published two books from past conferences (Byl & Visker, 1999; Van Andel, Heintzman & Visker, 2005). There are also a growing number of books (Benn, Pfister & Jawad, 2010), book chapters (e.g., Amara, 2007; Baker, 2007a; Hargreaves, 2000, 2007) and journal articles (e.g., Amara, 2008; Odibat, 1989; Walseth, 2006; Wiggins, Hillyer & Browning, 2005) that have examined the relationships between Islam and sport, in particular the subjugation and exclusion of women in sporting circles. The foundation of organizations such as the *Islamic Countries Women Sports Federation* and the visibility and enduring legacy of Muslim professional athletes, such as NBA basketball star Hakem Olajuwan, and boxing legend Muhammad Ali, also has served to raise awareness of the dynamics between the Islamic faith and sport.

Links between sport and Eastern religious traditions have a long and fascinating history in the martial arts. It is, however, the foundational work of Eugen Herrigel (1999/1971), *Zen in the Art of Archery*, that sparked significant interest amongst sports scholars on the relationship between Eastern religious ideas and sport, in particular Zen Buddhism and Hatha Yoga (e.g., Cooper, 1998; Hyland, 1990; Mahoney, 1999; Murphy & White, 1995). Zen Buddhist techniques have also been adopted by sport psychologists to enhance the performance and spiritual well-being of athletes (e.g., Ravizza, 2002; Watson & Nesti, 2005).

Well-being, health and wholeness through sport are also one theme (esp. in Simon Robinson's chapters) of a recent authored book, *Sport and Spirituality: An Introduction* (Parry et al., 2007), that has created a new avenue of research which wrestles with religious and secular definitions of spirituality in sport and how they can be used to combat the 'win-at-all-costs' ethic of modern sport, understanding the evolution and current direction of the Olympic movement and elements of sport psychology consultancy and physical education practice. Scholars such as Susan Saint Sing (2004), Kevin O'Gorman (2010b), Thomas Ryan (1986) and Edward Hastings (2004), in a similar fashion, have provided interesting analyses of 'spirituality in sport' within the Catholic tradition. Interestingly, then, it was a Catholic philosopher, Professor Paul Weiss (and Professor Warren Fraleigh), who helped found the closely related subdiscipline of the philosophy of sport in 1972.

The discipline of sport philosophy, a subdiscipline of philosophy in which sport (gymnastics) was important during the classical Greek period (Plato, *The Republic*), is closely tied to the study of sport, spirituality and religion (see Deardorff, 2000a). And although the analytical tradition has dominated the philosophical study of sport (Kretchmar, 1997; McNamee, 2007), other schools such as pragmatism (esp. Jamesian) and phenomenology, although largely underrepresented, are certainly more compatible with spiritual ideas. This said, articles published in the two professional journals of sport philosophy, on the ethics of prayer in sport (Kreider, 2003), the *athletae Dei* (Hoffman, 1976) and the application of Eastern religious notions in sport (Abe, 1986; Wertz, 1977), indicate an openness to nonrationalistic and humanistic work. Further evidence of this is shown by the recently launched journal, *Sport, Ethics and Philosophy*, publishing a fascinating article by Pete Hopsicker (2009), which examines the notion of miracles in the sporting realm. Although from a different perspective, this idea is an element of Ian Lawrence's original chapter on sectarianism in professional Scottish football, based upon extensive interviews with ex-Rangers F.C. footballer Marvin Andrews, who reported the miraculous healing of his badly injured knee (see also Slot, 2005).

On the fringes of the discipline of sport philosophy, Howard Slusher's controversial book *Man, Sport, and Existence* (1967) explicitly addressed the religious and spiritual dimensions of sporting experience—controversial, in that Higgs (1982: 205) suggests that this '. . . book is an ontological binge, a shot in deep space where wonders abound for those brave enough to look'! One of the founders of analytical philosophy of sport, Scott Kretchmar, has also pushed the boundaries of his discipline in publishing work on the philosophy and theology of play. His chapter in this book is a good example of this, and extends the philosophical enterprise in sport beyond the power of human reason, neat and tidy divisions, dichotomies and logical relationships—something I believe is required if we are to more holistically understand the complexities of sport across the disciplines. A more holistic approach is something that is also long overdue in the academic discipline of sport psychology, which was founded in the late 1960s.

Sports psychology is arguably 'hanging on to the coattails' of its parent discipline in terms of introducing and accepting spiritual and religious psychologies, Watson and Nesti (2005) have argued in their review of literature. The existence of a division in the American Psychological Association (APA) for spiritual and religious issues and a section for transpersonal psychology in the British Psychological Association (BPS) and academic textbooks published by the APA (e.g., Shafranske, 1996) indicate the growing acceptance and need for this area of study in sport. To date, sport psychology has been largely dominated by humanistic and positivistic research and cognitive-behavioral consultancy *techniques*. Although, since Rainer Martens's (1987) important paper that challenged the accepted canons of quantitative methodology and positivist epistemology in sport psychology and related disciplines, there has been a gradual shift in research and consultancy methods. This has been supported by radical scholarship within the social science of sport that documented the 'paradigm wars' of the 1980–90s and raised awareness of the need for, and credibility of, qualitative research (e.g., Sparkes, 1992, 2002). In support of this shift, Graham McFee (2009, 2010) emphasizes the intimate link between 'epistemology and ethics' and thus the need for 'person-centred epistemologies,' which has, and should, impact upon methodological choice in all psychological and sociological sport research. Specifically, in sport psychology, both consultants and researchers have then slowly acknowledged this need for more qualitative studies and have used approaches such as phenomenology (Dale, 1996, 2000; Nesti, 2004) to explore the existential and spiritual in sporting contexts.

Sport psychologist Mark Nesti, who has worked in a number of British Premiership Football Clubs and with Olympic athletes, provides a fascinating insight into the 'real world' of *doing* sport psychology in his chapter, by drawing on existential psychology and a range of Catholic writings. Also, within the Catholic tradition, Patrick Kelly's chapter examines how Mihaly Csikszentmihalyi's well-known psychological concept of 'flow' can be used to develop what he calls a "spirituality of sport," in which people can experience optimal performance and well-being. Personal meaning and well-being are also something that is addressed in the increasing number of studies that have examined the use of prayer in sport (e.g., Czech & Bullet, 2007; Czech et al., 2004; Kreider, 2004; Murray et al., 2005; Watson & Czech, 2005). Shirl Hoffman's chapter, provocatively titled "Prayer Out of Bounds," adds further critical insight as to how athletes' religious rituals like prayer should, or should not, be brought to the field of play.

John Corlett (1996a, 1996b) and the well-known American sport psychologist Ken Ravizza (2002), who was a keynote presenter at the IICSS, have both advocated the need for more holistic, spiritual and philosophical approaches to consultancy that can accommodate spirituality and religion. The chapter by Irena Martínková is an excellent contribution to this small corpus of writings, by discussing links between Zen states and performance and wrestling with nonempirical concepts such as trust, faith and meaning in sport. My own contribution to this book is a psychological and theological analysis of 'identity in sport' that similarly investigates themes such as faith and personal meaning in sport from a Christian perspective, and thus also challenges the narrowness of the discipline at present. Nonetheless, cognitive-behavioral techniques (mental skills training), such as imagery, thought-stopping, goal-setting and relaxation methods, are foundational to the theory and practice of the discipline of sport psychology and thus are invaluable in many consultancy situations where performance enhancement is the only goal. Nevertheless, it is the lack of consultancy approaches that allows for deeper existential and religious concerns to be addressed (e.g., identity boundary situations, such as retirement from sport and career-ending injuries) and the exploration of the meaning of sport (and life) for the athlete that I would argue is a major omission from the discipline and which is in part addressed in this volume. As 'an individual life cycle (psychological) cannot be adequately understood apart from the social context in which it comes to fruition' and as 'individual and society are intricately woven, dynamically in continual change' (Erikson, 1959: 114), we must also briefly assess how, if at all, the discipline of sport sociology has accommodated religious and spiritual ideas.

Built on the foundations of 19th-century mainstream atheistic anthropology (e.g., Feurbach) and sociology (e.g., Comte, Marx and Durkheim et al.), the discipline of sport sociology evolved mostly in North America and the United Kingdom during the mid-1960s and has grown exponentially during the past decade (see Coakley & Dunning, 2000: xxi–xxxviii; Dunning, 2004). Within this broad and diverse corpus of research and scholarship in the field, there have been a number of informative analyses of the sport-religion relationship, for example, the excellent edited book of Magdalinski and Chandler (2002) and Jay Coakley's (2007) chapter, which provide a good general overview. These could be described as sociohistorical analyses of the sport and religion relationships that have no serious theological reflection (not the aim of the authors). Sociologists of religion, in particular James Mathisen (2005), a leading authority on the sport-religion interface (esp. muscular Christianity in America), and theologian Michael Wittmer (2008) have, however, both provided a sound foundation for others wishing to understand how religion and sport intersect in modern culture. In this regard, Mark Hamilton's chapter in this book adds to this small handful of writings. He critiques the problems evident in the modern world of sport through the theology and philosophy of church father St. Augustine, asking the question, 'Is there something inherently wrong with sport . . . Can we possibly look to metaphysical solutions to these problems?'

One challenge that this book offers to readers is an acknowledgment of the importance of sociohistorical context, and an acceptance that theories and ideas before the evolution of all modern sports studies disciplines (approx. 1960–1970s) may have something to contribute to understanding sport (for a new idea read an old book!). The sociologist of sport Eric Dunning (2004: 22) goes some way to acknowledging this, in his conclusion to a recent overview of the sport sociology field, '. . . the history of sport is fast coming to rival its sociological counterpart' and 'it would be fruitful for historians and sociologists of sport to engage more in cross-disciplinary . . . research.' I agree, but would add that theologians and religious studies scholars also need to come to the table, if we are to gain a deeper understanding of both the positives and negatives of modern sport and how we might go about affecting practical change and legislation.

Arguably, the most comprehensive and balanced account of sport and religion in the sports history literature is Allen Guttmann's book *From Ritual to Record* (1978), which is based largely but not exclusively on Max Weber's sociology. There are of course scores of sports history books and articles that touch on the relationship between sport and religion (see Deardorff , 2000b, Chs.1, 12), but the works of Holt (1990) and Mason (1989) on British sport and Baker (2007b) on the American sporting enterprise are useful for those wishing to ensure sociohistorical rigor in studying this area. Within the confines of sports history there is of course the well-researched topic of muscular Christianity and many books on sport and religion that have chapters that have addressed this topic (e.g., Chandler, 2002; Higgs, 1992; Watson, 2007) and journal articles. For example, a recent special edition of the *International Journal of the History of Sport* (2006, Issue 5) is devoted to this topic. The key scholarly analyses in this topic are, however, Ladd and Mathisen (1999), Putney (2001), Erdozain (2010), Hall (1994), Mangan (1981/2000), Macaloon (2009) and Vance (1985). The fact that the founder of the Modern Olympic Games in 1896, Baron de Coubertin (1863–1937), was heavily influenced by the muscular Christian ethos articulated in these books highlights another important research avenue in the sports-religion literature that has received significant attention, that is, the relationship between religion and the Olympic movement (e.g., Kortzfleisch, 1970; Miller, 2004; Parry, 2007; Weir, 2004).

With the 2012 London Olympics and Para-Olympics on the horizon, the religious and spiritual dimensions of the Olympic Games may well be *one* theme of the Second International Conference on Sport and Spirituality. Let us hope that new avenues of research will be presented at the conference, for example, following the original and fascinating presentation by Graeme Watts at the IICSS, which explored the role of spirituality and religion when working with athletes who have physical or intellectual disabilities.

The aim of this book is to provide a multi- and interdisciplinary examination of the relationship between sport, spirituality and religion. Although the continued 'scientization' of sport since the 1960s (Beamish & Ritchie, 2006; Hoberman, 1992) is certainly not a negative thing in itself, perhaps it is time to reconsider the deeper meaning of sport in terms of human purpose and spiritual value. As Gregg Twietmeyer (2008: 461) recently suggested in what I would argue is a 'landmark paper' for this embryonic field, 'science (a necessary, although not sufficient, good in Kinesiology) ends up overwhelming the field. Consequently the study of human movement is unalterably crippled.' Theology, as the founding discipline of the academy in the 13th century at the University of Paris, is a discipline that this book argues has a place in challenging this worldview in sport.

Let us hope that we can move away from this and towards the foundational educational notion of 'knowledge as its own end,' as articulated by the scholar Jaroslav Pelikan (1992: 78), who has reexamined Cardinal Newman's classic work, *The Idea of a University* (1854/1996). On this note, valuable ethical, sociological and psychological research, scholarship and practical initiatives have abounded in the last two decades, but I ask: has the world of sport, especially big-business professional sport, actually changed significantly? Is there evidence of any reduction in cheating, financial irregularities, racism, violence, drug doping, eating disorders and alienation in the sports world? This is of course a difficult thing to assess accurately, but I would argue there has been little change. Perhaps, then, 'knowledge as its own end' (ultimately leading to practical change), through theology and religious studies, may have an important role to play in the study of sport, if we want to stimulate radical change in this domain. Jürgen Moltmann (1997: 256, 258) provides a rationale for why this could be a good idea in the study of theology and sport, arguing that if 'theological faculties have any eye to *the common good* of the whole of society . . . and not just to look to their own religious communities . . . theology has its place in the university because, and in so far as, it supports universal concerns. . . .'

So, in conclusion, I hope that this text will challenge the past dominance of humanistic and quantitative research in sport and, in turn, open a pathway for students and academics, to think beyond secular monodisciplinary research (of course sometimes wholly appropriate) and rationalistic and narrow conceptions of sport—thus allowing them to play, teach, administer and coach sport with a greater passion, love and depth of understanding.

Nick Watson, chair, Inaugural International Conference on Sport and Spirituality, 2007, York St. John University.

## NOTES

1. St Olaf's College, Minnesota, Minneapolis, USA, hosted two excellent conferences on Sport and Religion, organized by Dr Gary Wicks.
2. It is hoped that the academic-practice link that was emphasized at the IICSS will be maintained at the second conference (2011), through a strand that focuses on practitioners, such as sports coaches, physical educators, sport chaplains (e.g., Boyers, 2000; Heskins & Baker, 2006) and those involved in sport ministry (e.g., Mason, 2003; McGown & Gin, 2003).
3. The term 'theology' originates from two Greek words: *theos* (God) and *logos* (word). The term 'theology' then means 'discourse about God' (McGrath, 2001: 137). The term was traditionally used to apply to Christian theology in its many manifestations (e.g., Biblical theology, systematic theology, liberation theology etc.), although it is used more broadly in the modern world, e.g., Islamic theology. Religious studies evolved from the time of the Enlightenment, in part due to the formation of the disciplines of anthropology and sociology—the study of the human phenomenon of religion, e.g., the beliefs and practices of adherents of any of the world's religions: Buddhism, Judaism, Christianity, Hinduism etc. See McGrath (2001, Chapter 5) for a detailed explanation of the historical usage and development of these terms.
4. Examples are Centre for Sport, Spirituality and Religion (http://www.glos.ac.uk/research/shsc/cssr/Pages/default.aspx), SCORE (Sport Chaplaincy), The Centre for Sport and Jewish Life, The Mendelson Centre for Sport, Spirituality and Character Development (Catholic), Athletes in Action, Christians in Sport (UK), Verite Sports (the last three are all sports ministry organizations), the Islamic Countries Women Sports Federation and the Christian Society for Kinesiology and Leisure Studies.

## BIBLIOGRAPHY

Abe, S. (1986) Zen and Sport, *Journal of the Philosophy of Sport, XIII*, 45–48.

Amara, M. (2007) An Introduction to the Study of Sport in the Muslim World, in B. Houlihan (Ed.), *Sport and Society: A Student Introduction* (2nd ed.), London: Sage, 532–553.

Amara, M. (2008) The Muslim World in the Global Sporting Arena, *The Brown Journal of World Affairs*, 14(2), Spring/Summer: 67–76, Available Online from: http://www.bjwa.org/index.php?subpage=currentissue

Bain-Selbo, E. (2008a) *Game Day and God: Football, Faith and Politics in the American South*, Macon, GA: Mercer University Press.

Bain-Selbo, E. (2008b) Ecstasy, Joy and Sorrow: The Religious Experience of Southern College Football, *Journal of Religion and Popular Culture*, XX, Fall: 1–2.

Baker, W.J. (2007a) Athletes for Allah, in W.J. Baker, *Playing with God: Religion and Modern Sport*, Cambridge, MA: Harvard University Press, 218–239.
Baker, W.J. (2007b) *Playing with God: Religion and Modern Sport*, Cambridge, MA: Harvard University Press.
Baum, G., and Coleman, J. (Eds.) (1989) *Sport* (Religion in the Eighties, Concilium 205), Edinburgh: T & T Clark.
Beamish, R., and Ritchie, I. (2006) *Fastest, Highest, Strongest: A Critique of High-Performance Sport*, London: Routledge.
Begbie, J. (Ed.) (2000) *Beholding the Glory: Incarnation through the Arts*, London, UK: Darton, Longman and Todd.
Benn, T., Pfister, G., and Jawad, H. (2010) *Muslim Women and Sport*, London: Routledge.
Bernardi, L., Sleight, P., Bandinelli, G., Cencetti, S., Fattorini, J.W., and Lagi, L. (2001) Effect of Rosary Prayer and Yoga Mantras on Autonomic Cardiovascular Rhythms: Comparative Study, *British Medical Journal*, 323: 1446–1449.
Boff, L. (1989) Anti-Communism: End of an Industry, in G. Baum and J. Coleman (eds.) (1989) Sprt (Religion in the Eighties, Concilium 205), Edinburgh, UK: T and T Clark: xi–xiii.
Boyers, J. (2000) *Beyond the Final Whistle*: A Life of Football and Faith, London, UK: Hodder & Stoughton.
Byl, J., and Visker, T. (Eds.) (1999) Physical Education, Sports, and Wellness: Looking to God as We Look at Ourselves, Sioux Center, IA: Dordt College Press.
Chandler, T.J.L. (2002) Manly Catholicism: Making Men in Catholic Public Schools, 1954–80, in T. Magdalinski and T.J.L. Chandler (Eds.), *With God on Their Side: Sport in the Service of Religion*, London: Routledge, 99–119.
Coakley, J.J. (2007) Sport and Religion: Is It a Promising Combination?, in J.J. Coakley (Ed.), *Sport in Society: Issues and Controversies* (9th ed.), Maidenhead, UK: McGraw-Hill Education, 528–563.
Coakley, J.J., and Dunning, E. (2000) *Handbook of Sports Studies*, London: Sage Publications.
Collins, M. (2007) Editorial: Sport and Spirituality: An International Conference, York St. John University, 28–31 August, 2007, Implicit Religion: Journal of the Centre for the Study of Implicit Religion and Contemporary Spirituality, 10(3): 241–243.
Cooper, A. (1998) *Playing in the Zone: Exploring the Spiritual Dimensions of Sport*, London: Shambala Publications, Inc.
Corlett, J. (1996a) Sophistry, Socrates, and Sport Psychology, *The Sport Psychologist*, 10: 84–94.
Corlett, J. (1996b) Virtues Lost: Courage in Sport, *Journal of the Philosophy of Sport*, 23: 45–57.
Costantini, E., and Lixey, K. (Eds.) (2009) SAN PAOLO E LO SPORT: un percorso per campioni, Molfetta (BA) Italy: La Meridiana.
Czech, D., and Bullet, E. (2007) An Exploratory Description of Christian Athletes' Perceptions of Prayer in Sport: A Mixed Methodology Pilot Study, *International Journal of Sports Science and Coaching*, 2(1): 49–56.
Czech, D., Wrisberg, C., Fisher, L., Thompson, C., and Hayes, G. (2004) The Experience of Christian Prayer in Sport—an Existential Phenomenological Investigation, *Journal of Psychology and Christianity*, 2: 1–1.
Dale, G. (1996) Distractions and Coping Strategies of Elite Decathletes During Their Most Memorable Performance, *The Sport Psychologist*, 14: 17–41.
Dale, G. (2000) Existential Phenomenology: Emphasizing the Experience of the Athlete in Sport Psychology, *The Sport Psychologist*, 10: 158–171.

Deardorff, D.L., II. (2000a) Sport: Philosophy and Religion, in D.L. Deardorff, II, *Sports: A Reference Guide and Critical Commentary, 1980–1999*, London: Greenwood Press.

Deardorff, D.L., II. (2000b) *Sports: A Reference Guide and Critical Commentary, 1980–1999*, London: Greenwood Press.

Dunning, E. (2004) Sociology of Sport in the Balance: Critical Reflections on Some Recent and More Enduring Trends, *Sport in Society*, 7, 1: 1–24.

Eisen, G. (1998) Jewish History and the Ideology of Modern Sport: Approaches and Interpretations, *Journal of Sport History*, 25(3): 482–531.

Erdozain, D. (2010) *The Problem of Pleasure: Sport, Recreation and the Crisis of Victorian Religion*, Suffolk, UK: Boydell Press.

Erikson, E.H. (1959) *Identity and the Life Cycle*, Psychological Issues, Monograph No.1, New York: International Universities Press.

Feeney, F. (Ed.) (1995) *A Catholic Perspective: Physical Exercise and Sport*, Arlington, Virginia, US: Aquinas Press.

Grimshaw, M. (2000) I Can't Believe My Eyes: The Religious Aesthetics of Sport as Postmodern Salvific Moments, *Implicit Religion*, 3(2): 87–99.

Gurock, J.S. (2005) *Judaism's Encounter with American Sports*, Bloomington: Indiana University Press.

Guttmann, A. (1978) *From Ritual to Record: The Nature of Modern Sports*, New York: Columbia University Press.

Hall, D.E. (1994) *Muscular Christianity: Embodying the Victorian Age*, Cambridge: Cambridge University Press.

Hargreaves, J. (2000) The Muslim Female Heroic: Shorts or Veils?, in J. Hargreaves (Ed.), *Heroines in Sport: The Politics of Difference and Identity*, London: Routledge, 46–77.

Hargreaves, J. (2007) Sport, Exercise, and the Female Muslim Body: Negotiating Islam, Politics and Male Power, in J. Hargreaves and P. Vertinsky (Eds.), *Physical Culture, Power, and the Body*, London: Routledge, 74–100.

Hastings, E. (2004) Spirituality in Sport, *Spirituality*, May/June: 160–166.

Heintzman, P. (2003a) The Wilderness Experience and Spirituality: What Recent Research Tells Us, *Journal of Physical Education, Leisure and Dance*, 74(6): 27–31.

Heintzman, P. (2003b) Leisure and Spirituality: The Re-emergence of an Historical Relationship, *Parks and Recreation Canada*, 60(5): 30–31.

Herrigel, E. (1999/1971) *Zen in the Art of Archery*. London, UK: Random House.

Heskins, J., and Baker, M (Eds.) (2006) *Footballing Lives: As Seen by Chaplains in the Beautiful Game*, Norwich, UK: Canterbury Press.

Higgs, R.J. (1982) *Sports: A Reference Guide*, London: Greenwood Press.

Higgs, R.J. (1992) Muscular Christianity, Holy Play, and Spiritual Exercises: Confusion about Christ in Sports and Religion, in S.J. Hoffman (Ed.), *Sport and Religion*, Champaign, IL: Human Kinetics, 89–103.

Higgs, R.J. (1995) *God in the Stadium: Sports and Religion in America*, Lexington: University Press of Kentucky.

Higgs, R.J., and Braswell, M.C. (2004) *An Unholy Alliance: The Sacred and Modern Sports*, Macon, GA: Mercer University Press.

Hoberman, J. (1992) *Mortal Engines: The Science of Performance and the Dehumanization of Sport*, Caldwell, NJ: The Blackburn Press.

Hoffman, S.J. (1976) The Athlete Dei: Missing the Meaning in Sport, *Journal of the Philosophy of Sport*, III: 42–51.

Hoffman, S.J. (Ed.) (1992) *Sport and Religion*, Champaign, IL: Human Kinetics.

Hoffman, S.J. (2010) *Good Game: Christians and the Culture of Sport*, Waco, Texas, USA: Baylor University Press.

Holt, R. (1990) *Sport and the British: A Modern History*, Oxford: Clarendon Press.

Hopsicker, P. (2009) Miracles in Sport: Finding the 'Ears to Hear' and the 'Eyes to See,' *Sport, Ethics and Philosophy*, 3(1): 75–93.

Hutch, R. (2006) *Lone Sailors and Spiritual Insights: Cases of Sport and Peril at Sea* (Mellen Studies in Sport, Vol. 1), Lewiston, New York: The Edwin Mellen Press.

Hyland, D. (1990) *Philosophy of Sport* (chapter on psychoanalysis and Zen in sport), New York: Paragon House.

Koeing, H. (2001) *Handbook of Religion and Health*, Oxford: Oxford University Press.

Koeing, H. (2008) *Medicine, Religion and Health: Where Science and Spirituality Meet*, West Conshohocken, PA, USA: Templeton Foundation Press.

Kortzfleisch, S.V. (1970) Religious Olympism, *Social Research: An International Quarterly for Social and Political Science*, 37: 231–236.

Krattenmaker, T. (2010) *Onward Christian Athletes: Turning Ballparks into Pulpits and Players into Preachers*, New York: Rowman & Littlefield.

Kreider, A.J. (2004) Prayers for Assistance as Unsporting Behaviour, *Journal of the Philosophy of Sport*, XXX, 17–25.

Kretchmar, S. (1997) Philosophy of Sport, in J.D. Massengale and R.A. Swanson (Eds.), *The History of Exercise and Sports Science*, Champaign, IL: Human Kinetics, 181–201.

Ladd, T., and Mathisen, J.A. (1999) *Muscular Christianity: Evangelical Protestants and the Development American Sport*, Ada, Michigan: Baker Books.

Liberia Editrice Vaticana. (2008) *Sport: An Educational and Pastoral Challenge* (a series of studies edited by The Pontifical Council for the Laity), Citta del Vaticano, Italy: Liberia Editrice Vaticana.

Lynch, G. (2005) *Understanding Theology and Popular Culture*, Oxford, UK: Blackwell Publishing.

Macaloon, J. (Ed.) (2009) *Muscular Christianity and the Colonial and Post-Colonial World*, London: Routledge.

Magdalinski. T. and Chandler, T.J.L. (Eds.) (2002) With God on Their Side: Sport in the Service of Religion, London: Routledge.

Mahoney, J.F. (1999) *The Tao of the Jump Shot: An Eastern Approach to Life and Basketball*, Berkeley, CA, USA: Ulysses Press.

Mangan, J.A. (1981/2000) *Athleticism in the Victorian and Edwardian Public School*, London: Frank Cass and Co Ltd. (Taylor & Francis).

Martens, R. (1979) About Smocks and Jocks, *Journal of Sport Psychology*, 1: 94–99.

Martens, R. (1987) Science, Knowledge, and Sport Psychology, *The Sport Psychologist*, 1: 29–55.

Mason, B. (2003) *Into the Stadium: An Active Guide to Sport and Recreation Ministry in the Local Church*, Uckfield, East Sussex, UK: Spring Harvest Publishing.

Mason, T. (1989) *Sport in Britain: A Social History*, Cambridge: Cambridge University Press.

Mathisen, J. (2005) Sport, in Helen R. Abaugh (Ed.), *Handbook of Religion and Social Institutions*, New York, NY, US: Springer, 279–299.

McGrath, A. (2001) *Christian Theology: An Introduction* (3rd ed.), Oxford: Blackwell Publishing.

McFee, G. (2009) The Epistemology of Qualitative Research into Sport: Ethical and Erotetic? *Qualitative Research in Sport*, 1(3): 297–311.

McFee, G. (2010) *Ethics, Knowledge and Truth in Sport Research*, London: Routledge.

McGown, L., and Gin, V.J. (2003) *Focus on Sport in Ministry*, Marietta, GA, USA: 360$^0$ Sports.

McLeod, H. (2003) "Thews and Sinews": Nonconformity and Sport, in D. Bebbington and T. Larsen (Eds.), *Modern Christianity and Cultural Aspirations*, Sheffield, UK: Continuum International Publishing Group, 28–46.

McLeod, H. (manuscript in preparation) *Religion and the Rise of Sport in Modern England* (publisher TBC).

McNamee, M. (2007) Editorial: Sport, Ethics and Philosophy: Context, History and Prospects, *Sport, Ethics and Philosophy*, 1(1): 1–6.

Miah, A. (2004) *Genetically Modified Athletes: Biomedical Ethics, Gene Doping and Sport*, London: Routledge.

Miller, S.G. (2004) *Ancient Greek Athletics*, London: Yale University Press.

Moltmann, J. (1972) *Theology of Play*, New York: Harper.

Moltmann, J. (1989) Olympia between Politics and Religion, in G. Baum and J. Coleman (eds.) (1989) Sport (Religion in the Eighties, Concilium 205), Edinburgh, UK: T and T Clark: 101–109.

Moltmann, J. (1997) *God for a Secular Society: The Public Relevance of Theology*, London: SCM Press.

Murphy, M., and White, R.A. (1995) *In the Zone: Transcendent Experience in Sports*, London: Penguin.

Murray, M.A., Joyner, A.B., Burke, K.L., Wilson, M.J., and Zwald, A.D. (2005) The Relationship between Prayer and Team Cohesion in Collegiate Softball Teams, *Journal of Psychology and Christianity*, 24(3): 233–239.

Nesti, M. (2004) *Existential Psychology and Sport: Implications for Research and Practice*, London: Routledge.

Newman, J.H. (1854/1996) *The Idea of a University*, New Haven, CT, USA: Yale University Press.

Novak, M. (1994/1967) *The Joy of Sports: End Zones, Bases, Baskets, Balls and Consecration of the American Spirit*, New York: Basic Books.

Odibat, A.A. (1989) The Mind-Body Relationship as Related to Theories of Sport and Physical Education: The Islamic Philosophy in Comparison to Others, *Islamic Quarterly*, 33,(4): 263–276.

O'Gorman, K. (2010a) Saint Paul and Pope John Paul II on Sport, in K. O'Gorman (Ed.), *Saving Sport: Sport, Society and Spirituality*, Dublin: The Columba Press, 14–28.

O'Gorman, K. (2010b) *Saving Sport: Sport, Society and Spirituality*, Dublin: The Columba Press.

Pannenberg, W. (1985) *Anthropology in Theological Perspective*, Philadelphia: Westminster Press.

Parry, J. (2007). Peace and the *Religio Athletae*, in J. Parry, S. Robinson, N.J. Watson and M.S. Nesti (Eds.), *Sport and Spirituality: An Introduction*, London: Routledge.

Parry, J., Robinson, S., Watson, N.J., and Nesti, M.S. (2007) Sport and Spirituality: *An Introduction*, London: Routledge.

Paul, John II. (1986/1995) Sports Can Help Spread Fraternity and Peace, in R Feeney (Ed.), *A Catholic Perspective: Physical Exercise and Sport*, Arlington, VA, US: Aquinas Press, 78–81.

Pelikan, J. (1992) *The Idea of the University: A Reexamination*, London: Yale University Press.

Pfitzner, V.C. (1967) *Paul and the Agon Motif: Traditional Athletic in the Pauline Literature*, Leiden: E.J. Brill.

Pfitzner, V.C. (2009) We Are the Champions! Origins and Developments of the Image of God's Athletes, in G. Preece and R. Hess (Eds.), *Sport and Spirituality: An Exercise in Everyday Theology*, Adelaide: ATF Press, 49–69.

Pius XII (1945/1995) The Sporting Ideal, in R. Feeney (Ed.), *A Catholic Perspective: Physical Exercise and Sport*, US: Aquinas Press, 27–35.

Polkinghorne, J. (2005) *Exploring Reality: The Intertwining of Science and Religion*, New Haven, CT, USA: Yale University Press.

Prebish, C.S. (1993) *Religion and Sport: The Meeting of Sacred and Profane*, London: Greenwood Press.

Preece, G., and Hess, R. (Eds.) (2009) *Sport and Spirituality: An Exercise in Everyday Theology*, Adelaide: ATF Press.

Price, J.L. (2001) *From Season to Season: Sports as American Religion*, Macon, GA: Mercer University Press.

Putney, C. (2001) *Muscular Christianity: Manhood and Sports in Protestant America 1880–1920*, Cambridge, Mass: Harvard University Press.

Ravizza, K. (2002) A Philosophical Construct: A Framework for Performance Enhancement, *International Journal of Sport Psychology*, 33, 4–18.

Riesen, R.A. (2007) *School and Sports: A Christian Critique*, Monrovia, CA: Grasshopper Books.

Ryan, T. (1986) *Wellness, Spirituality and Sports*, New York: Paulist Press.

Saint Sing, S. (2004) *Spirituality of Sport: Balancing Body and Soul*, Cincinnati, OH: St. Anthony Messenger Press.

Savage, T.B. (1996) *Power through Weakness: Paul's Understanding of the Christian Ministry in 2 Corinthians* (Society for New Testament Studies Monograph Series 86), Cambridge: Cambridge University Press.

Seesengood, R.P. (2005) Hybridity and the Rhetoric of Endurance: Reading Paul's Athletic Metaphors in a Context of Postcolonial Self-Construction, *The Bible and Critical Theory*, 1(3): 1–14.

Shafranske, E.P. (Ed.) (1996) *Religion and the Clinical Practice of Psychology*, Washington, DC: American Psychological Association.

Slusher, H. (1967) *Man, Sport and Existence: A Critical Analysis*, Philadelphia, PA, USA: Lea and Febiger.

Slot, O. (2005) Why Marvin Andrews Believes He Is Walking Proof that Miracles Happen, *The Times* (Times online), Retrieved 28 September, 2009, from http://www.timesonline.co.uk/tol/sport/football/article571995.ece

Sparkes, A.C. (1992) Toward Understanding, Dialogue, and Polyvocality in the Research Community: Extending the Boundaries of the Paradigms Debate, *Journal of Teaching and Physical Education*, 10: 103–133.

Sparkes, A.C. (2002) *Telling Tales in Sport and Physical Activity*, Champaign, IL: Human Kinetics.

Twietmeyer, G. (2008) A Theology of Inferiority: Is Christianity the Source of Kinesiology's Second-Class Status in the Academy? *Quest*, 60: 452–466.

Van Andel, G., Heintzman, P., and Visker, T. (Eds.) (2005) *Christianity and Leisure: Issues in a Pluralistic Society* (republished), Sioux Center, IA: Dordt College Press.

Vance, N. (1985) *The Sinews of the Spirit: The Ideal of Christian Manliness in Victorian Literature and Religious Thought*, Cambridge: Cambridge University Press.

Van Kaam, A.L. (1975) *In Search of Spiritual Identity*, Denville, NJ: Dimension Books.

Walseth, K. (2006) Young Muslim Women and Sport: The Impact of Identity Work, *Leisure Studies*, 25(1): 45–60.

Watson, N.J. (2007) Muscular Christianity in the Modern Age: "Winning for Christ" or "Playing for Glory"? in J. Parry, S. Robinson, N.J. Watson and M.S. Nesti (Eds.), Sport and Spirituality: *An Introduction*, London: Routledge, 80–94.

Watson, N.J. (2009) Book Review of *Playing with God: Religion and Modern Sport*, Baker, W.J., 2007, London: Harvard University Press, *Journal of Contemporary Religion*, 24(1): 131–133.

Watson, N.J., and Czech, D. (2005) The Use of Prayer in Sport: Implications for Sport Psychology Consulting, Athletic Insight: The Online Journal of Sport Psychology, 17(4). Available from http://www.athleticinsight.com/Vol7Iss4/PrayerinSports.htm

Watson, N.J., and Nesti, M. (2005) The Role of Spirituality in Sport Psychology Consulting: An Analysis and Integrative Review of Literature, *Journal of Applied Sport Psychology*, 17: 228–239.

Weir, S. (2004) *The Ultimate Prize: Great Christian Olympians*, London: Hodder & Stoughton.

Wertz, S.P. (1977) Zen, Yoga, and Sports: Eastern Philosophy for Western Athletes, *Journal of the Philosophy of Sport*, IV: 68–82.

White, J., and Deardorff, D., II. (Eds.) (2008) *The Image of God in the Human Body: Essays on Christianity and Sports*, Lampeter, Wales: The Edwin Mellen Press.

Wiggins, M.S., Hillyer, S.J., and Browning, C. (2005) Pilot Study of Muslim Women's Perceptions on Religion and Sport, *Psychological Reports*, 96(3): 787–791.

Wittmer, M. (2008) *A Christian Perspective of Sport*, in D. Deardorff, II and J. White (Eds.), *The Image of God in the Human Body: Essays on Christianity and Sports*, Lampeter, Wales: The Edwin Mellen Press, 43–59.

# Part I

# Theological Ethics in Sport

# Part I Introduction

*Jim Parry*

## INTRODUCTION

A glance through the contents of the leading philosophy of sport journals reveals that the area of primary interest and work is the field of ethics. This part explores what light can be shed on the enterprise of sport by the discipline of theological ethics, which we define as any ethical position or argument that makes theistic assumptions. In the West this includes, of course, Christian ethics (dominated by Divine Command Theory), but is not limited to it, since each of the major ethical theories has a theological version (Paley's utilitarianism, Aquinas' natural law theory, the virtue ethics of both Aristotle and MacIntyre, etc.).

In addition, theological ethics may adopt a variety of approaches to sport, including:

- The application of the insights of theological thinkers to ethical issues in sport (e.g., Augustine)
- The understanding of religious practices in relation to sport (e.g., prayer)
- The clarification and exploration of theological concepts, and their relevance in sporting environments (e.g., evil, sin and redemption)
- The significance of religious beliefs in terms of social and lifestyle issues (e.g., Christian beliefs and sporting identity)
- The application of religious morality to sporting practices
- The interpretation of sporting events, institutions and relationships in religious terms
- The critique of sport from a theological point of view

All of these approaches are to be found in this part. In Chapter 1, Mark Hamilton observes the range of ethical problems that seem to arise on almost a daily basis in contemporary sports. These problems range from heavy-handed pressure placed on children by parents who will sacrifice all for their child's athletic opportunity and success, to many different forms of cheating including the use of banned performance-enhancement methods, to the growing influence of the sport business industry.

Each of these problems brings unique issues of its own to the fore, but we should pause and question whether there are any fundamental or foundational problems that cause all of these manifestations of trouble in sport. Maybe there is something inherently wrong with sport (such as its competitive nature), or maybe we could identify some common failure that with some effort we could improve upon so as to correct moral errors in sport? Might we even look to metaphysical solutions to these problems?

Hamilton's response to such questions is to suggest that the ontology of evil and the account of immorality presented by the ancient philosopher-theologian Augustine can provide us with an explanation for the supposed evils in sport, with the hope that sport might yet be redeemed if practiced properly within the framework of Augustinian thought.

In Chapter 2, Shirl Hoffman takes a hard look at the role and meaning of prayer in sporting contexts. He begins by noting that prayer has become a conspicuous part of many athletes' competitive lives, often under evangelical influence. For these athletes, private prayers, often cojoined with team recitations of the Lord's Prayer, are incorporated as essential parts of both pregame and postgame rituals. In recent decades, though, Hoffman observes that sport prayer has taken on a more public face. Football players join hands at center field with evangelical teammates and opponents in highly visible postgame rituals. Prayerful gestures by athletes during the course of the game have become commonplace; when a football player kneels in the end zone after scoring a touchdown or a baseball player points skyward after hitting a home run, most Americans no longer find it a curious accompaniment to the spectacle.

However, Hoffman asks whether what happens in play and sport is truly worthy of the divine's interest. Is it possible that God really doesn't 'care' whether or not one plays to the best of his ability, sinks the free throw, scores the penalty kick or wins the game? Is it possible that God would prefer not to be dragged into our sport spectacles? What theological conundrums arise when 'competing prayers' are offered up by opposing sides in a contest? And, more to the point, are athletic prayers consistent with the theology evangelicals claim to believe? These are just some of the issues discussed, as Hoffman suggests that evangelicals should think more carefully before introducing the solemn act of prayer into athletic contests.

In Chapter 3, Tracy Trothen reflects upon the age-old propensity for humans to enhance their capacities, and the recently developed biotechnologies that promise genetic improvements in the enhancement of sporting performance. Cases such as that of the sprinter Oscar Pistorius cause us to reconsider our concept of 'normalcy,' the adequacy of the therapy/enhancement distinction and the whole notion of transhumanism. Meanwhile, "gene doping" is already recognized as a banned method by the World Anti-Doping Association (WADA), whilst ethicists such as Andy

Miah have constructed persuasive arguments supporting the use by athletes of genetic-modification technologies that could alter the shape of the meaning, value and virtues of sport.

Trothen seeks to develop a particular theological perspective on these issues. Some previous theological analyses of genetic technologies have focused on the dangers of "playing God," whilst others, most notably theologian Ted Peters, have challenged this focus and its attendant assumptions in a general sense, arguing that a reconsideration of the idea of 'sin' is required, in the particular context of sport and genetic technologies. Her chapter explores the ethical implications of sin, understood primarily as a giving up of power, a resistance to vulnerability, and a denial of human dependency as a virtue. She suggests that redemption is often located in those very things that we seek to avoid as part of the human condition, and asks us to rethink what it means to be human in the context of the moral complexity and ambiguity of a radical relational ethic.

Trothen concludes that, although there are persuasive moral goods relating to the use of such technologies for purposes related to athletic performance, the potential harms outweigh the potential benefits.

In Chapter 4, Ian Lawrence explores the distinctive Christian identity of the Jamaican professional footballer Marvin Andrews, within the context of Scottish professional football. It has been argued that, with increasing modernization in contemporary British society, religious belief has become implausible for increasing numbers. However, Lawrence suggests that, while Christian 'belonging' has clearly declined, Christian 'believing' seems nonetheless persistent, and in the case of Marvin Andrews the two are embodied in a somewhat unconventional public figure.

Marvin Andrews, as a black Christian, presents a significant challenge to preconceived notions of what constitutes a role model in the context of religious intolerance in the west of Scotland. This case study of Andrews, based on a series of interviews by the author, seeks to analyze his personal perceptions as a practicing Christian, and to provide a historical and social background to the issue of sectarianism. In so doing, it examines the notion of religious identity and its expression as sectarianism (especially in relation to singing and chanting practices), and documents Andrews's responses as expressions of his Christian idealism and his belief in the church as 'a mission to the world.'

# 1 An Augustinian Critique of Our Relationship to Sport

*Mark Hamilton*

Much of the discussion in contemporary sports ethics involves analysis of the actions of athletes and coaches regarding how the game is played. Most of the papers, presentations and discussions about sports ethics heard at sport philosophy conferences focuses on criteria used to create, determine or evaluate fair play often involving examination of questions about doping or other attempts to enhance performance, cheating as it relates to fairness, gender issues, sportsmanship, sports wagering or the business of sport, analyses of overinvolvement or interference by parents, fan misbehavior, or issues of violence in sport. No doubt sport is saturated on a daily basis by these moral tensions.

As I have thought about or even taught on these issues, one question has continued to disturb me, and that is whether there is a root cause of all these problems. What is it that is really wrong with sports, not just what is it that we do that is wrong in our sport practices, but is there anything essentially wrong with sport? What is it about sport itself that creates so many wrong actions? How come there are all these accumulated problems in sports? Why is there: doping? cheating? violence? So much overly aggressive parental intrusion? Is there any reasonable explanation? And, if there is something fundamentally flawed with sport, why should we continue to pursue such an activity so essentially destructive or even evil? If there is so much wrong in sports and there are so many problems created by it, shouldn't we simply give up on it altogether and expel it from our collective lives? Or if there is nothing essentially wrong, then why is there so much misbehavior? And if we are unwilling to abandon sport and believe it contributes to our quality of life, that it has human significance and competition has value to it, then maybe we should forget about attempting to solve its problems through piecemeal solutions and endeavor to determine whether there is something much greater, more profound, or even metaphysical which lies at the core of our current moral failures in sport and work to correct this.

Many reject even probing in this direction but it seems to be a necessary question if behavioral improvement is to be successfully sought. Broader, more general ethical questions must be raised by Christians examining these sport and competition issues from a cosmic, eternal perspective with a realistic understanding of the ontology of evil and how that evil is translated to sport.

Back in the 1960s and 1970s there was much discussion and debate over the nature and value of competition, since it is obviously at the heart of all sports. The problem of sports, according to many of these critics, became simplistically the problem created by the inherent evil of competition. These critics were contending that competition is itself inherently immoral and intrinsically negative and so sport being competitive is unavoidably immoral. It was generally argued that since competition involves a zero-sum contest where the goal is to defeat an opponent and since the goal cannot be secured by all competitors that sport must necessarily breed selfishness and egoism. Writers such as John Schaar and Michael Fielding put forth this criticism of competition where there is a "selfish concern for oneself at the expense of others" (Simon, 2004: 20).

This has been countered by numerous apologists for competition such as Robert Simon, who argues that competition is no longer a zero-sum game if one sees competition as a personal challenge and one competes as part of a "mutually acceptable quest for excellence through challenge" (Simon, 2004: 27) or as ethologist Konrad Lorenz argues that it is our competitive aggressive instinct "far from being the diabolical, destructive principle that classical psychoanalysis makes it out to be, is really an essential part of the life preserving organization of instincts" (Lorenz, 1963: 44). This spirited drive allows us to combat disease and survive as a species, resulting in the good of competition outweighing the bad.

Today the greater appreciation for competition is based on the widely accepted utilitarian belief that more good (social benefit) than evil comes from our competitive instincts and practices. Though with all the current negatives found in sport this is certainly vulnerable to challenge. And though most of us who are involved in sports or sport philosophy are in it because we are sympathetic to sport and competition and agree with many of the traditional arguments supporting the value of competition, often because of our emotional attachment to sport we fail to question whether there might be something essentially wrong within sport which creates this multitude of ethical problems associated with it even if competition itself is not a sufficient cause of all the immoral maladies. The remainder of this chapter will probe into this question of what is wrong with sport and attempt to answer it within an updated ancient framework by making use of the analysis of evil and immorality put forth by Augustine and applying it to contemporary sport.

Augustine's understanding of evil can provide a comprehensive explanation for the ethical problems in sport today. It is argued that the primary ethical problems with sport are not the nature of competition, not how the games are played, nor the behavior in the games but rather how people relate to sporting competition, thus putting the locus on humanity.

Early in his life, Augustine embraces Manichaeism, a form of dualism. But after his conversion to Christianity, he rejects dualism and strongly emphasizes God as the author of all that exists and that everything originally made by God was created essentially good. Yet Augustine acknowledges that evil exists as a reality in the world. In seeking the origin of evil, He asks, "Where then evil, and what is its source, and how has it crept into the Creation? What is its root, what is its seed?" (Augustine, 1993: 111). For Augustine, evil is essentially a perversion or corruption of the good. He writes, "But in certain of its parts [of Creation] there are some things which we call evil because they do not harmonize with other things" (Augustine, 1993: 111). This is not a strict Platonic concept of disharmony which sees the metaphysically lower as the cause of evil, but it is rather a type of dissonance ensuing from the human choice of making the lower things higher. Evil is taking something which is by nature good and twisting it in a way that it becomes evil. The cause of evil is in humanity not in the things. Augustine observes that evil is not a thing and thus could not be chosen because there is no evil thing to choose. He states, "Evil has no being of its own but is only an absence of good, so that it simply is not" (Augustine, 1993: 41). Since all things are essentially good as created, one can only turn away from the good, from a higher good to a lower good in this Augustinian hierarchy. The tree in the Garden of Eden was not an evil tree but the disobedience in desiring it more than desiring obedience to God creates evil. This is the origin of evil portrayed in Adam's sin and is repeated in virtually every subsequent sin. Immorality is a hierarchical perversion as the act of choosing the lesser good over the higher. And the effect of this is disharmony, disorder, evil.

For example, animals and humans were both originally created good with innate value, but only humans are in the image of God, which makes them ontologically higher and greater in both being and value. It is therefore immoral to place more value on an animal's life over a human's life.

Augustine distinguishes three types of evil: metaphysical, physical and moral; and each of them consists in a deficiency in being, a descent toward nonbeing. Metaphysical evil is the lack of perfection due to a given nature and hence is not actually an evil. In this sense all creatures are "evil" because they fall short of full perfection being finite but this does not make them morally evil. This is a very loose usage of evil and not the traditional orthodox notion of evil as grounded in moral evil. Only God alone is good in this sense of full perfection. Corporeal evil consists in the privation of perfection owing to nature; for example, blindness is the poverty of sight in a person who ought to have sight according to the essence of its nature. This ontological difference between the created and the creation is not a moral cause of evil. The cause of moral evil is not God, nor is it matter, as the Platonists would have it, for theism matter is part of creation and hence good. Neither is the will as a faculty of the soul evil, for it too has been created by God. The only true evil is moral evil, an action contrary to the will of God, a misuse of an essential good. It is choosing to make the ontologically lesser as superior in value. It loves the lower more than the higher.

Augustine sees the universe as an ordered structure where the levels of being are also levels of value, where the lower must be subordinate to the higher because this is its due as God has structured it. This is both a metaphysical and ethical hierarchism. Humans must make an accurate assessment of the established value and rational order in nature. A good life is lived by a person who loves what ought to be loved properly. Evil and disharmony occur in loving things the wrong way or out of order. Evil is a perversion of the will turned aside to lesser things. This gives evil a reality—negative in the sense of rejection of the established order, and hence a decadence of being or descent toward nonbeing. Humans fall from what they were made to be and ought to be.

Augustine holds to voluntarism, the primacy of the will over the understanding. Love as he describes it is not a mushy feeling but an active choice. He assumes we have control over our affections and believes our first love must be God and all other loves are to be subordinated to this first love. The possibility of evil makes possible a greater good. This is a world in which true moral decision making and cultivation of virtues are possible by humans as character is formed through growth and struggle. This is his proposed end for humans.

Evil exists as a deficiency of goodness. Augustine states, "When accordingly it is inquired, whence is evil, it must first be inquired, what is evil, which is nothing else than corruption, either of the measure, or the form, or the order, that belongs to nature. Nature therefore which has been corrupted, is called evil, for assuredly when incorrupt it is good; but even when corrupt, so far as it is nature it is good, so far as it is corrupted it is evil" (Augustine, 1993: 352). To say that something exists is to say it possesses a definable character. Deprivation of form, order and harmony can only exist as long as there exists something having form, order and harmony (these can be used interchangeably). Whatever has a definable nature possesses a natural order that is good. Corruptive moral evil is created when there is a deficiency of form, order and accord, which exists in a thing only as a lesser degree of goodness and being than the thing might otherwise possess. So evil is the state of a thing that is good essentially, but not supremely and unchangeably good. In this Augustinian tradition Thomas Aquinas has assessed evil in the following. "Now, what is evil in itself cannot be natural to anything. For it is the very definition of evil that it be a privation of that which is to be in a subject by virtue of its natural origin, and which should be in it. So, evil cannot be natural to any subject, since it is a privation of what is natural. Consequently, whatever is present naturally in something is a good for it, and it is evil if the thing lacks it. Therefore, no essence is evil in itself" (Aquinas, 1975: 49). A privation is not an essence, but is a negation in a substance. In Aristotelian language, he adds that evil, as such, is not a direct cause but an accidental cause (1975: 67).

When Augustine sins he describes himself as falling toward lower things. He writes of his past, saying, "But these things I did not at that time know, and I was in love with those lower beauties . . ." (Augustine, 1993: 61). The apparent conclusion of this is to set forth a medieval hierarchy of substances, but a closer evaluation of Augustine should consider this a hierarchy of value even if it is grounded in a metaphysical framework. We should make valuable, not just what is higher in a metaphysical sense since he sees the material world equally possessing good substance, but rather higher in value. So for Augustine hierarchical order is a necessity and a good. Our moral responsibility is to understand the nature of the universe and to order our affections toward things in it properly.

If Augustine was with us today he would, of course, not be a great sportsperson. In fact, he gives the impression that too much time is wasted on leisure activities, but a close inspection of Augustine can provide us with a way to understand what is wrong with sport as we apply his approach to the cause of evil in the broader cosmic universe to the problems in sport.

In looking at the object of the disordered affections one might ask what is the good of the lower ordered object the person wished to gain or to avoid losing. For humans the quest for happiness consists in attaching ourselves through love to objects of our affections that we think will bring us happiness. But in order for this to properly occur there must be a real knowledge of the value of objects of love so that our love might be properly ordered. Otherwise we are prone to seek satisfaction in things that are metaphysically and morally incapable of providing it.

Athletes often fail to maintain this standard of love and then turn to themselves as the focus of attention and appreciation. This gives rise to all forms of evil in sport. Our love for sport becomes distorted through loving the lower things more than the higher. We love winning more than virtue so that there is an overemphasis on winning, thus disordering our affections resulting in evil. Winning matters but it should not matter disproportionately to things that must matter more. But unfortunately we assess its value as more than it is really worth, resulting in it producing an alluring hold on us. Why we even allow athletics to dictate to us what school districts we will live in, what jobs to hold, how to spend our leisure time, whom we marry, what activities we place our children in, how we will spend large sums of money, or with whom to socialize. It reaches into every nook and cranny of life. We give it a power over us and, through our preoccupation with it, we lose our moral compass and it distorts our nature and the nature of sport, resulting in sin.

Have you ever asked what it means to love sports and that maybe our problem is simply that we love sport too much or we love in ways that we should not? What does it mean when we say "I really love sports"? Do we love sport when it should not be loved? In his book *The Four Loves*, C.S. Lewis says analogously that we can never love another person "too much" . . . we can only "love him too much in proportion to our love for God"

(Lewis, 1960: 148). Lewis is arguing that love for another human has a rightful expression to it but that we must have our love for another understood in proportion to our other loves. For example, if one loves another but loves the self more, the likelihood is that the love will become an obsession rather than true love because one will love for one's own sake rather than for the sake of the other. So that obsession, an evil, is a distortion of love created by a disordering of one's affections. In applying this concept to sport, we find that evil in sport is also created by making the lower things higher and the higher things lower. One cannot love sport, the body, or competition too much; one can only love them too much in proportion to the other objects of love in one's life. Love for sport must be properly prioritized.

Jesus once told his disciples that they must hate their father and mother (Luke 14:26). Did he really mean hate? No, he was using hyperbole in this statement. What he meant was that compared to one's love for God the love for one's family should look like hate. He was emphasizing the importance of loving God first not on hating one's family. The danger is not loving God as much as necessary. Augustine is consistent with this approach. One's loves must be prioritized properly.

Augustine specifically makes observations about the gladiatorial games of his day and despite the fact that there is no precise parallel of violence in our current sports activities (though one may argue that some of the tough man or ultimate fighting contests are getting close), some of the observations Augustine makes regarding the games have usefulness in our current ethical assessment of sport. Some of the general observations that Augustine makes about the social relationship of these games by the fans and participants can be applied to the modern social phenomena of sport and the way people relate to sport in order to identify and clarify the cause of the immoral practices in sport today.

In a famous passage in Book VI of his *Confessions*, Augustine describes his friend Alpius's attraction to the gladiatorial games. Augustine says that "the passion for idle spectacles—had sucked him in his special madness being for gladiatorial shows" and that Alpius was in the "grip of this wretched craving" (Augustine, 1993: 94). Because of this obsession he was "fatally devoted to the Games" (Augustine, 1993: 94). Augustine believed Alpius was throwing away much promise on such an "empty pastime" (Augustine, 1994: 95). One day, however, Alpius is in Augustine's class when Augustine is mocking the Games and Alpius sees the light and because of this he "braced his mind and shook it until all the filth of the Games fell away from it and he went no more" (Augustine, *Confessions*: 95). But then at a later date Alpius is forced by a group of his friends to again attend the Games. He tells them they cannot make him watch and that he will remain detached while sitting in the stands. However, he refuses to watch; and as the noise and frenzy grows he weakens and his curiosity gets the best of him and he begins to peek. Before long he falls "more miserably than the gladiator whose fall had set the crowd to that roar—a roar which had entered his ears and unlocked his eyes, so that his soul was stricken and beaten down . . . Seeing the blood he drank of the savagery . . . He drank in all the frenzy, with no thought of what had happened to him, reveled in the wickedness of the contest and was drunk with lust for blood. He was no longer the man who had come there but one of the crowd to which he had come, a fit companion for those who had brought him" (Augustine, 1993: 94).

His condition is described as a type of madness. He forgets what it was doing to him and he loses the ability to reflectively think on the topic. Of course it is nearly absurd to compare most contemporary sport with the gladiatorial games due to the great degree of difference in the area of violence. But there is a parallel element in these passages to how many approach sports today as they are "sucked in," "in the grip of the craving" and "fatally devoted." Few do deliberation on the effect their passion for sport has upon them and thus fail to realize how shallow it makes them when sport is the all-consuming passion of life. A type of self-deception occurs which prohibits the person from analyzing their own relationship to sport, how much time and energy they put into sport, and how other things which are obviously more important are neglected for the sake of sport. There is also a naïve belief that one could abstain from sport if one wanted to but that it is harmless to love sports and spend all of life consumed by it.

Relating to sport in this distorted devoted manner affirms a reductionist view of humans, that we are only our bodies. As physical activities and love for sport and competition overtake love for family or friends, God or even personal mental or moral development, sport becomes the primary passion or affection and the consequence for many individuals or families is that success in sport becomes obsessive and the only family life they have centers around sport. All they can speak to one another about is sport. The only relationship a father may have with a son or daughter is the bond of sport. Now the bond of sport can be good and can enhance a relationship, and there have probably been many families saved by their common bond of sport. This value cannot be downplayed. There are probably many families who would not have anything to speak to one another about were it not for sports. But does a relationship really have great substance to it if it is only based on the common interest in sport and the child's success in it? It is less than the best and distorts sport and ourselves. It becomes a surrogate point of reference binding shallow masses of humanity together.

One example of this came to my attention through my work as NCAA faculty representative and compliance officer at our university. We had a football player enter our university but early in football practice he suffered a concussion. We soon discovered that he had a hidden history of this type of injury and that he was having short-term memory loss. None of our athletic trainers, physicians, coaches or administrators had been notified of any previous injuries or any preexisting condition. After the player returned home we received a call from his father notifying us that the son would soon be returning to action. We refused to permit this due to the danger of permanent damage. We were looking out for the athlete's best interests, yet his dad still insisted that the son would play. This certainly is a clear example of a father's disordered affections. Sure he loves his son and yes he loves sport. But does the father love his son playing sport and what it does to his ego more than he loves his son? This is not uncommon immoral action by the father. In the Augustinian hierarchy of affections others must come before self. The son must be loved more by the father for his own sake than for the father's sake or more than for the glory brought by sporting success.

When love for winning becomes more important than it ought, it creates a distortion, a disharmony, vice or evil. How often have we heard stories of coaches who cared more about winning than the character of their athletes and thus allowed numerous indiscretions? A parallel perversion is described in C.S. Lewis's novel *The Great Divorce*. He describes an artist who once loved art and being creative who now only loves what recognition he receives from doing the art (Lewis, 1996: 78–82). So the contemporary athlete goes from love of the sport to love of the accolades given to him for his success. When this occurs he becomes arrogant and full of self-importance when it is only sport. This athlete may mistakenly think himself a better person because he can run faster, jump higher, or shoot better than anyone else. This is a perversion of human nature and an expectation of sport that it cannot satisfy.

Augustine's concept of disordered love can help us understand today's moral problems in sport. Augustine notes "that all men desire happiness is a truism for all who are in any degree able to use their reason. But mortals, in their weakness, ask, "Who is happy? And how is happiness gained?" (Augustine, 1984: 371). What object or objects should one seek in order to obtain true happiness so that human longing and satisfaction will be fulfilled in the quest for contentment and the greatest good? "For one who seeks what he cannot obtain suffers torture, and one who has got what is not desirable is cheated, and one who does not seek for what is worth seeking for is diseased" (Augustine, 2004: 42). The fallen human seeks happiness in the lower objects and prioritizes the lower over the higher, and when this happens in our sporting behavior the consequence is that our sports activities begin to become distorted, resulting in the incalculable harms described at the beginning of this chapter.

Augustine believes that love is the force which truly moves people. He says, "My love is my weight: wherever I go my love is what brings me there" (Augustine, 1993: 266). The true quest for happiness consists in attaching our affections on objects of desire that we think will make us happy. But for this to occur, wisdom is needed. An understanding of the metaphysical order and value of objects of love is necessary so that love might be properly ordered. The parent who pushes the child beyond what is appropriate has demonstrated more self-love than love for the child. The father who only relates to the child on the basis of sport has loved sport more than loving the child.

Which is the higher moral activity, winning a game or cultivating virtue? For the person who loves winning more than being good, a disordering of affections occurs, resulting in evil. It is a perversion of sport and of human nature. The problem is that many prefer the lower over the higher, winning over being good or virtuous. As a result, cheating and doping occur. People would rather be losers than lose; they fail to realize there are things worse than losing, like a loss of character or virtue or becoming a jerk. This model of understanding provides a basis for understanding the nature of the core problems in sport culture and that our primary problem is not necessarily inherent to sport but rather extrinsic expressions toward sports, or how the human heart and will relate to sport.

The advantages to this approach are the following:

1. It affirms creation and allows one to maintain that competitive sport is something good, that it is not inherently evil. All that has been made is essentially good and competition exists in creation so it is good. It is not a necessary evil, nor is the body evil in itself. This should not diminish our view of sport. It does not reduce sport to simply a form of entertainment or recreation. One can take seriously the idea of sport as a significant human activity, as a form of self-improvement, or even as a profession. We can still see it as what sport philosopher Spencer Wertz describes as a truly "human enterprise" (Simon, 2004: 34).
2. Evil is not glossed over. It takes seriously the problem of evil and recognizes the real existence of evil and the evils in sport. It is the perversion of the good. It is like rust that corrodes good metal. Since competition is not intrinsically evil, the evil in competition is a corruption of sport, a corruption caused by humans who love it disproportionately by loving the lower things more than the higher, by loving winning more than virtue, by loving self more than others, by loving the body more than the soul, by loving what is made more than the Maker.
3. Because evil is dependent on good as a parasite or perversion of the good, there is real hope that evil can be overcome by good and sport can become better, more moral, redeemed. Though it may seem nearly impossible, there is a philosophic and ethical basis to work for change and to know what sport ought to be. We can continue to pursue the ideals of sport.
4. This paradigm is comprehensive and explains the obsession we have with sport. It explains the violence resulting from lack of love for other people or from loving self or loving winning more than loving people; it explains the difficulties created by the sport gambler who

does not really love the game at least not as much as the rush he feels from betting. It explains the desire to cheat or dope due to disproportionate affection. And there would certainly be implications for this affecting the issues of running up the score or for crowd behavior and violence.

There is no doubt that our sports have taken on a type of idolatrous religious zeal that presents a true moral danger. In *The Four Loves*, C.S. Lewis writes, "We may give our human loves the unconditional allegiance which we owe only to God. Then they become gods: then they become demons. Then they will destroy us, and also destroy themselves. For our natural loves that are allowed to become gods do not remain loves. They are still called so, but can become in fact forms of hatred" (Lewis, 1960: 10). The result, says Augustine, is that "Every soul is wretched that is bound in affection of mortal things: it is tormented to lose them, and in their loss become aware of the wretchedness which in reality it had even before it lost them" (Augustine, 1993: 55–56). Finally, one must recall the two great commands by Jesus to first love God and then to love your neighbor as yourself (Matthew 22:36–39). If sport is to be practiced Christianly and morally, and in ways that reduce the multitude of problems and evils in sport, then these two commands must be the central guidelines to our sporting practices.

## BIBLIOGRAPHY

Aquinas, T. (1975) *Summa Contra Gentiles*, Notre Dame, IN: Notre Dame Press.
Augustine (1984) *City of God*, New York: Penguin Books.
Augustine (1993) *Confessions*, Indianapolis, IN: Hackett Publishing Co.
Augustine (2004) *The Writings against the Manichaens*, in P. Schaff (Ed.), *Nicene and Post-Nicene Fathers*, Vol. 4, Peabody, MA: Hendrickson Publishers, Inc.
Lewis, C.S. (1960) *The Four Loves*, London: HarperCollins.
Lewis, C.S. (1996) *The Great Divorce*, New York: Macmillan Publishing Co.
Lorenz, Konrad (1963) *On Aggression*, New York: Harcourt, Brace, and World.
Simon, Robert (2004) *Fair Play*, San Francisco: Westview Press.

# 2 Prayers Out of Bounds[1]

*Shirl Hoffman*

## INTRODUCTION

Homer's *Iliad* contains what modern sportscasters would call "a color commentary" of a footrace held as part of the funeral games honoring slain warrior Patroclus. Ajax breaks out in the lead at the start, followed closely by Odysseus, so close in fact that Ajax can feel him breathing down his neck as he runs "lightly and relentlessly on." It doesn't look like Odysseus has a chance. Then, coming down the home stretch, Odysseus does what many contemporary athletes would do in this situation: he prays. And his prayer is answered. The goddess Athena not only gives him a supernatural boost of adrenalin; she causes Ajax to slip and fall in a pile of cow dung, assuring Odysseus' victory. After the race, Ajax accepted the second prize of an ox, but not graciously. As he spat out cow dung he complained: "Curse it, that goddess tripped me up. She always stands by Odysseus like a mother and helps him."

That the gods of ancient Greece would intervene in something as mundane as a footrace doesn't seem all that unusual in a society in which the gods were undependable and frivolous. But asking the omnipotent, omniscient, omnipresent Christian God to help in the arena is also an accepted practice, dating back to when the church first began its flirtations with big-time sports. When chariot racing, once despised and reviled by the early church, was "Christianized" in third-century Rome, some charioteers began visiting chapels to say prayers before the start of the races. In fourteenth-century England and France, vengeful, bloodthirsty knights often resorted to prayer, kneeling with their "chaplains" before taking part in bone-jarring and often fatal contests in the lists. Prayer was also part of Siena's 16th-century Palio, where both jockeys and their horses received the priest's blessing on the day of the race, a practice continued to this day.

But in no age has prayer become so woven into the fabric of sports as in the modern era. Surely the pace has quickened since Joseph Marbeto's 1967 survey of college and university athletes and coaches in which 55% acknowledged praying in connection with athletic events, usually at the beginning of the game and usually to ask God to bless their performance and help them win (Marbeto, 1967). At church-related colleges Marbeto found the incidence of prayer even higher: 82% of coaches said they prayed before games, 51% of whom believed that their prayers affected the outcome of the contest. Today, prayer has become a familiar part of the pre-and postgame rituals of professional, college teams, high school teams, youth league teams and church league teams. The ritual of NFL players and their opponents gathering at the center of the field to pray after the game has become so common it no longer is regarded as a curiosity by sportswriters or television cameras.

Prayers in sports take many forms. Team prayers, offered in locker rooms before and after games, are often supplemented by the private petitions of individual athletes. Pregame invocations offered over the public address system are part of pregame ceremonies at many Christian schools. Some athletes regard their performances as prayerful gestures; others insert gestures into the game as a way of recognizing God's presence. Making the sign of the cross before foul shots, pointing to heaven after hitting a home run, or kneeling in the end zone have become as familiar in big-time sports as the ubiquitous "chest bump." The trend of praying in sports has been on the rise for at least 30 years. By 1995 so many football players were praying in the end zone after scoring touchdowns that the NCAA sought to ban it under the provisions of a rule banning "showboating," defined as "any delayed, excessive or prolonged act by which a player attempts to focus attention upon himself." Enraged televangelist Jerry Falwell saw a world of difference between a player praying in the end zone and the strutting, taunting and gloating that the rule seemed designed to target, and he brought suit against the NCAA under the provisions of the 1964 Civil Rights (Reed, 1995).

In fairly short order the NCAA caved in, agreeing to allow end zone prayers provided the players do not kneel in such a way that it "is delayed" and "excessive," "doesn't focus attention on the player," and if, in the opinion of the referees, the prayer is "spontaneous and not in the nature of a pose." Both the original and revised rulings set off a firestorm of controversy. Critics and sportswriters wanted to know: "Why must these players pray *in the stadium*?" "What is "*excessive* prayer?" and "How can such prayers *not* be focused on the player?" "If one player is allowed to kneel to pray, why are others banned from wiggling their fannies; might this not also be a way of praying"? Little did Philadelphia Eagle Herb Lusk know, when he first knelt and prayed in the end zone more than 30 years ago, that he was at the vanguard of a movement that would make prayer the legally and religiously preferred alternative to "boogaloos," cartwheels, and backflips (NCAA Clarifies Prayer Stance, 1995).

There is something about sports, and particularly football, that whets the appetite for prayer. Everybody wants to get into the act. Band members and referees sometimes pray before games; so do cheerleaders and dancers who provide the entertainment. The Top Cats dancing team which performs at the North Carolina Panthers football games, for example, gather in a circle to say a pregame prayer for "health, good memories, and boundless energy" before taking the field to gyrate to hard-edged music in what often aren't always pious routines (Rowe, 1996). Fans feel the need to pray too. Soon after Ohio State University hired Jim Tressel to coach its football team, a local Columbus church posted a message on the church marquee asking the public to "Pray for the OSU football program and [coach] Jim Tressel." A market for athletic prayer fetishes has emerged: Internet access and a credit card will get you Christmas ornaments decorated with "The Coach's Prayer," "The Athlete's Prayer," "The Golfer's Prayer," the "Fisherman's Prayer" ($6.95), the "Coach's Prayer Plaque" (with laminated front and fancy frame for $26.95) and a T-shirt emblazoned with "A Baseball Coach's Prayer" for $5.95 (King, 2002).

Precisely how implanted prayer is in the sports mentality surfaced a few years ago after the Supreme Court handed down its decision banning invocations at high school football games, a venerable tradition at southern high schools. The reaction of fans was organized, swift and bitter. Nationwide protests erupted. Ad hoc groups such as "No Pray, No Play" mobilized. The family that had brought the original suit against the Santa Fe school district seeking to stop pregame prayers became the object of death threats. In Hattiesburg, Mississippi, 4,500 fans stood at a high school football game and recited the Lord's Prayer in unison; 25,000 attended a similar rally in a football stadium in Asheville, North Carolina. A popular New Jersey high school football coach, forbidden by his principal to lead pregame prayers for his team, quit his job in protest and became a *cause celebre*. The president of FCA blasted the court's ruling, pronouncing it hostile "to all things religious in public life," and promised that athletes and fans everywhere would continue to pray (Sheehy, 2000). Almost overnight, clever innovations for circumventing the ruling cropped up, including a plan at Alabama schools to have fans bring portable radios to the game and turn up the volume while a local minister said a prayer over the local radio station before the game (Firestone, 2000; Hiskey, 2003).

## PRAGMATIC PRAYERS

In truth, most of these invocations had been marginally sectarian at best, severely hedged by sensitivities to religiously pluralistic audiences. Many of them resembled the ecumenical supplications offered at political conventions and Washington prayer breakfasts; expressions of Christian secularity. Precisely how generic they could be came to light when officials at University of Oklahoma, after consulting with their lawyers, decided to permit the local Presbyterian minister to continue offering an invocation before football games because, in their opinion, his prayers weren't "identifiable with any religious faith" ("No comment department," 1993).

Similarly, when the Santa Fe school district pled its case before the court to allow prayer to continue to be offered at its football games, it did so not by arguing that its pregame prayers were fitting tributes to a Christian God, or meaningful expressions of athletes' faith, but on grounds that they were civic and nonsectarian rituals intended to "solemnize the event," "promote good citizenship" and "establish the appropriate environment for competition" ("Excerpts from the Supreme Court Decision," 2000).

Such pragmatism flavors much of the prayer uttered in the world of big-time sports. Some pregame prayers by coaches and athletes seem more suggestive of gimmickry than helping to evoke "a deep consciousness of the place of man in relation to the Deity," less likely to "express, awaken, and sustain piety" than ready the team for competition (Lovelace, 1979: 167). Former Washington Redskins coach George Allen, a man touted by sport-faith organizations yet uniformly described by those who knew him as pathologically obsessed with winning, insisted on locker room prayers on game days because "it does more to produce togetherness and mutual respect than anything else I've found in 21 years of coaching" (Levitt, 1972: 33 ). Sounding the same note, Grant Teaff, former Baylor head football coach and executive director of the American Football Coaches Association, suggested that the reason "well over 50 percent of the coaches have prayers before a game" is to strengthen team bonds (Shulman, 2007). Unity isn't the only quality sought through prayer. There is a growing interest among sport psychologists in using prayer "as a type of pre-competition awareness training that helps center the performer and alleviate(s) performance-related anxieties" (Watson & Nesti, 2005). Athletic prayers have also been pushed as a way of checking the profligate lifestyles of players that hamper the team's performance and reflect badly on the reputation of the team. "Why not see prayers on the fifty-yard line (in NFL games) as evidence of an antidote to the social irresponsibility that professional athletes too often display?" asked a writer in the Catholic journal *Commonweal* (Douglass, 1991). But prayer organized around ulterior motives is too easily exploited, something that became apparent when the Labrador Tigers, an Australian Rules football team, signed a contract with the Christian Community Church on the Gold Coast. After being repeatedly embarrassed by reports of sexual misconduct of several of its stars, the team contracted to require team members to attend at least one church service each season. In return the church would provide a pastor who would pray for the team's success. Such crassly opportunistic approaches to prayer may raise eyebrows in certain evangelical circles, but in the world of sports, everything, including prayer, must be harnessed to the overriding goal of winning (Amid Sex Scandals, One Aussie Team Turns to God, 2004).

Locker room prayers offered in an atmosphere of urgency and high anxiety can easily become inseparable from the coach's pep talk. H.G. Bissinger's description of the prayer offered by a Permian (Texas) high school football coach, for example, suggests that it was aimed more at readying the team for the big game against an archrival as it was at God (Bissinger, 1992). As Bissinger describes it, the coach had just finished a private session with defensive ends in which they were told to "knock the hell out of 'em," (the opposing team) and to "put some helmets on 'em" (the opponent's star player). Gathering his entire team around him in the locker room, he said that "a supreme, fanatical, wild-eyed effort" will be required to win the game, and then, abruptly, he knelt on the floor: "Dear God, we're thankful for this day, we're thankful for this opportunity you've given us to display the talent that you've blessed us with. Heavenly Father, we thank you for these men and these black jerseys, thank you for the ability that you've given 'em and the character that you've given 'em. We ask your blessings on each one of them this afternoon. Help them, dear God, to play to the very best of their ability. Help them to play with some quality that they've never played with before, give them that something extra that they've never had to call up before" (Bissinger, 1992: 273).

Prayer may indeed foster team unity, help players cope with anxiety, and help athletes gird for rough competition, but exploiting it for such practical purposes seems a gross misuse of a godly gift, if indeed it is proper to speak of "using" prayer at all. Indeed, at least one philosopher has objected to using prayer in this way on grounds that it is cheating; the athletes who pray, he says, are not much different from cyclists who ask their coaches to help push them up a hill (Kreider, 2003). Advocating prayer as a way of solidifying team unity is only shades removed from recommending it as a means toward a host of other ends: lowering blood pressure or improving flexibility in the knees, for example. Team unity is essential for success in team sports, but prayer designed to foster it seems a bit off track. Praying for unity in the spiritual life, of course, is an entirely different matter. Unity was the focus of Jesus' longest prayer ("that all of them may be one, Father, just as you are in me and I am in you"), and of the Apostle Paul's repeated urgings in his letters to young churches. But there is a vast difference between unity of team spirit and the spiritual unity that Paul had in mind. When Paul exhorted the Ephesians to unity he was talking about exercising spiritual gifts, not trying to psych them up for a weekend track meet against the church at Corinth.

Craftily inserting prayers into pregame locker room rituals as a way of elevating team spirit may be a bit disingenuous, but it is shades of hypocrisy apart from using them to stoke the fires of competition. When fierce physical battles await athletes in the arena, appeals to the Almighty aren't always easily distinguished from war cries. In the NFL-sponsored film *Religion and Football,* just before taking the field team members gather in circle, hold hands, and bow their heads while a teammate offers a call to arms with a revivalist fervor:

> Oh Lord we thank you for the opportunity to come before
> you Lord. Father you said that you will answer our prayers.

> Now we come to ask for wisdom, power, and might, God
> to dominate because Lord you're on our side and you give
> us strength . . .
>
> (*Religion and Football*, 2004).

This tradition of mixing war rhetoric with prayer hasn't escaped the eye of novelists, some of whom have experienced sports up close and personal. In *North Dallas Forty*, Peter Gent, the Dallas Cowboy turned novelist, offers an especially satirical vignette of a locker room prayer offered by a sports-crazed chaplain who's "amen" was quickly followed by a player's vulgar exhortation to violence. "Its OK," says the chaplain; "I know how you feel" (Gent, 1973: 247–248). In *The Great Santini*, Pat Conroy, a former athlete who is no stranger to basketball locker rooms, describes the transformation that came over "Coach Spinks" ("a generalissimo in the land of the jock") before a big game. "I want you to feast on some medium rare West Charleston High School *****. I want us to win. Win. Win." Then his face suddenly mellowed, "his eyes glistened, his gaze became beatific. 'Let us pray,' he said and all the heads on the team dropped floorward as though they were puppets strung on the same wire" (Conroy, 1987: 251).

If some athletic prayers seem inauthentic it's because they are so contrived and calculated. God may not be worth centering one's life around, but it's good to know that He's there in the gut-wrenching moments before the big game or race. "I don't pray daily," NASCAR star Dale Earnhardt, Jr., told a reporter, "but I ask God for strength in certain situations . . ." And then he added: "Most of the time right before qualifying" (Dale Earnhardt Jr., In His Own Words, 2005). The fact that the locker room piety of so many coaches so often isn't matched by a reciprocal piety in the coach's private life led curmudgeonly former Michigan State University football coach Duffy Daugherty to suggest that "all those coaches who require pregame prayers by their players ought to be made to go to church once each week" (Hoffman, 1985: 67).

Viewed against the backdrop of money-grubbing, scandal-riddled big-time sports it's tempting to accept any sort of prayer, any acknowledgment of a higher power, as a breath of fresh air. Even a coarse blend of God, guts, glory and profanity, some might say, is better than no prayer at all. Some evangelicals, attuned to cultural theology, might even see in these prayers, however facetious and hypocritical, the specter of common grace. But it's hard not to look upon entreaties inflamed with zealotry and bent on transmogrifying high school football games into World War III as bordering on spiritual fraud. When Jesus taught his disciples The Lord's Prayer—hands down, the most popular prayer in locker rooms—it's doubtful he anticipated its being coupled to athletic jingoism to be incanted by testosterone-fueled gladiators as a way of psyching themselves up for the mock wars that pass for some of our most popular forms of sporting entertainment.

Lutheran theologian Olle Hallesby chose two words to describe the "heart attitude" that God accepts as prayer: "faith" and "helplessness." "Only he who is helpless," said Hallesby, "can truly pray." At prayer, he said, "God crushes our self-conceit and self-sufficiency" (Hallesby, 1994: 18). Encounters with "the wholly other," said renowned theologian Rudolf Otto, leave one awestruck by majesty, overcome with a diminished sense of self, a feeling of littleness, weakness, and dependence (Otto, 1923: 50). "The diminution of the self into nothingness" was how he phrased it. Such a disposition may be fine for a quiet morning's meditation, but the athlete who has just put on his or her "game face" is likely to view it as an inappropriate attitude for "taking care of business" on the athletic field. They may be correct. Conjuring up a diminished sense of self in the dressing rooms of sport palaces built as testaments to the glories of human power, strength and self-sufficiency quite likely will lead to a diminished score.

## THE TRIVIALITY OF ATHLETIC PRAYER

It is against this backdrop of concocted piety that committed evangelical athletes and coaches seek the proper role for prayer in sports. Prayer for most evangelical athletes isn't confined to the tense moments before big games. Prayer is part and parcel of their holistic spiritual life, its importance underscored by the more than 600 prayers recorded in the Bible and the fact that Jesus prayed often and instructed his followers to do the same. Since more than two-thirds of evangelicals pray daily—usually before meals, as part of their devotional life, before making important decisions, and when facing crises in life—it is hardly surprising that athletes of their number also pray before athletic contests.

But the athletic setting isn't like most other settings in which evangelicals pray. One difference is that sport, a derivative of play, is what some philosophers call "an activity of maintaining an illusion." "Play," says philosopher Kenneth Schmitz, "reveals itself as "a transnatural, fragile, limited perfection" (Schmitz, 1979). Its rules, traditions and customs are human devices fabricated for the sake of our amusement. Former commissioner of major league baseball and renaissance scholar Bart Giammati once described sport as being based on "a practical joke, . . . a conscious agreement to enjoy, a pleasurable self-delusion" (Giammati, 1989: 71). Sports manipulate images and create drama much like that served up in television soap operas, but it isn't the drama of real life. We play sports "as if" they had ultimate importance, in a world philosophers have described as being "outside and beyond the world of nature . . . a new totality." Sport requires players to adopt a state of mind that philosopher Eugene Fink called "non-pathological schizophrenia" (Fink, 1979: 79).

When the game is on, "the affairs of everyday life recede into the background," says philosopher William Morgan (Morgan, 2006: 19). Softball players willingly "play along" with the fiction that failing to step on a base or swinging and missing a pitch or dropping a fly ball really matters, all the while cognizant that these rules and customs are only relevant within the mental constructs of the game. To suggest that pretending is essential to the playing of games doesn't mean that athletes don't or shouldn't play seriously. Being serious *in* the game means you are invested and absorbed in it, unhitched from everyday life, caught up in its air of pretense. Being serious *about* the game, however, more often than not leads to trouble. It is this "set-apartness" of the sports world that enables players "to telescope all their attention, effort, and concentration and to summon as much strength and energy as they can muster to meet the competitive challenges presented to them" (Morgan, 2006: 19).

A fair portion of the criticism of athletic prayers has to do with their insertion into this illusory environment. How can prayers, expressions of the Ultimate, offered in the context of an activity of illusion, be taken seriously? One answer posed by religion scholar Joseph Price is that prayer and play share certain similarities (Price, 2009). Both, for example, are set off from real life, both are voluntary, both are bound by spatial and temporal limitations; so much so that Price suggests that in a definitional sense at least, prayer might be understood as a form of play. Prayer like play is set apart, secretive, voluntary, bracketed from everyday life and sometimes even "entertaining" (60). However, while the play of athletes may take place divorced from everyday life in a theoretical sense, in reality their prayers represent umbilicals to the serious world of their faith. As such the aim of prayer seems intended to puncture the illusion. But the real question is whether prayer, having been interjected into the world of play, can avoid being influenced by the illusory nature of sports themselves. This is what makes athletic prayers so difficult for many people to take seriously. Richard Wood, former dean of Yale Divinity School, summed up the opinion of many critics when he said: "To suggest that God has a direct involvement in athletic contests trivializes the whole notion of God's involvement with the world." "It doesn't seem odd that God would know in detail what happens in football games," said Wood; "what seems to me odd is that God would care" (Nack, 1998: 23; Wood, personal communication, 2007).

Most evangelicals—especially athletes and coaches—would be less willing than Wood to say that God doesn't "care" about our games; some would even argue that He takes a direct hand in determining the winner. "According to Jesus," writes popular evangelical author Philip Yancey in his best selling book *Prayer*, nothing is too trivial to bring to God in prayer. "Everything about me—my thoughts, my motives, my choices, my moods—attracts God's interest" (Yancey, 2006: 121). Obviously, to suggest that humans are able to put themselves in environments where prayers can't be answered or to suggest that God is locked out of the stadium when the game is on doesn't fit well with evangelical visions of an omnipresent God. But the critical question isn't whether God is present at big-time athletic contests but whether or not the unfolding of events in a sports contest are matters sufficiently important in the divine scheme of things to be prayed over. The undeniable fact that God is present in nature doesn't necessarily mean that it is appropriate to pray that a particular leaf will fall from a certain tree in a certain hour. Asking whether or not God *could* intervene in an athletic contest is not the same as asking whether it is appropriate to ask Him to intervene.

The passionate sports fan finds it nearly impossible to imagine that God is less interested in popular sports than he or she is. It is easier for a sports fan, for example, to imagine that the World Series weighs heavier on the mind of God than the outcome of a backyard game of badminton, simply because most of us are more interested in the former than the latter. It might strain the fan's credulity to imagine that God invests Himself in the World Cow Chip Throwing Contest held each year in Beaver, Oklahoma, as much as He is invested in the NCAA's March Madness. It seems entirely plausible to the religious sports fan that prayers of Olympic contestants will be granted direct access to the divine throne, but not those of, say, Joey Chestnut, winner of the 2007 Annual Nathan's Famous Fourth of July International Hot Dog Eating Contest. Evangelicals empathize when a player kneels in the end zone amidst the warmongering, trash-talking and incredibly dangerous game of football, but had Joey Chestnut prayed before polishing off 66 hot dogs in twelve minutes or if, after ingesting the final bun, he knelt to thank God for helping him find that additional niche in his stomach, it would have given most of them indigestion.

The point isn't that sports can't be appropriate places for prayer; it is that our models of sport, the settings and circumstances with which we surround them, aren't well suited for prayer. This isn't to say that sport contests, properly framed and celebrated, couldn't be. Prayers offered, for example, in the context of what Josef Pieper has described as a feast would seem fitting places for prayer. In *In Tune with the World: A Theory of Festivity*, Pieper shows how even secular festivals—properly celebrated, and springing from "the praise of God in ritual worship"—can be important occasions for deepening spiritual lives and focusing participants' visions on eternity. But the festival succeeds, says Pieper, only when we accept the divine gift lying behind the busyness of the festival (Pieper, 1963).

Even in the mid-20th century, Pieper believed the festival was in steep decline, gradually being replaced with what he called "pseudo-festivals." As Pieper described them, pseudo-festivals sound a great deal like our sports spectacles: "virtually purchasable surrogates which convey a counterfeit of the things that can be had only with true festivals." Instead of rapture, oblivion of ills and a sense of harmony with the world, our sport spectacles give us cheap thrills, noisy pomp and titillation. Instead of helping us see through the excitement to "the fundament of existence," our spectacles, with their unbridled commercialism and media overkill, hog all the attention for themselves. Almost without thinking participants become enamored with the tinsel on the package rather than the festive gift itself. In place of unity and assent to the Creator our games thrive on combat and partisanship, borrowing, as Eisner has put it, "the means from war and the mood from festivals" (Eisner, 1963).

Prayer at a festival, as Pieper described it, would be a natural thing; prayers at the pseudo-festivals of our sports spectacles come off like the proverbial brown shoes mistakenly worn with a black tuxedo, fundamentally out of synch with the partisan, militant spirit of the stadium. Some have suggested that prayer can be a way of solemnizing the spectacle, of domesticating its barbarous impulses. But prayers are no more likely to help in this regard than playing hymns before soccer games will reduce hooliganism and on-field violence, a tack recently taken recently by the owner of Bucharest's professional soccer team. Adding a few hymns or prayers to a pseudo-festival is unlikely—at least as Pieper saw it—to convert it into the real thing (Soccer: Steaua Paymaster Calls Religious Tune, 2007).

In fact, experience enables us to predict with a fair degree of accuracy that the opposite will happen. More often than not, when prayer is inserted into pseudo-festivals it is prayer itself, not the moral and spiritual tenor of the game, that changes. Pseudonymous festivals have a way of rubbing off on religion in the most remarkable ways. Sportswriters' humorous but sacrilegious characterizations of the mural of Christ with upraised arms that looms over Notre Dame football stadium as "Touchdown Jesus," the priest in Grove City, Pennsylvania, an ardent Pittsburgh Steeler fan, who conducted part of the liturgy waiving the team's fetish—the yellow "terrible towel"—are a mere sampling of ways in which the triviality of pseudo-festivals trivialize religion (Kindred, 2006).

One is tempted to call them "clown prayers," those instances in which athletes reveal perceptions of prayer that are so elemental and twisted that one must laugh if only to keep from crying. Former New York Yankee Reggie Jackson ("Mr. October"), known not only for his overbearing persona but for his knack at elevating his game in playoff and World Series competition, once waxed theologically to reporters on the benefits of prayer after belting three homers in game 6 of the 1977 World Series: "Man is not big enough to handle these intense pressure situations by himself," said Jackson. "In a no-deposit, no-return game like this, you have to find some sort of way to key down, to find an inner peace so that you can let your native talent express itself . . . I ask the Big Man Upstairs for a good pitch to hit, and then whatever happens happens." Like many who pray, Jackson was not a particularly religious man, but after hitting an especially important home run on the way to winning the World Series, he admitted to having sent up a prayer in the on-deck circle, something on the order of Jacob's promise to follow God if he kept him safe, and fed, and clothed when he was hightailing it from his enraged brother Esau. "I told Him," said Jackson, "that if he let me hit a home run, I'd tell everyone he did it" (Boswell, 1978: E1).

But Jackson was not any further off base than the late evangelist Jerry Falwell, whose sport fanaticism could prompt some bizarre comments not only about prayer but the entire relationship between sports and faith. He once told a *Sports Illustrated* reporter that one method he used to recruit pitchers for the school baseball team was to invite coach and former Yankee great Bobby Richardson to be a guest on his television show. Then, said Falwell, I'd ask him, "Bobby, if God could grant you one wish, wouldn't He send you a 6′ 4″ left handed pitcher who can throw the ball 100 miles per hour and know where its going?" The reporter asked: "But what if Richardson said he would ask God for world peace instead?" "Well, that would be all right too," said Falwell. "Either that or the pitcher" (Montville, 1989: 87).

Asked if God favored the Irish, Notre Dame theologian Richard McBrien said if God intervened in human affairs it would probably be in something more important than a football game. Still he averred that it's okay to pray for one's team "as long as these things aren't taken too seriously. Once it's taken seriously, then you are on dangerous ground" (Sherman, 1990). But discerning the line between the serious and nonserious isn't always easy. Was a popular evangelical minister in the Pittsburgh area being serious when he delivered the pregame sermonette and prayer for the Houston Oilers before their upset of the heavily favored Steelers in 1978? And was he serious when he declined the Oilers' request for him to pray for them when they returned to Pittsburgh later in the season for a critical playoff game, telling them "this time my heart is with the Steelers. The Oilers aren't losers anymore. They've proven themselves and *don't need me*"? (Wayne Alderson, Oilers huddle with God for Extra Point, 1978: S2). The Steelers won the playoff game, thus extending the minister's streak to 2–0. When a well-regarded evangelical minister hints that his prayers—and apparently his alone—might have accounted for victories on the football field, we get an idea of how frivolous sport prayers can be. Even Yancey seems prepared to accept certain limits on God's patience with our praying: "Surely, some prayers go unanswered," he says, "because they are frivolous." Among the frivolous prayers he mentions are those offered by athletes (Yancey, 2006: 222).

The way sport can erode the serious foundations of prayer reached something of a climax when silly invocations, offered before football and hockey games for purposes of amusing spectators, became the rage in the 1970s. In a particularly noteworthy case, Rev. Richard Bailar, minister of a United Church of Christ in Miami, offered this prayer over the stadium loudspeakers in a televised game between the Miami Dolphins and the Cincinnati Bengals in 1974:

> Creator God: Father and Mother of us all, we give you thanks for the joy and excitement occasioned by this game. We pray for the physical well-being of all the gladiators who run the gamut of gridiron battle tonight . . . but, knowing that the tigers are voracious beasts of prey,

> we ask You to be especially watchful over our gentle dolphins. Limit if You will, the obfuscations of (sportscaster) Cosell's acidulous tongue, so that he may describe this night truly and grammatically as it is . . . A great game, in a great city, played before Your grateful children, on whom we ask peace and shalom. Amen (Michener, 1976: 384).

Bailar's prayer brought scathing criticism from evangelicals across the country; some described it as unadulterated blasphemy. Not all fans, however, thought the prayer inappropriate. It was, after all, interrupted by a total of 26 seconds of applause, and Bailar was showered with letters and phone calls, most of them supportive. He became a minor celebrity. His photo was displayed in sports bars; he was stopped on the street for autographs and flooded with requests for copies of the prayer, "all of which," said Bailar, "says something about the sterility of religion and idolatry of sports in America" (Michener, 1976: 385). Was it sacrilege, blasphemy? Perhaps it was. A writer to the *Miami Herald* called it a mockery of prayer, betting that "the invocation didn't make a dent in the mind of God." There was a time when I would have agreed with the writer, but now I wonder if rather than a mockery of prayer, it pointed to the mockery of *most* prayers offered at bombastic athletic spectacles. Silly, irreverent, and banal: the prayer seemed to me to have been the perfect supplication for the spiritually vacuous events transpiring in the stadium that night, and perhaps that's what Balair's prayer was pointing to all along.

## GESTURES, PRAYER CIRCLES AND END ZONE PRAYERS

The ebbing of public invocations at sports events has brought with it a perceptible rise in on-field prayer gestures by athletes. These gestures (chest thumps followed by index fingers pointed skyward, usually after an especially successful performance, bowing the head or kneeling in the end zone, etc.) have come to be accepted as a normal part of athletics. Performed in other contexts, the same gestures would lead to a great deal of head-scratching. We wouldn't quite know what to make, for example, of an evangelical professor who bumps chests with students and points skyward when they perform well on his or her exam. These rituals are familiar parts of a religion tailored specifically for sport spectacles. Typically they express thanksgiving; hence they are rarely seen when the tide of events has turned against the player or his team. Heisman trophy winning quarterback at University of Florida, Danny Wuerffel, for example, always made a gesture of prayer after each touchdown pass that he threw, but a quarterback who has just thrown an interception isn't likely to point an index finger skyward; neither is the soccer player likely to fall on his knees after being yellow-carded. (One exception was Tony Fernandez in Cleveland, who claimed to have thanked God after hitting a game-winning home run in the playoffs—and then again after making a decisive error in the World Series.) Prayerful gestures on the sports field are always in response to things having gone one's way, markedly different from the place given to prayer in ordinary life.

Some evangelicals view these gestures as "witness" but others regard them as an inelegant mixture of teeth-gritting competition, violence, self-promotion and a religion that trifles with the deeper messages of the gospel. "Somehow that post-game (prayer) huddle leaves me feeling uncomfortable," said former Cincinnati Bengal Chris Collinsworth (Kellner, 1999: 76). For every evangelical who believes such demonstrations advance the faith, scores of others regard them as inappropriate intrusions of a player's religious preferences into a secular event. "In my faith as a Christian," says Hall of Fame quarterback Terry Bradshaw, "I am not called to put on a display and call attention to myself. . . . I don't look at it [on-field gestures] as religion, I look at it as selfish" (Football and Religion). Even outspoken evangelical coach Tom Landry thought on-field gestures were inappropriate: "I'm afraid these little 'God helped me score a touchdown' and 'God helps me be a winner' testimonials mislead people and belittle God" (Landry, 1990: 293.

If the intent of these demonstrative gestures is to give witness to the players' faith, some rethinking might be in order. They seem as likely to alienate as convert. Even sportswriters and narrators who have been sympathetic to evangelical athletes have grown weary of what they see as two-bit theologizing and staged piety. One television reporter quipped: "There's a rule with me. You get one 'I thank the Lord Jesus Christ.' The next one we're going back to the booth. I'm not waiting for the director to cut away" (Smith, 1997). The unwelcome reception given them shouldn't always be interpreted as the price the Christian bears for costly witness. Theologian Bryan Stone's assessment of those who regard trendy T-shirts with Christian slogans or witty bumper stickers as "witness" is just as aptly applied to public sport prayers: "If those around us take offense at our witness," said Stone, "it is not because they have taken seriously the import of our beliefs; they just find us annoying" (Stone, 2007: 284).

There also is the charge that on-field or on-court religious gestures are too theatrical, too showy, reflecting what theologian Carl Henry called "the righteousness of ostentation" exhibited in the prayer of the Pharisee which Christ condemned (Henry, 1957: 575). There is no reason to believe that Christ's words—"When thou prayest, enter into thy room and when thou has shut thy door, pray to thy Father in secret" (Matt. 6:5)—are any less incumbent on modern athletes than on His ancient followers. Regardless of the athlete's sincerity or intent, prayers and gestures offered in full view of the crowd and television audiences are inherently demonstrative, intended to "be seen by men." An NCAA attorney defending the association's short-lived ban on end zone prayers in college football games saw this as an irrefutable fact: "When a person kneels in the end zone," said the lawyer, "nobody but that person and God knows whether he is praying or not. But *everyone* is looking at him and that is the point" (Reed, 1995: A8).

Many evangelical athletes would agree. When reporters asked NFL player Howard Cross why he and his teammates didn't save their prayers for the locker room rather than kneel at midfield following games, he said it would defeat their purpose: "We *want* people to notice," he said (Reed, 1995). Praying in the less public, more anonymous atmosphere of informal pickup soccer games, sandlot softball games or playground basketball is much less common. In fact, such gestures are likely to confuse and even irritate fellow players. Let a Saturday morning golfer kneel for a quick prayer after sinking critical putts or belting a long drive and it's likely he will find himself looking for different playing partners the next weekend.

Defenders of public athletic prayers see Jesus' admonition to his followers to "let your light shine before men that they may see . . ." (Matt 5:16) as softening his injunction to avoid showy prayers. Yet the verses appear to point to two different sins, the temptation to cowardice and the temptation to vanity. To pray as a way of seeking attention is vanity, yet not to bear witness for fear of harm or punishment is cowardice. Are athletes who *refuse* to engage in these public prayers guilty of spiritual cowardice? An evangelical seminarian has suggested as much, likening athletes' prayers in the arena to those offered by first-century martyrs in the Roman coliseum. "Picture that while crowds roared, the believers bowed and prayed as a witness to their faith. Do I think such an action would have been approved by the apostles and leaders of the early church? I suspect it would" (Walker, 1997).

But the good professor's analogy fails in several respects. First, the hulking men who play sports aren't slaves; they aren't forced to play—indeed, they have substantial economic interests in the spectacle's promotion—and they certainly don't face cruel persecution if they don't pray. They aren't bystanders; they are predominant actors. Under the circumstances the temptation to vanity seems a far greater danger than the temptation to cowardice.

More to the point, perhaps, prayers enacted as propaganda, whether to self-identify as a Christian athlete on the athletic field or to register opposition to abortion on the courthouse steps, too easily become victims of their ulterior motives. Such prayers beg entrée into God's presence but never forget the cause to which they have been harnessed. Few things are more irritating in social intercourse than talking to someone who is looking over your shoulder hoping to catch the eye of a passerby. Demonstration prayers strike me as being very similar: petitioners talking to God but all the time, trying to look over His shoulder to catch the eye of the crowd.

This isn't to say that all prayer is cheapened simply by being offered in public. In a gem-filled little book titled *Praying at Burger King*, Richard Mouw describes his well-established custom of asking the blessing for his food, whether at home or in the public environment of a fast food restaurant. Part of the reason he does it, says Mouw, is to acknowledge God's presence; even in a noisy Burger King "there is indeed a God whose mercy reaches out to me . . ." (Mouw, 2007: 4). Certainly the evangelical athlete recognizes God's presence in the stadium and understands that His mercy reaches out to those who are there, but beyond this the analogy begins to fall apart. Mouw's are private not public, prayers offered in an otherwise inattentive environment. (If he were to spread his napkin on the floor, kneel on it and pray aloud we might have a different opinion.) In acknowledging God's presence at Burger King, Mouw isn't part of the show; his prayers, for example, don't glorify the consumption of French fries, hamburgers or other high-cholesterol food. But the on-field prayers of athletes aren't private and disinterested, and that is the point. Inserted into the spectacle by its central figures, they become inseparable from the spectacle itself. Mouw's prayers *just happen* to be offered in a Burger King; athletes' prayers are offered *because* they are in a stadium. Mouw's prayer in Burger King is an affirmation of his faithfulness, but athletes' are affirmations not only of their faithfulness but an affirmation of the spectacle itself. Jason Kelly, writing in the *US Catholic*, hit the proverbial nail solidly on the head:

> . . . players who pray on the playgrounds should realize that they aren't glorifying God when they kneel in the end zone or cross themselves in the batter's box. They are glorifying the game itself by invoking the name of the Lord in an otherwise insignificant instance . . . Save the prayers for the locker room, or the bus, or better yet the bedroom or some other private place where the words of thanks won't be lost amid the din of cheering multitudes, where the prayers won't seem so much like shameless preening. (Kelley, 2001)

Martyred theologian Dietrich Bonhoeffer was conscious of how easily prayers, even when done in private, could degenerate into "empty noise." Even *private* prayers, he said, risk that the supplicant will become "the one who at the same time prays and looks on." To his way of thinking prayer was "the supreme instance of the hidden Christian life," and for this reason "it is never given to self-display, whether before God, ourselves, or other people." In fact, prayer is, he said, "the antithesis of self-display," the "perfect example of undemonstrative action" (Bonhoeffer, 1978: 181). What Bonhoeffer would have thought of prayer offered up by devout athletes in the heat of battle before teeming crowds and television audiences is anybody's guess, but it seems more than likely that he would have joined Kelley in suggesting that they save it for the locker room.

## PRAYING FOR SAFETY

In their interviews with evangelical athletes, Daniel Czech and his associates found that prayers for safety were among the most common pregame petitions (Czech et al., 2004). One athlete told them: "I felt after praying I was safe. Not only did I pray for my safety, but I prayed for my teammates, in fact, I would specifically pray for each individual player's safety and health before each game. As someone who has experienced many injuries, I always have a fear of getting hurt. The fear subsides after I know God will be my co-player so to speak" (p. 3). Aware of the risks of their sport, race car drivers are specialists in foxhole praying. Says veteran NASCAR driver Mark Martin: "One of the reasons there are so many Christians involved in motor sports versus some other sports is that we deal with risk. The risk factor is a little bit higher in our sport than some sports. We understand that. And I personally want to be prepared" (Bentz, 2000). Even in less publicized venues of dimly lit dirt tracks, chaplains minister to drivers, praying with them through the netted windows of their cars just before they start their engines, and often offering an infield invocation, asking God to protect the drivers (Orozco, 2007).

The risk of being injured in sports is a fact of the athletic life, but some sports pose much greater dangers than others; thinking too much about the risks they pose can distract, inhibit, even paralyze the athlete "When you're going 100 miles an hour and you're doing your assignment," said former University of Washington football player Greg Carothers, "you really can't think about it. It's a risk that we take" (Kelley, 2001).

Suppressing this reality is part of the athlete's psychological bag of tricks, and prayer often plays a role. The realization that what they are about to do is dangerously irrational is why the cliff divers of Acapulco kneel at the shrine of the Virgin of Guadeloupe before diving into a narrow channel of water 150 feet below. The same fear drives football players, boxers, hockey players, bullfighters and rodeo bull riders to their knees before they enter arenas where they will push their bodies beyond reasonable limits, or expose themselves to spectacular collisions. Prayers in these cases are solicitations for protection from the harms that lie in wait for those who do unreasonable, even foolish things. There is a remarkable similarity between a player asking God to protect him or her before engaging in dangerous, even brutal sports and the man or woman who prays for protection before engaging in high risk sex. When a football player asks God to keep him safe before running onto the field where injuries are virtually guaranteed, he isn't all that unlike the person who pauses to beg God's protection from lung cancer before lighting up another cigarette.

Surely God, if He chooses to, can protect athletes, just as he could protect the person who elects to wrestle alligators or walk a tightrope stretched over a deep gorge. But the issue is whether or not it is appropriate to ask God to save one from the predictable results stemming from his or her own willful, dangerous actions. Are athletes about to submit their bodies to the violence of sports like football, boxing and hockey for the sake of money, fame or enjoyment justified in asking God to prevent what a reasonable person would conclude to be the logical result of their actions? Isn't asking God to keep you safe before getting in a race car and driving 200 miles per hour in rush hour traffic, or voluntarily participating in the body-crush of tackle football, an unbiblical testing of God, asking Him to prevent the playing out of the natural chain of cause and effect? Should Christians dare God to help them even when they don't help themselves? If the old adage is true that "God helps those who help themselves," does the inverse follow: "God doesn't help those who don't help themselves"?

Judging from the scourge of athletic injuries besetting sports like football, God, in His infinite wisdom, hasn't chosen to honor many of these prayers for safety. This hasn't stopped evangelicals from not only asking God for protection, but asking Him to heal their bodies after the predictable has occurred. My point here isn't to overlook the many injuries that occur in sports that can be truly defined as "accidents," nor am I diminishing the physical and psychological suffering athletes endure as a result of those injuries. At the same time, it's fair to ask if those who take unreasonable risks in order to meet the demands of brutal games, in some sense, waive their right to ask God to come to their aid after being injured.

The scene football fans witnessed several years ago of evangelical football star Mike Singletary praying over the crumpled body of quarterback Steve Pelluer, after Singletary had knocked him unconscious with a ferocious tackle, simply defies any satisfactory explanation, theological or otherwise. One wonders what religious scheme can make sense out of players joined in a circle asking God to save the life of Curtis Williams as he lay comatose on the football field at University of Washington after a helmet-to-helmet collision left him paralyzed and destined for an early death at age 24, or when players and coaches from the New York Jets and Detroit Lions paused to pray and cry for Reggie Brown's survival as he was given CPR, his head having been driven into his shoulders in a brutal collision with Jet's lineman Lamont Burns (Kee, 2001). Thankful that "God turned (his) head just right so that I wouldn't die" and no doubt equally thankful that spinal surgery kept him from paralysis, Brown would never again don a football uniform.

Only Sportianity can try to make theological sense out of this, although that hasn't kept those in the evangelical sports community from trying. Asked about Brown's injury, former Detroit quarterback Frank Reich and active worker in sports evangelism ministries told a reporter: "There's no doubt sports is violent. It requires warfare, but if you want to read about warfare, you can read all about it in the Bible (Kee, 2001: 9).

Such scenes are so breathtaking in their drama and so moving in the sympathy shown by players and coaches that the fundamental ethical point can easily be overlooked. Prayers looked upon as insurance policies are dubious at best, but even an insurance company won't offer loss protection unless the insured does his or her part by following safe practices. If it seems presumptuous for athletes to ask God to protect them before they engage in sports known to be injurious, it seems doubly presumptuous that, after injuries have been inflicted, for them to ask God to heal the injured party. And it seems triply presumptuous for them—before their prayers have drifted out of the stadium and the injured player having been carted from the field—to return to the same activity which led to the injury.

The wisdom of ethicist R.E.O. Smith may point the way to Christian athletes who play dangerous sports. Smith pointed out that prayer is always morally conditioned, something he considered an important safeguard against its misuse. A petitioner's prayers for forgiveness, for example, are conditioned by the supplicant also demonstrating a spirit of forgiveness, prayers for fruitfulness upon abiding in Christ. By the same token it might be asked if prayers for protection and recovery from injury be conditioned by the supplicants' having acted as wise stewards of their bodies, even if it might mean avoiding dangerous sports altogether (Smith, 1979).

## Praying to Win

When unheralded golfer Zach was interviewed following his surprising victory at the 2007 Masters, he touchingly gave Jesus "all the credit," tearfully mentioning that "Jesus was with me every step," a comment that gave rise to a few irreverent jokes on the Internet about the strict "no robes and sandals" policy at Augusta National. A few months later, after the glow of winning had dimmed, Johnson thought better of his remarks, declaring that he didn't really think "God cares how I do out there," adding, "I don't know if He has anything to do with golf" (Truss, 2007: 64). Whether Johnson's initial impulse to credit God for the win, or his more reflective conclusion that God doesn't care how he performs and may not even have "anything to do with golf," is the proper way for evangelical athletes to position winning in their theological *zeitgeist* has long been a source of debate. Does God control events of a game like he controls other events in the universe? Does he really determine who will win a game? Is it appropriate to pray for victory? For the Christian athlete, such questions are important because they arise with the advent of every game.

Many of those immersed in the subculture of sport find it unthinkable that God doesn't control events of a game, including picking the winner. If St. Louis Ram All-Pro receiver Isaac Bruce is to be believed, his team's victories were secured days before the game was played, "down on our knees praying for it." After catching the game-winning pass in the 2000 Super Bowl, he told the media: "That wasn't me. That was all God. . . . I had to make an adjustment on the ball, and God did the rest" (Plotz, 2000). (And "the rest" seemed to have included blinding referees to the fact that the Rams illegally had an extra man on the field during the play.)

And who can forget the confident prediction of former champion Evander Holyfield—outspoken Christian whose purple fight robe is embroidered with Philip 4:13 ("I can do all things through Christ who strengthens me.")—before his celebrated fight with Mike Tyson in 1997: "There is no way I cannot win. I believe in God, so I will surely beat Tyson" (Blank, 1997: 9). As it turned out, Holyfield won, perhaps because God helped him, but as far as the judges were concerned it was because Tyson, in a not very prayerful mood, bit a large chunk out of Holyfield's ear and was disqualified.

Over and against such sentiment are the opinions of an increasing number of Christian athletes—though probably still a minority—who are aware that glib references to God's involvement in games can come off as theologically naïve. They go out of their way to set reporters straight on the issue. Former New York Yankee player Chad Curtis, for example, told reporters that the devotional meetings among team members is not to try to get favor from God on the field: "I mean God doesn't care how many wins I have. That's not a concern of his. What matters is that I'm being a good servant to him; and I'm helping other people" (Plotz, 2000). Even some sports evangelists see it this way. "I think God could care less who wins or loses," remarked James Mitchell, former Tennessee Titans chaplain and national director of outreach for Pro Athletes Outreach. "God may intervene at times when it truly matters—when Hitler threatens to conquer the world—but He doesn't concern Himself with boys' games" (Plotz, 2000).

The question hasn't figured prominently in the agendas of theologians, even those known to take more than an occasional interest in sports. A few years ago a *Sports Illustrated* article asked several theologians if "God cares who wins the Super Bowl." Evangelical scholar Richard Mouw offered that he doesn't believe that God is aloof from it all, and that He cares about how people play the game, but he cautioned against "identifying God with any partisan cause." "God isn't a Michigan or Notre Dame fan," said Mouw (Nack,1998: 46). But for many in the sports subculture it is but a short step from believing that God is present in the arena to believing that he will honor requests to have them turn out in a particular team's favor. For this reason many athletes and coaches pray unabashedly for victory. Super Bowl winning coach Tony Dungy, for example, told a reporter: "I pray I will give every effort and when I've done that, I don't see anything wrong with praying for victory (Nack: 46).

Others, like Joseph C. Hough, president of the faculty at Union Theological Seminary, view the issue differently. Hough calls prayers for victory "religiously offensive" and "anti-Christian at [their] core (Nack: 47). Such prayers "make God look immoral and arbitrary," he says. An even harsher judgment is rendered by Christopher Evans and William Herzog, authors of *Faith of Fifty Million*. Believing that God grants divine favor to a specific individual or team, they wrote, is not only "non-sensical, but a form of the worst marriage between pseudo-faith and self-centeredness" (Evans & Herzog, 2002: 218).

Theological opinions notwithstanding, it is extraordinarily difficult for athletes, whose training, sacrifice, planning and practice are all directed at winning, to imagine that God, somehow or in some way, doesn't share their concern about the outcome. Despite familiar evangelical platitudes about the "most important thing is to play to the best of my ability" or to "glorify God with my effort," winning remains the object of every athlete's training, practice and sacrifice. Winning and the desire to win shape the athlete's worldview. In the Darwinian world of competitive athletics, scoreboards don't display "percentage of effort"; players aren't elected to all-star teams because they "gave 110%" or because "they glorified God." Being a perennial loser won't get you a scholarship, a trophy or invited to the church supper to give a talk. It won't get you on the cover of *Sports Illustrated*; in fact, it won't even get you on the hero-graced covers of *Sports Spectrum*, or *Sharing the Victory*, evangelical magazines whose writers adamantly, though ironically it would seem, emphasize that Christian athletes don't place a premium on winning. Suggesting to the dedicated athlete that God isn't interested in the outcome of a sport contest is tantamount to saying that He isn't interested in the full fruition of the athlete's sacrifice, training, and practice. If so, we might wonder if he is equally uninterested in the fruition of the teacher's, the businessman's, the plumber's, the author's labors. And then there is this: if sports are "boy's games," as Chaplain Mitchell suggested, how is it possible for evangelical athletes to glorify Him with their talents, a belief deeply ingrained in the evangelical sports culture, through participation in something in which He has no interest?

Sorting out answers to these questions requires theological competence well beyond that of the author, but a few observations here may help frame the issue. As a matter of first importance I would remind that sports, as already described, are derivatives of play and, as such, are part of an illusory experience. The illusion sustains the integrity of the game, yet praying for victory seems to intrude upon it, destroying its charm and threatening to rob it of it of adventure and uncertainty. "How will the game turn out, how will it unfold; what role will I play in the game?" are the questions that spark the adventure. Praying for victory reflects an unhealthy impatience with the gifts that sport has to offer; it attempts to shortcut the adventure, much like reading the end of a novel before reading its beginning. Such prayers of course are not always answered, so some sense of adventure remains, but it is the spirit behind such prayers that counts, an unwillingness to take the best of what the game offers. In this limited respect, praying to win a game isn't a great deal different from praying that the heroine be saved in the last pages of the novel, or that a movie ends with justice being served up to the good guys. Honors, not its conclusion.

Religion Professor Joseph Price has suggested that connecting athletic success to divine favor may represent a reintegration of athletic and religious rituals (like prayers), a "restoration of metaphysical and mystical impulses that generated or characterized early forms of play and expressions of piety" (Price, 2009: 70). I would the first to applaud that idea, but I am not convinced that connecting athletic success to divine favor will do this, nor am I convinced that the type of sports that fill our arenas and stadiums of the land nurture the play spirit that Price's vision rests upon. Over 70 years ago Huizinga lamented the demise of the play spirit, a development he labeled *puerilism*—a blend of "adolescence and barbarity" which (among other things) manifests itself in "the insatiable thirst for trivial recreation and crude sensationalism" (Huizinga, 1955: 205). Authentic play is a perfect place for authentic prayer; it can inspire, nurture and guide it. But as history has shown, puerilistic play has a way of evoking puerilistic prayer.

Second, prayers for victory inevitably come to be interpreted within the context of the competitive worldview of athletes, coaches and fans. Like most prayers, they reflect "the implied or implicit theology of those that offer them" as well as a "vision of God" and that typically is of a muscular Christ who plays favorites. In the hyped-up partisanship of modern sports, prayers offered by one team invariably come off as partisan appeals to a partisan God, set off against competing prayers by its opponents. This begs the adolescent image of God as a fan with loyalties to both teams caught in the middle, agonizing over which set of prayers he will honor. Even uneducated Beau Jack, lightweight boxing champion of the 40s, understood the futility of this. Asked if he ever prayed to win, he answered: "I pray nobody get hurt." "Don't you ever pray to win," asked the interviewer? "No," he said, "I would never do that. Suppose I pray to win. The other boy, he pray to win, too. Then what God gonna do?" (Smith,1979).

This elementary conception of a God torn between team loyalties dangerously anthropomorphizes Him by reducing Him to a "Superfan" whose interests in the event, like those of spectators, are wrapped up only in its conclusions. It overlooks the possibility that God may not buy into the antagonisms that frame our play, that His interests might center on the experience of playing rather than its conclusion, that he is more interested in sport as a way of *being* than a way of *doing,* or that his entire conception of sport and play may be foreign to that prescribed by the NCAA rulebook or ESPN. Our fascination with winning is a self-inflicted pestilence; God surely is present at our games, but how they end may not even be a blip on His celestial radar screen.

The uncomfortable but rarely talked about reality of victory prayers is that they are backdoor requests for your opponents' defeat. Sport competition is zero-sum in nature; it is impossible to pray for your own victory without implicitly petitioning for your opponent's defeat, a request difficult to imagine being honored in the reality of war, much less in the illusory world of sports. Even where stakes to the winners are low, winning brings with it an elevated reputation, a boost to self-esteem, and a sense of having proved oneself. Asking God to bless you with these socially derived fruits of victory while he inflicts discouragement and disappointment on others makes sense only in the minds of those whose worldviews have been contorted by incessant competition.

Some athletes and coaches prefer going through the proverbial front rather than backdoor, asking God directly to hamper the efforts of their opponents. During the 1991 Super Bowl, for example, a group of New York Giants knelt on the sidelines while their opponents prepared to kick what turned out to be the game winning field goal. They later admitted that they had been praying for kicker Scott Norwood to miss it, just as University of Oregon coach Mike Belotti acknowledged praying for UCLA's kicker Chris Griffith to miss a 50-yard field goal as time expired (Griffith's kick was short and wide right). Viewed from this angle, praying to win seems an insufferably selfish act, only a shade removed from praying to be the prettiest, the richest or, like Janis Joplin, asking the Lord to buy you a new Mercedes-Benz. If such prayers aren't answered, it is because they are unanswerable (Nolan, 1998; Rosenblatt, 2001).

The idea that God would grant the wishes of athletes with an aching need to be recognized, who prefer it be them rather than their opponents who are objects of adoration, won't sit well with evangelicals mindful of the cross believers are called to bear. But to those washed in the tidal wave of the prosperity gospel, victory prayers make a great deal of sense, and the prosperity gospel thrives in the world of sports. Bruce Wilkinson's enormously popular book *The Prayer of Jabez,* an extrapolation of a few words uttered by a minor biblical character, didn't sell over nine million copies—mostly to evangelicals—by reminding readers of the arduous struggle of the Christian life or elaborating on the unending list of prayer requests God, in his divine wisdom, has chosen not to grant. "If Jabez had worked on Wall Street," writes Wilkinson, "he might have prayed, 'Lord, increase the value of my investment portfolios' " (Wilkinson, 2001: 24). On the athletic field the prosperity gospel urges athletes to pray for touchdowns. It is the theological opinion of former San Francisco 49er Darnell Walker that "it's never His will for us to lose. He wants us all to prosper" (Nack: 49).

Without doubting God's Old Testament promises or New Testament verses promising believers that what they pray for in faith they shall receive (Mark 11:24), one can question whether God is likely to align Himself with such sublimated selfishness. Such a naïve faith in the power of prayer, says Judith Shulevitz, "grants the supplicant full access to the American cult of success, an adoration of power and material satisfaction untroubled by any sense that the world may be a tragic place or the fear that the enlargement of one's territory might leave others diminished" (Shulevitz, 2001). Every deathbed, every war, every famine and plague and especially Christ's unanswered pleas in Gethsemane are reminders that prayer isn't the infallible gimmick so often celebrated by "name it and claim it" prosperity gospel proponents. Evangelical theologian Carl Henry called prayer "the great school of selflessness" that "militates against selfish motives" and few things seem quite as selfish as praying for victory to assuage a thirst for recognition (Henry, 1957: 577). Evans and Herzog view such prayers in even more dubious terms: "The very fact that so many contemporary athletes see God's hand as the primary reason why they hit a home run, or make an impossible catch, goes to show that Augustine and other theologians were right to suggest that the essence of our 'fallen nature' is personal selfishness:

perhaps the pattern of athletes invoking the Deity every time they win is just another illustration of original sin" (Evans & Herzog: 218).

The Lord's Prayer—the most common locker room invocation—has been called "relentlessly plural" (Smith, 1979: 69). By reinforcing community and solidarity of life through such plural phrases such as 'our daily bread,' 'our debts' and 'our debtors,' it guards against selfish motives. There is no room in the prayer for special favors or for furthering personal agendas. It is a prayer intended to meet the needs not simply of the petitioner but of everyone. For the athlete this means not only teammates but opponents as well, but the athletes' prayers for their opponents, hedged by the agonistic structure of sports, can be only so generous, only so other-minded. They may truly want the best for them and may pray, as many do, that they will come out the game uninjured or even that they may play well, but it is extraordinarily difficult for an athlete to ask the Lord to make one's opponents the winners, even when such prayers seem enjoined by one's faith.

As noted in our discussion of prayers for safety, logic dictates a certain concert between the supplicant's prayers and his or her behaviors. It would seem hopelessly cynical for one to pray that "Event A" will occur, all the while working one's hardest to bring about "Event B." If on one hand athletes were to ask God to give victory to their opponents, the logical consequence would seem to be that he or she would not try to win, thus committing the sin of deception and violating the near sacred oath of the athlete to do his or her best. Athletes, after all, who don't try to win are the most detested athletes, one reason why "throwing a game" is such a difficult sin to forgive. If, on the other hand, athletes were to respect the sacred athletic code and try their best to win, their prayers would seem to be a mockery. But there is no disjunction between asking God to allow the joys of victory to be enjoyed by one's opponents and, at the same time, insuring that one's efforts are in the *direction of winning*—that is, aimed at the goal of winning. Unless each team gives their best effort to secure victory there is no enjoyment in playing, and there is no joy for the team that ultimately wins. The commitment to playing as hard as one can is to insure that there is a good game; it is not necessarily connected to securing the victory for oneself. That humans might have trouble making this critical distinction shouldn't surprise us. Perhaps the more important point is this: there would seem to be no grounds on which Christians could presume to involve themselves in a leisure pursuit which makes it self-contradictory to ask that his favor fall on others.

## PRAYER AS MAGIC AND SUPERSTITION

Finally, a brief word must be said about prayer and superstition, two rituals so intertwined in big-time sports that it often is difficult to disentangle them. Imploring help from "the other side" is as old as sport itself. Although athletes, coaches and fans might dismiss them as quaint and even silly, magic and superstition infest big-time sports. When Clemson alum "Pitchfork" Ben Tillman was governor of South Carolina (1893), he was said to have placed a curse on the University of South Carolina that has been blamed for a long list of athletic disappointments at USC. In 1992 some USC fans took matters into their own hands by hiring a witch doctor to perform rituals designed to remove the curse. The New Orleans Saints had long labored under a curse thought to have been placed on their home field (the Superdome) because it was erected on an ancient burial ground. Before a critical 2000 playoff game against St. Louis, the team hired a Yoruba priestess who, along with her associate "Voodoo Macumba," incense, and a serpent, performed a cleansing ritual at the 50-yard line beseeching the spirits to "rid the dome of all curses." The Saints won their first playoff game in 34 years (Kennedy et al., 2002). And sportswriters still puzzle over golfer Sergio Garcia's thinly veiled reference to sinister forces conspiring against him when he lost the playoff in the 2007 British Open: "I'm playing against a lot of guys out there," he said, "more than the field (meaning his fellow competitors; Hack, 2007: C15).

Tales of players' superstitions are legion, ranging from their refusal to change their socks or shirts or underwear or shave when they are on a winning streak, to eating the same meal before each game, traveling the same route each day to the stadium or parking in the same spot. Baseball players may be the most superstitious of all. Most, for example, refuse to step on the first and third base foul lines when taking the field. Mentioning that a pitcher has a no-hitter going is strictly taboo. Hall of Fame third baseman Wade Boggs always traced the Hebrew symbol *chai* in the dirt at the plate before he batted, just as he religiously ate chicken before every game. Basketball players often try to be the last to shoot the ball during pregame warm-up or to make sure that their last warm-up shot before leaving the court goes in the basket. Some hockey players believe that crossing their stick with a teammate's during pregame warm-up or looking at the red goal light when referees test it is bad luck. Famed race car driver Mario Andretti would never sign an autograph in green ink (McCallum, 1988).

According to British anthropologist Sir James George Frazier, who, quite literally, wrote the book on the subject, magical practices are based in a mechanical conception of the universe in which human acts dictate the course of the universe, a line of thinking miles apart from the evangelical conception of a God who controls the order of nature. Christian prayers propitiate a supernatural, conscious, personal agent while magic takes for granted that the course of nature is determined by the operation of immutable natural laws. Magic may or may not—Frazier said it was rare—include a belief in a supernatural power (Frazer, 1922).

Anthropologist Bronislaw Malinowski described magic as a practical art consisting of acts (such as locker room and on-field rituals) which are viewed entirely as a means to well-defined ends that are expected to follow later on (winning). Magic, said Malinowski, is simple, trite and predictable, while religion is complex, serious and more uncertain (Malinowski, 1954: 31). Unlike magic, which is always a means for bringing about some subsequent end, prayer and religious ritual may not be a means but an end in itself. Practitioners of magic manipulate forces entirely for self-serving ends; in contrast, prayers may be prayers of praise and thanksgiving that spring from adoration and godly fear. Malinowski and Frazier might have short-changed the reach of Christian prayer a bit but they did capture one important difference. Prayers that are crassly manipulative and self-serving, performed mechanically in a routine fashion with a specific end in view, risk crossing the barrier from religion to magic.

Although evangelicals as a group shun magic, paranormal beliefs, UFO's, astrology, communication with the dead and other forms of psychic activity, evangelical athletes flirt, often unwittingly, with the boundaries of magic and superstition. Painting crosses on their shoes, carving scripture references into their equipment, or performing pregame rituals are very magic-like acts, even though difficult to reconcile with a Christian conception of the universe. When evangelical quarterback Kurt Warner brought his St. Louis Rams back to the Superdome following the Saints' voodoo priestess incantations, he was reported to have stopped in the tunnel to read scripture his pastor had given him and to pray with his teammates as a way of counteracting the spell she was thought to have cast (Kennedy et al., 2002).

Straight-laced former UCLA coach John Wooden would seem to be the least likely person to practice superstitious rituals, yet during his legendary career he was said to have made it a practice to walk around campus looking for hairpins which he always stuck in a special tree. Whether he recognized it or not, the ritual dated back to the days of witchcraft when witches were thought to use bits of metal to cast spells. "See a pin and pick it up/All the day you'll have good luck" is an ancient rhyme. Some athletes seem to believe that incorporating prayers or religious references into such rituals rids them of their magical undertones, but it is more likely that prayers themselves will become magical. On balance there is little difference between the United States Olympic Softball Team—after experiencing a three-game losing streak in the 2000 Olympics—throwing their bats and equipment in the shower to rid them of an alleged "voodoo curse" and the NFL player who tapes his wrists exactly the same way and writes "Jesus" on it, or another who wears his "Jesus bracelet" because "it protects me, I think," or another who writes "LENTIL" on his wrist tape as a reminder of an Old Testament account of a warrior sent to protect a lentil bean field who slew more than 100 men by himself, and the major league baseball player who, unable to make the pregame chapel, sent his bats along nevertheless (Kennedy & Schecter, 2005; Tom, 1990).

When prayer is woven into superstitious pregame routines, when they must be said in a certain way, in certain orders, or in combination with other rituals, they verge on the kind of "vain repetition" and mechanical prayer that evangelical theologian John Stott labeled hypocrisy and a sin and ethicist R.E.O. Smith labeled as "unanswerable" (R.E.O. Smith: 69; Stott, 1978: 145). One of Marbeto's interviewees told him: "I never play my best if I haven't recited the Lord's Prayer first," a difference in kind perhaps from the athlete who must always lace his shoes the same way before each game, but arguably, not so different in intent. The evangelical NFL player who inserts prayer into his game-day routine of first having prayer with his wife then driving to the stadium, drinking one cup of coffee, eating three pieces of French toast, then some pasta with sauce and then Bible study—in that order—blurs the edges between prayer and superstition, in spite of claims that "it's more routine than superstition." When an athlete prays because she fears what might happen if she doesn't, her prayers become manipulative, done not so much to express her interior relation to God, but to coerce the future turn of events, again, not unlike the practitioner of magic (Winkeljohn, 2001).

Likewise, when an NFL kicker says he pauses before each kick to recite Philippians 4:13 ("I can do all things through Christ who strengthens me"), it is difficult not to view it as what Malinowski called an effort "to master the elements of chance and luck" (Malinowski, 31). If they aren't magic, prayers said only for the prospect of personal reward, without gratitude for goodness, grace, forgiveness or the plight of others on the opposing side, certainly seem to move in that direction. Athletic prayers lacking the safeguards of orthodoxy are easily shaped by the vanities of the sports culture, becoming nearly indistinguishable from those of Ajax, Jabez or the Yoruba priestess.

In the final analysis the opinion one holds regarding prayers offered in the locker rooms and arenas across the land will hinge largely on his or her impression of how big-time sports fit into the larger Christian worldview. Those counseled by chaplains who tell them to pray in the locker room like it's all up to God, but to play the game like it's all up to them, will find it difficult to navigate these two fundamentally different worlds. Those who believe that the imperfections in big-time sports are merely minor sins of overemphasis that are more than compensated for by the enjoyment they bring will be less bothered by prayers in the arena than will those who believe big-time sports rehearse us in ways that are antithetical to the Christian creed. Those whose concerns run in the latter direction will continue to regard insertion of prayer into big-time sports as a ticklish affair at best.

Having said this, I would venture one unqualified role for prayer in sports, although not one likely to figure prominently in the locker rooms and arenas of our day. It is characteristic of evangelicals, says Richard Lovelace, to pray about their own vocational world, about their own responsibilities, and the conversion of their coworkers but rarely about "the moral shape of the corporation they work for" (Lovelace, 1979: 393).

Unlike the leaders of the Second Awakening who prayed fervently for cultural and social renewal, American evangelicals organize prayer primarily around their needs and evangelistic ventures. Lovelace could have been talking about evangelicals in sport where prayers almost always are self-referential, thematically shaped to help athletes conform to the dynamics of a morally suspect social institution. In years of studying sport and religion I have yet to hear an athlete or coach pray for the redemption of the NFL, the NCAA or the Premier League. My suggestion is this: evangelical athletes and coaches who insist on praying should make it a practice of including in every pregame or postgame or on-field prayer a petition for the redemption and restoration of sport to its divinely created design. But having uttered such prayers, some might find it difficult to walk out into the arena.

## NOTES

1. This chapter is adapted from: Shirl James Hoffman, *Good Game: Christianity and the Culture of Sport*, Baylor University Press, 2010.

## BIBLIOGRAPHY


Amid Sex Scandals, One Aussie Football Team Turns to God (2004) *Agence France Presse*, March 17.

Bentz, R. (2000) Survival of the Fittest, *Sports Spectrum on Line*, retrieved June, 20, 2000, from http://www.sportsspectrum.com.

Bissinger, H.G. (1992) *Friday Night Lights*, Reading, MA: Addison Wesley.

Blank, J. (1997) *U.S. New and World Report*, The Greater Struggle, 122(25): 9.

Bonhoffer, D. (1978) *The Cost of Discipleship*, New York: Macmillan.

Boswell, T. (1978) Reggie's Fate: Bluster Takes Luster off Work at Plate, *Washington Post*, October 6, E1.

Conroy, P. (1987) *The Great Santini*, New York: Bantam Books.

Czech, D.R., Wrisberg, C.A., et al. (2004) The Experience of Christian Prayer in Sport: An Existential Phenomenological Investigation, *Journal of Psychology and Christianity*, 23(1): 3.

Earnhardt, Dale, Jr. (2005) In His Own Words, *The Roanoke Times* (April 10) (Martinsville Speedway Race Insert, p. 4).

Douglass, R.B. (1991) Keep Your Prayers to Yourself?, *Commonweal*, June 14, 395.

Eisner, K. (1905) *Feste de Festlosen* Dresden: Kaden (p. 9) [quoted in Pieper, 62].

Evans, C.H., & Herzog, W.R. (2002) *The Faith of Fifty Million*, Louisville, KY: Westminster John Knox Press.

Excerpts from Supreme Court opinions on prayer (2000) *New York Times*, June 20, A22, retrieved October 22, 2008, from F82FF7F796DB61&d_place=CTRB&f_subsection=sSPORTS&f_issue=1990–09–27&f_publisher=

Fink, E. (1979) The Ontology of Play, in E.W. Gerber and W.J. Morgan (Eds.), *Sport and the Body: A Philosophical Symposium* (2nd ed.), Philadelphia: Lea & Febiger.

Firestone, D. (2000) South's Football Fans Stand Up and Pray, *New York Times*, August 27, 1.

*Football and Religion* (2004) NFL Films, Show 18, Tape ID 137444, retrieved from http://www.nflfilms.com/specialorders/spcat_presents.html
Frazer, J.G. (1922) *The Golden Bough*, New York: Colliers Books (Macmillan).
Gent, P. (1973) *North Dallas Forty*, New York: William Morrow & Company.
Giammati, B. (1989) *Take Time for Paradise*, New York: Summit Books.
Hack, D. (2007) Garcia Bemoans Bounces That Didn't Go His Way, *New York Times*, July 25, C15.
Hallesby, O. (1994/1931) *Prayer*, Minneapolis: Augsburg Publishing House.
Henry, C.F.H. (1957) *Christian Personal Ethics*, Grand Rapids, MI: Baker.
Hiskey, M. (2003, December 15) Issue of Religion and Sports Hits Home for Georgia School, *Spartburg (S.C.) Herald-Journal*, B1–6.
Hoffman, S.J. (1985) Evangelicalism and the Revival of Religious Ritual in Sport, *Arete: The Journal of Sports Literature*, II:2, Spring, 61–87.
Huizinga, J. (1955) *Homo Ludens: A Study of the Play Element in Culture*, Boston: Beacon.
Isaacson, M. (2002) Religion Looms as Part of Ram's Team Spirit, *Chicago Tribune*, February 2, B5.
Kee, L. (1998) Lions and Christians, *The Nation*, August 10/17, 37–38.
Kelley, S. (1997) Keep God Out of the Big Leagues, *US Catholic* 62(4): 26.
Kelley, S. (2001, November 4) One year later, one bad hit later, teams had vision of Williams agaian, *Seattle Times*, C–1.
Kellner, M.A. (1999) God on the Gridiron, *Christianity Today*, 43(13): 76.
Kennedy, K., and Schecter, B.J. (2005) Doing It My Way, *Sports Illustrated*, 103(2): 2.
Kennedy, K., King, P., White, R., Deitsch, R., and Kim, A. (2002) Curses! *Sports Illustrated*, 96(21): 21.
Kindred, D. (2006, February 10) A different breed, praying for the same result, *The Sporting News*, p. 26.
King, K. (2002) Winning Ugly, *Sports Illustrated*, 97(21): 97.
Kreider, A. (2003) Prayers for Assistance as Unsporting Behaviour, *Journal of the Philosophy of Sport*, 30, 17–25
Landry, T. (1990) *Tom Landry: An Autobiography*, Grand Rapids, MI: Zondervan.
Levitt, A. (1972) *Somebody Called Doc*, Carol Stream: IL: Creation House.
Lovelace, R.F. (1979) *Dynamics of Spiritual Life: An Evangelical Theology of Renewal*. Downers Grove, IL: InterVarsity Press.
Malinowski, B. (1954) *Magic, Science and Religion*. New York: Anchor Books Doubleday.
Marbeto, J.A. (1967) *The Incidence of Prayer in Athletics as Indicated by Selected California Collegiate Athletes and Coaches*, master's thesis, University of California, Santa Barbara.
McCallum, J. (1988) Green Cars, Black Cats and Lady Luck, *Sports Illustrated*, February 8, 88–93.
Michener, J. (1976) *Sports in America*, New York: Random House.
Montville, L. (1989) Thou Shalt Not Lose, *Sports Illustrated*, November 13, 87.
Morgan, W.J. (2006) *Why Sports Morally Matter*, New York: Routledge.
Mouw, R. (2007) *Praying at Burger King*, Grand Rapids, IL: Eerdmans.
Nack, W. (1998) Does God Care Who Wins the Super Bowl? *Sports Illustrated*, January 26, 46.
NCAA Clarifies Prayer Stance (1995) *Charleston Daily Mail*, September 2, 2B.
No Comment Department (1993) *Christian Century*, January 27, 76.
Nolan, B. (1998) Mass Raises Questions of Ethics, *The Times-Picayune*, January 10, B-4.
Orozco, R. (2007), Prayer a Pre-Race Ritual for Some Race Car Drivers, *Star News* (Wilmington, NC), August 4.
Otto, R. (1923) *The Idea of the Holy*, Oxford, England, Oxford University Press.

Pieper, J. (1963) *In Tune with the World: A Theory of Festivity*, New York: Harcourt, Brace & World.

Plotz, D. (2000) The God of the Gridiron: Does He Care Who Wins the Super Bowl? *Slate*, retrieved January 30, 2007, from http://www.slate.com/id/74294/

Price, J.L. (2009) Playing and Praying, Sport and Spirit: The Forms and Functions of Prayer in Sports, *International Journal of Religion and Sport*, 1(1): 55–80.

Reed, D. (1995) Falwell Seeks to Block NCAA No-Gloating Rule, *The Patriot News*, Harrisburg, PA, September 1, A8.

Rosenblatt, R. (2001) Highs and Lows from Saturday's Games, *Associated Press*, November 11.

Rowe, J. (1996) You Guys Are so On! Cats in Hats, *Greensboro News and Record*, November 23, D3.

Schmitz, K. (1979) Sport and Play: Suspension of the Ordinary in *Sport and the Body: A Philosophical Symposium* (2nd ed.), E.W. Gerber and W.J. Morgan (Eds.), Philadelphia: Lea & Febiger, 22–29.

Sheehy, D. (2000) FCA, retrieved July 25, 2000, from http://www.fca.org/

Sherman, E. (1990) Holt's Logic on God's Role More Holey Than Holy, *Chicago Tribune*, retrieved September 27, 2002, from http://libproxy.uncg.edu:2524/iw-search/we/InfoWeb?p_product=NewsBank&p_theme=aggregated5&p_action=doc&p_docid=0F Shulevitz, J. (2001) The Close Reader, retrieved May 20, 2007, from http://www.nytimes.com/books/01/05/20/bookend/bookend.html

Shulman, R. (2007) Case Tests Boundaries of Prayer in Sports, *Washington Post*, October 7, A14.

Smith, R. (1979) They Heard the Cheers, *New York Times*, August 26, S3.

Smith, C. (1997) God Is an .800 Hitter, *New York Times*, July 27, SM26.

Smith, R.E.O. (1979) *Biblical Ethics*, Atlanta: John Knox Press.

Soccer: Steaua Paymaster Calls Religious Tune (2007) *International Herald Tribune*, June 7, 8.

Stone, B. (2007) *Evangelism after Christendom*,Grand Rapids, IL: Brazos Press.

Stott, J.R.W. (1978) *Christian Counter-Culture*, Downers Grove, IL: InterVarsity, 142–152.

Tom, D. (1990) Superstition Bowl, *USA Today*, January 18, D-1.

Truss, L. (2007) Have Faith in the Power of Prayer (and a Good Putter), *The Times (London)*, July 18, 64.

Walker, K. (1997) Feel the Real Power, *Today's Christian*, November/December, retrieved August 22, 2002 from http://www.christianitytoday.com/tc/7r6/7r6015.html

Watson, N.J., and Nesti, M. (2005) The Role of Spirituality in Sport Psychology Consulting: An Analysis and Integrative Review of Literature, *Journal of Applied Sport Psychology*, 17: 228–229.

Wayne Alderson, Oilers Huddle with God for Extra Point (1978) *Pittsburgh Post Gazette*, Dec 1, 2.

Wilkinson, B. (2000) *Prayer of Jabez: Breaking through to the Blessed Life*, Sisters, OR, USA: Multnomah Publishers.

Winkeljohn, M. (2001) Pro football: Serious Routine: Falcons Players Prepare in Different Ways as They Seek the Edge of Mayhem on Sunday, *The Atlanta Constitution*, December 7, 15F.

Yancey, P. (2006) *Prayer: Does It Make Any Difference*? Grand Rapids, MI: Zondervan.

You guys Are so On!: Cats in Hats (1996) *News and Record*, Greensboro, NC, November 23, D3.

# 3 Better Than Normal?

## Constructing Modified Athletes and a Relational Theological Ethic[1]

*Tracy J. Trothen*

Athletes have long pursued enhancement of their abilities. As genetic and machine technologies become increasingly available, many wishing to be stronger or faster will seek out these means of enhancement.

An adequate ethical analysis of the use of genetic modification technologies in sport must go beyond issues of cheating or safety and address larger questions, including what it means to be relational humans and what about our humanness makes sport a persistent sociocultural force. Sport, as a significant and persistent cultural expression, manifests many socially dominant assumptions about what is most desirable and admirable about being human. Intertwined with these questions are foundational epistemological issues. In particular, the moral relevance of dualistic thinking, essentialism and the often uncritical acceptance of dominant cultural values must be examined. In this chapter, I will contribute to that task from a relational theological perspective, acknowledging that this is but a moment in this widening moral discourse.

I argue for the moral complexity and ambiguity of the issue and conclude that although there are persuasive moral goods, in most cases the potential harms outweigh the potential benefits of the use of emergent genetic modification technologies for athletic performance. Further, when approached through a relational ethic, redemption is often located in those very things that are avoided in the human condition. Most important is the way in which the issue is defined; this dictates the shape of the ensuing moral discourse and thus is a powerful political act.

I will begin with an introduction to some of the emerging genetic technologies and related science that either will influence or are already influencing athletes and sport. Next I critique how the issue has been defined and posit an alternative approach based on a relational theological ethic. Finally, I will begin to apply a relational theological ethic to sport and genetic technologies.

### EMERGING GENETIC TECHNOLOGIES AND SCIENCE

Scientists involved in the internationally funded Human Genome Project completed the mapping of genes of human DNA in 2003. This mapping provides the foundation for diagnostic testing and medical interventions. Although progress in these two areas has been limited, effective gene therapies are anticipated.[2] This science is relevant to everyone as we "are all carrying . . . forty to fifty faulty genes" that may or may not manifest as a disease (Collins, 2002: 5). It is expected that the knowledge afforded by the mapping of the human genome eventually will yield answers to many diseases; there is much debate regarding how long this will take.

Further, other scientific progress will add to genetic technologies. Recently, scientists announced they have discovered how to reprogram "somatic cells to pluripotency, thereby creating induced pluripotent stem (iPS) cells" (*Nature*, 2009). This breakthrough paves the way to regenerative medicine; a goal is to "grow" replacement organs and tissue from existing cells in one's body, thus avoiding autoimmune problems as well as the shortage of organ donors.

In preparation for the upcoming 2012 Olympic Games, England's House of Commons, Science and Technology Committee on Human Enhancement Technologies in Sport produced a report in which it is stated, "Gene doping, or the modulation of an athlete's genetic material or its expression to improve performance, is . . . thought of as a potential threat to the London 2012 Olympics. . . . there have already been reports of use of gene therapy in this fashion" (House of Commons, 2007: 40; McCrory, 2003: 193).

There are different categories of gene transfer technologies that either will or already do affect sport, including somatic cell modification, germ line cell technologies and genetic profiling. The greatest ethical objection to germ line interventions, aside from immediate physical harms, is that autonomy is superseded as such interventions will be passed on generation to generation (Anderson, 1999: 584; Chapman 2001: 74–76; Cole 1998: 63). Somatic cell technologies target a particular set of cells and only the individual treated. However, the distinction between somatic cell and germ line interventions is not so clear: it is possible somatic cell interventions can affect germ line cells (McCrory, 2003: 192; Sweeney, 2004; Unal & Unal, 2004: 358).

Somatic cell genetic modification technologies that are of potential use by athletes have been tested primarily on animals thus far. The preferred method of delivery is an ordinary adenovirus such as the virus for the common cold; the cold-causing genes within the virus are removed and replaced with the synthetic genes that direct the body to produce the desired proteins. The newly configured vector is then injected into the animal or human body (Eassom, 2001).

Perhaps the most enticing emergent genetic technology for athletes is Repoxygen—"the tradename for a type of gene therapy which induces controlled release of EPO in response to low oxygen concentration in mice" (House of Commons, 2007: 40). This genetic modification of the erythropoietin (EPO) receptor has been a technology pursued primarily for the medical treatment of diseases such as anemia resulting from chronic renal failure. Exogenous EPO has been available legally since 1989 for this purpose, and has been used illegally by some athletes, notably in the 1998 Tour de France (Gaudard, Varlet, Bressolle et al., 2003: 187–212; McCrory, 2003: 192). The EPO receptor provides feedback control of red blood cells' oxygen-carrying capacity. The ability to genetically modify the EPO receptor could significantly increase athletes' endurance abilities (Zhou, Murphy, Escobedo et al., 1998, cited in Unal & Unal, 2004: 359).

Although still in preclinical development, Repoxygen is suspected as a banned substance used by some elite athletes. Thus far, it is only detectable through muscle biopsy which is too invasive an approach to be viable for testing purposes. However, samples from elite athletes are stored for as long as eight years during which time they can be retested as other methods of detection are created. This practice is communicated to athletes as a deterrent (Associated Press, 2008).

Being developed for degenerative muscle diseases such as muscular dystrophy, insulin-like growth factor 1 (IGF-1) could be used by athletes to increase muscle bulk and repair muscle damage, increasing recovery time (Swift & Yaeger, 2001: 86; Unal & Unal, 2004: 357, 359). In 1998, scientist H. Lee Sweeney found that IGF-1 gene therapy increased muscle bulk in sedentary mice by 15 to 30% (Sweeney, 2004). In a later study, Sweeney found that rats could increase their strength further through weight training (Brownlee, 2004). Sweeney also reports that Rosenthal's follow-up study, using the same gene therapy, found that the mice had an increased muscle bulk of 20 to 50%. Additionally, the mice "retained a regenerative capacity typical of younger animals," indicating the possibility of not losing muscle mass due to aging (Sweeney, 2004). Sweeney has received several requests from athletes interested in IGF-1 (Brownlee, 2004: 280).

The remaining most oft cited example of emerging somatic cell genetic technologies attractive to athletes is vascular endothelial growth factor (VEGF), which could increase the development of blood vessels, thus increasing blood flow to muscles and organs, which would delay exhaustion (House of Commons, 2007: 81; Unal & Unal, 2004: 357, 359).

Genetic profiling is another technology relevant to elite sport. Children could be genetically mapped and assessed for possible excellence in sport. Further, genetic predisposition to sports injuries or other vulnerabilities could be assessed (for example, see House of Commons, 2007: 82). Genetic profiling could end dreams of being or not being a top-caliber athlete, if one takes a genetic determinist view.[3]

This leads to a brief mention of genetic mutations or abnormal genetic coding that enhance athletic performances. The most well-known case is that of Finnish athlete Eero Mantyranla, who, in the 1964 Winter Olympics, won two gold medals in cross-country skiing. A rare mutation in the gene coding for his EPO receptor resulted in a 25–50% increase in the oxygen-carrying capacity of his red blood cells causing him to have superior endurance (Aschwanden, 2000: 24–29; McCrory, 2003: 192). More recently, one has only to consider the example of swimmer Michael Phelps. Phelps has several genetic advantages including: disproportionately long "wingspan"-to-height ratio; disproportionately large shoe size and hand size; a "greater-than-average lung capacity"; and "his muscles produce 50% less lactic acid than other athletes" (Dvorsky, 2008). Such discrepancies have always existed. What has changed is that we now have the ability to know who possesses these advantages; a natural level playing field has never existed.

## DEFINING THE ISSUE

However this issue is approached, usually the moral discourse is shaped by a desire to argue for or against the use of genetic transfer technologies by athletes. Often the respective arguments are at least partially informed by repugnance or, on the other side, excitement over the sheer possibility of knowing more. Neither cause is ethically sufficient. An awareness of one's biases or loyalties is important to the ethical task. As Christian ethicist Grace D. Cumming Long observes, passion without reason is "ineffective" and reason without passion is rudderless (Cumming-Long, 1993: 6).[4] Heart surgery, when it first was attempted in the middle of the 20th century, was perceived as tampering with the core of human life. Often fueled by the religious conviction that we were messing with what we ought not, it took time before heart surgery was eventually seen as 'normal.' Now we are messing with genes—that which is often now seen as the core of human life. As an issue is being defined, a critical understanding of context is morally relevant and can assist in widening one's perspective. Based on history, it is reasonable to expect that genetic technologies will not be regarded as shocking or repugnant in the future; in fact, as they become safe, many will be seen as part of normal medical care.

The International Olympic Committee's (IOC) 2003 list of banned substances and methods identified "gene doping" as a category, and it remains on the more recent list. The World Anti-Doping Agency (WADA), an IOC organization created in 1999, defines gene doping as "the non-therapeutic use of genes, genetic elements and/or cells that have the capacity to enhance athletic performance" (WADA, 2003; Swift & Yaeger, 2001).[5] WADA has held three Gene Doping Symposia to date—in 2002, 2005 and 2008. IOC and WADA are concerned with the "integrity of sport," which is understood largely to mean fair play, including abiding by the rules (e.g., not cheating) and the well-being of athletes (WADA, 2009). As relevant genetic technologies become medically safe, the criterion of fair play, if that concept assumes a 'level playing field,' is not sufficient to justify the banning of gene transfer technologies in sports.

As others have argued, the use of these technologies must be considered in context with other means of performance enhancement (Miah, 2005:

51). For example, vitamins, vaccinations, advanced training techniques, and cutting-edge equipment such as titanium tennis racquets, and fastskin swimsuits all enhance athletic performance and usually raise the dominant perception of what is normal. Even the criterion of whether or not physiological change is caused by the technology in question has become to some degree unhelpful as a moral assessment tool since some such changes have been defended as normal, including the changes caused by vitamins, vaccines, and even the controversial hypobaric training chambers. These enhancements have become considered therapeutic treatments or justifiable ways to 'even the playing field' in the case of hypobaric chambers.

The world of sport has been challenged by the use of more extreme means. The "Bladerunner"—21-year-old Oscar Pistorius—was approved in 2008, by the Court of Arbitration for Sport, to compete in Olympic Games. Pistorius was born without fibulae in his lower legs. Both legs were amputated below the knee when he was 11 months old. Some experts contend that the carbon-fiber prosthetics have given him an advantage over able-bodied athletes (Sutcliffe, 2008; UltraFuture, 2009). However, as I have demonstrated, the concept of a level playing field has existed only at the level of the popular imagination: some countries chose to or are able to allocate greater resources to the training and support of athletes than others; some athletes are born with favorable genetic abnormalities. Genetic transfer technologies undoubtedly will be expensive as they become available; in a world characterized by wide economic disparity, the gulf between the haves and have-nots will only deepen. The issue cannot be defined such that it assumes a 'level playing field' amongst competing athletes.

Transhumanists see this uneven playing field as a significant problem and seek to resolve it by advocating for the development and use of technology to bring humans into a posthuman state in which there is greater equality, less prejudice if any and all people are moved into a new state in which certain human traits are maintained and heightened while others are overcome as unnecessary limitations or harms. This evolution is not only desirable, according to proponents, but necessary to our long-term survival. With advances not only in biotechnology including genetic technology, but also in nanotechnology, information technology and cognitive science, the transhumanist movement has arisen.[6]

Already we add pieces of machinery to enhance or enable life: witness pacemakers, plates and other hardware and high-tech prosthetic limbs. Some argue many of us are, therefore, partial cyborgs (e.g., the integration of humanity with machine) already. Certainly Pistorius would be considered a cyborg athlete. Even the addition of corrective eyeglasses arguably brings us closer if not to a cyborg state (Campbell, 2006: 65). Certainly the collective understanding of what is 'normal' has been adjusted as medical interventions and technologies have developed over the centuries. The transhumanist way of defining the issue, which will only become more pervasive as technology increases options, rests on assumptions regarding what is most valuable and what human features are obstacles at best or threats at worst.

When the use of genetic technologies is framed as a performance-enhancement issue instead of a narrowly and pejoratively defined doping issue, often the ethical assessment has relied on a distinction between therapy (good) and enhancement (bad), and/or natural (good) and artificial (bad). These distinctions rest on the essentialist concept of 'normal' as the dividing point. What is considered normal and normative are defined largely by dominant cultural values. Normal is code for what is acceptable if one desires to 'fit in' or 'succeed' within the dominant context and reap the most widely prized rewards including social status and money.

Gregor Wolbring, biochemist and bioethicist, provides a helpful critique of 'normal' through his analysis of ableism: "Ableism exhibits a favouritism for certain abilities that are projected as essential while labeling real or perceived deviations from (or lack of) these 'essential' abilities as a diminished state" (Wolbring, 2007). An uncritical reliance on the concept of normal reflects an acceptance of dominant sociocultural values and perpetuates existing systemic power distributions and attendant distributive justice implications. For example, it is considered normal to be hearing: medical interventions usually are sought to 'correct' deafness. However, many deaf people do not wish to become hearing people as they value deaf culture and themselves. In sports, for example, female athletes are often pushed to fit the 'normal' profile of the thin body with eating disorders or other health issues often resulting (Lelwica, 2000). A relational ethic must take seriously these systemically marginalized voices and critique the underlying values that promote and sustain the normalizing of one group at others' expense.

An essentialist understanding of what it means to be human underpins any claim of 'normalcy.' Yet no one way to be human has persisted from the beginning of humanity; humans have changed longitudinally and have been diverse within the species. This does not mitigate claims for a 'human condition' but it does raise cautions. In an earlier anthology, I argue that from a theological perspective humans are created in the image of God and understandings of the *imago dei* rest on the underlying theologies of the nature of God (Trothen, 2008). Most important to this discussion is the debate regarding God's nature as static or dynamic and changing in response to relationships while remaining true to covenantal promises. God, as Trinitarian community, is movement grounded in relationship. Thus, to claim that humans are created in God's image does not necessarily mean a static essentialist view of humanity. Thus, while there is no one 'normal' except as it is a concept constructed based on dominant normative values that reflect the current unjust systemic power patterns, there are shared human experiences such as those experiences connected to human finitude and creatureliness.[7]

Although we must discard arguments that rest solely on the concept of normal, I would argue that we need not reject the therapy/enhancement distinction entirely. Rather, we must approach it for what it is: a continuum that relies, for moral evaluation, on culturally constructed values. It is a perspectival and therefore partial way in which to define the issue. Rarely are there clear conceptual divides unless these are constructed around dominant values such as the concept of normal; a dialectic or continuum are more accurate concepts with which to describe seeming opposites that are in relationship. However, the ethical caveat is that a critical examination of the values that undergird any division of genetic technological applications is necessary to a relational ethic of justice.

Pistorius's case is accordingly complex; the amputation of his lower legs was for therapeutic purposes but in so doing he is now partly 'artificial' and this stirs concerns of 'fairness,' which seem to have been at least partially conflated with concerns of 'sameness.' Pistorius's prostheses are very visible, unlike the advantage yielded by the greater availability of resources or a congenital genetic condition. In his case, arguably what is natural for him are amputated lower legs and prostheses. Yet, how does one assess whether or not his cheetah legs are therapeutic or enhancing—surely they are both. Further, why should the question of whether they are therapeutic or enhancing be the litmus test for whether or not he can compete in the 'normative' Olympic Games?

Appeals to *the* human *essence* or *the nature* of sport presume an anti-Darwinian stance that fails to recognize the changes that have occurred in our presumptions of what is meant by normal or acceptable regarding human health (Moritz, 2007). A further trap is the tendency attached to such essentialist claims: to subscribe—intentionally or not—to a genetic or environmental determinism, or a combination of the two (Peters, 2003). Such definitions of the issue rely on essentialisms, and the moral elevation of that which is perceived as natural over artificial camouflage the moral relevance and indeed centrality of our dominant operative values. In short, humanity's nature or a distinction between enhancement and therapy are not the formative questions, although they may help deepen the analysis after other assumptions are critiqued; rather, how we approach the issue of genetic technologies and sport is shaped largely by a relational dimension that includes current dominant values that shape and reflect how we approach our neighbors.

The preceding argument poses a challenge to ethicist Andy Miah's contention that genetic modification, if developed to the point of physical safety, could allow people to become more authentic in their humanities by maximizing their choices via genetic technologies, and that this should be the criterion by which the use of such technologies in sport is evaluated (Miah 2005: 109). Miah argues the use of genetic technologies or any other means to enhance performance is unethical unless the "motivation behind using it implies something meaningful about being human. Thus, unless the use of the technology is constitutive of our humanness, then it is not a justifiable method of altering (rather than enhancing) performance" (Miah,

2007: 151). I agree to an extent with this contention; if it were possible to access what it means to be "authentically human" this would be a sufficient ethical criterion. Miah explains his position further:

> To embrace genetic modification entails making a statement about what is valuable about being human, which might be little more than acknowledging that humans are a kind of being that seeks to transcend the limitations of biology. Thus, in relation to genetic modification or other methods of human enhancement in sport, the important point is that the justification of using genetic modification is not to enhance performance or to gain an advantage. Rather, it is to approach a way of being human that is more reflective of our authentic selves (Miah, 2004). It is this basis that should be the criterion against which performance modification is evaluated.
>
> (Miah, 2007: 155)

This could imply an essentialist claim about what it means to be 'authentically' human or more probably a normative expectation that all are able to access their authentic selves. The latter case fails to appreciate the moral relevance of systemic power imbalances that can impinge on one's agency. Also, before we can determine adequately how to be authentically human, again we must evaluate how we know; as Gebara observes, "All epistemology can be seen as ethics, and all ethics is epistemology" (Gebara, 2002: 73). Miah presumes a sufficient critical and imaginative capacity to discern what it is that constitutes best our authentic selves. Socialization carries significant moral weight; dominant social values often are uncritically assumed as best and therefore most closely aligned with the selves we wish to be. In a world that rewards those with most money and status, it is difficult not to conflate these prizes with our true heart's desires. Thus, while transcending some biological limits that stop our bodies from going 'further' may seem like removing obstacles to what it is that we feel compelled to pursue or achieve or be, the removal of these barriers fails to address adequately the underlying reasons for this desire or compulsion to go 'further.' The question of what it means to be relational humans is one to which we must return again and again in this discussion. It is inextricably related to the issue of motive.

One must ask how possible is such a quest for authenticity in a global context that is shaped by a dominant acceptance of a value system that manifests in systemic marginalization. In such a context, moral agency is compromised or unduly shaped by dominant sociocultural normative values. A counterargument that must be considered is that this is an unduly paternalistic claim; people generally are able to identify and assess relevant contextual factors. However, one needs to consider that historically humans have tended to buy into the dominant values of the day. For example, for many decades slavery was widely accepted as normal. As oppressed voices gain force, humanity has also demonstrated an ability to change but often not until after much damage has been done.

I suggest a re-visioning of dominant values from the perspective of a radical relational ethic informed by Christian faith claims. Sources of authority, including science, media, experience (both personal and global), faith claims and sacred texts, are intertwined with and formative of our values and ethical claims. From a Christian perspective, scripture is a formative source of authority. Many of the values that emerge from this source of authority point to relationship, particularly the directive to do unto others as you would yourself, and to love God with all your heart and your neighbor as yourself; the "golden rule" continues to carry much weight in Christian faith communities. Further, Hebrew Scriptures point to the importance of covenant and hospitality as overarching norms. Relationship is at the core of Christianity.

## RELATIONSHIP: A THEOLOGICAL ETHICAL ANALYSIS OF GENETIC TECHNOLOGIES AND SPORT

I will identify and briefly explore the following issues raised by a relational theological ethic by considering briefly an imagined transhumanist case, followed by a more probable case concerning the use of Repoxygen: imago dei, extreme individualism, the body, distributive justice, motive and hope.

Transhumanists, as stated earlier, understand humans to be on a desirable journey towards a posthuman state. Along the way, the world will have to contend with the ramifications of this transition, including the escalating use of genetic-modification technologies and the interfacing of such technologies with implanted machinery.

Pistorius's case will become 'normal'; the elite sporting world will be faced with cases, instead, of athletes who chose to have their limbs amputated in order to gain new limbs that are considered more adaptable to sport competition than are human limbs. Or, perhaps, if such surgical interventions are against the rules, undetectable genetic technology will be used to cause such amputation to become medically necessary. Or genetic modifications will be made that increase muscle bulk in particular areas, bone growth in others, in addition to various uses of machinery when the human body, no matter how genetically tweaked, will not suffice to provide the desired performance. Further, perhaps we will gain the technology—genetic or otherwise—to change brain function such that distracting emotions are prevented. These modifications will reflect what is most valued in both elite sports competition and in the wider sociocultural systems that provide the context for elite sport.

Historically, the dominant theological interpretation of the imago dei has centered on rational thought; the primary criterion of being created in God's image has been seen as the capacity to reason. This elevation of reason has reinforced and reflected a hierarchical understanding of: men over women, adults over children, the cognitively able over the cognitively impaired, and human over creatures and creation. This prizing of reason parallels the transhumanist focus on cognitive function as the defining feature of human identity.

However, there are other understandings of the imago dei including understandings that center on relationship rather than reason. When the relational nature of God is emphasized, rational thought cannot be the primary criterion. An emphasis on the Trinitarian and covenantal nature of God points to the centrality of mutual relationship (not a hierarchical valuing) and interdependence; this understanding puts both limits and expanded obligations on the use of genetic enhancement technologies.

For example, understood in the context of God who *is* community, humans as created co-creators (Hefner, 1999) have the duty to create for beneficent purposes, in the knowledge that humans are fallible. Theologically, we must grapple with the awareness that sin and evil will not disappear as we create new technologies; and so new technologies will be free neither from evil nor salvific dimensions. Because humans are fallible, and both good and evil are part of humanity and creation, ongoing accountability and ethical analysis in communities of diversity are necessary. Further, good purposes must be understood to attend to the well-being of the wider community as well as, but not only, one's self-interests. In particular, from a Christian liberation perspective, the marginalized or least powerful must receive most attention; autonomy must be understood in radically relational terms, and not conflated with extreme individualism as is the dominant global tendency (see, for example, Johnson, 1992: 68).

"Individual freedom and choice" are care transhumanist values (World Transhumanist Association, 2002). Again, if it is true that most of us internalize society's message regarding the ideal pictures of beauty, status, success, then individual choosing will be driven towards achieving these internalized, socially constructed and contextually driven ideals. A cyborg-genetically-enhanced elite athlete will then choose to be fat free, endurance designed, optimally strong for their particular sport, and intellectually and psychologically focused on the task of winning. Such a task-oriented, designed being risks becoming a performer, not a person who competes as an athlete. Performance records will get better and better, but there will be losses.

The thrill of knowing the competition is between persons who have good and bad days, who have more or less heart to drive them, who might need help or be moved to give help even at the possible cost of winning, who might become ill or heal from illness, and whose vulnerability stirs compassion will be lessened greatly or be gone altogether. A just relational perspective demands that one not assume that finitude, dependence, fragility and mutable bodies are wholly undesirable, even if one is an athlete.

Christian ethical analyses of the issue have tended to be defined mostly by concerns regarding excessive human pride and the folly of a desire to 'play God.' In relational terms, excessive human pride and undue self-centeredness have come to be manifest in North American extreme individualism in which 'my rights' are exalted over the rights of others. This worldview hinges on a denial that all life is intertwined and that 'I' cannot truly thrive without 'you.' Without reconceptualizing interdependence as a moral good, it is very tempting to the elite athlete to seek only to win and to do so at almost any cost.

The conflation of excessive pride with the meaning of sin has received a much needed critique by feminist theologians; many women and other systemically marginalized people tend more toward an undue giving up of power and sense of self rather than undue pride. For these, it could be tempting either to embrace genetic and cyborg technologies as a means of escaping and losing oneself or to refuse the use of such technologies because one does not feel deserving or sufficiently valuable. Excessive pride and resulting self-centeredness,[8] and a lack of love or even regard for self, are inadequate and arguably evil reasons from a theological relational perspective to use genetic modification technologies; neither foster mutual relationship as they impede access to one's authentic humanity.

The transhumanist quest to lose the boundary between what is human and what is machine also brings into greater relief the question of the meaning and value of the body. Embodiment has long been a Christian concern. Although early Christians were clear, particularly through their understanding of Gnosticism as heretical, that the body is a gift of God and therefore good, how to approach embodiment has continued to raise challenges. Christians have long tended to fear the body and sexuality in part due to recognition of its power. Notable work to reconstruct "sexual theologies" (Nelson, 1987) and to heal the constructed chasm between spirit and body has been done in the last 40 years. Feminist theologians, in particular, understand the body and spirit to be intertwined, both parts of what it means to be created in God's image. Much more than the "first prosthesis we all learn to manipulate," the place of the body in Christian theology is very different from the transhumanist understanding of the body as defined by a set of limitations that the human brain can and ought to overcome (Hook, 2004: 38).

To complicate the issue further, one must ask if cognition located only in the brain is the sum total of human knowing and intelligence; the mind, indeed, seems much larger than such a reductionist approach to intelligence would allow. Significant parts of our human ability to know and develop are located in our capacities to build and engage in relationship.

If theologians such as James Nelson are correct, then to realize more fully human potential, one must embrace much more deeply a way of approaching life that understands human physicality as deeply intertwined with and inseparable from the human mind and spirit. Even writing or speaking about these components as if they are separable is misleading;[9] what makes us human is this fusion of elements—body, mind, spirit. As

Gebara insightfully concludes, "I am suggesting that the very imperfection of the human person is what constitutes it, what makes it human. To say 'human' is to say 'fallible,' and *fallible* is not just the possibility of doing evil but also the possibility of doing good" (Gebara, 2002: 135). As it is, we live in a human world in which scientific technology is creating new possibilities for both good and evil and much in between.

Repoxygen is expected to make an undeclared appearance at the 2012 Olympic Games, increasing athletes' endurance capacities. Besides being against WADA's rules, are there adequate ethical reasons against the use of this emerging genetic technology? Although Repoxygen has not yet passed the clinical trials necessary to insure safety, some see autonomy as a sufficient justification. From a relational perspective, this argument is faulty because it assumes that individual freedom of choice trumps a consequentialist argument that minimizing harms when possible is necessary; relational autonomy means that individual rights must be weighed in the context of communal well-being.

Communal well-being also includes distributive justice concerns. The allocation of resources must be addressed in a global context that is characterized by great disparities of power. The world continues to groan under the weight of injustice; many still do not have enough food to eat or shelter or basic medical care. In such a context, the allocation of scarce resources to athletic performance seems frivolous. However, one must also consider that the primary purpose behind the development of Repoxygen is the treatment of renal failure, not athletic performance. While it may be the case that limited resources will be used to tailor Repoxygen and produce it for athletes, one must also consider whether it—once determined safe—would be equally accessible to all athletes including those from poorer countries and families.

In addition to safety and distributive justice arguments, from a relational perspective, motive and hope must also be considered. The primary motive for using genetic technologies is winning and usually winning not by achieving one's perception of a level playing field but by gaining a covert edge on one's competition. However, there are also those athletes who are convinced that other competitors are using the technology and therefore they too must use it if they are to maintain the same chance of winning.[10] Still others will use the technologies motivated by patriotism; they will do almost anything to win for their country. Systemic power imbalances and an attendant pervasive tendency to pit us against them suggest that nationalism often mitigates global relationships.

Many athletes are so motivated to win that self-violence is not uncommon, including: the use of performance enhancing drugs and genetic modification technologies; excessive thinness for female athletes; overtraining; and competing or training while injured. As I have argued elsewhere, violence is normative in our culture, including most of our mainstream religions and professional sport (Trothen, 2009). Complicating the issue, not all violence is more evil than salvific; violence must be assessed relationally. For example, some degree of violence is done by pushing oneself to overcome feelings of exhaustion, yet the euphoria experienced by surpassing what might have been one's limit is inspiring. On the other hand, the violence that causes serious injury either to self or others is destructive.

I do not find it convincing that all motivation to use genetic technologies will be or is reducible to the dominant value of winning for either oneself or one's country. Miah identifies the possibility of an athlete finding genetic modification technologies to provide them with a way to be more authentically themselves. I understand this to mean the potential removal of a block to more fully engaging the rest of one's self in competition. Competition, in and of itself, is not counter to relationship; in fact I argue that competition can—but will not necessarily—help build more authentic relationship through the increased realization of one's own power and beauty; a certain amount of self-love is necessary if one is to love others. To realize one's potential, some technologies could be helpful. Potentially, if one's body does not absorb oxygen to such a degree as to match the complement of the rest of one's physical, emotional and intellectual self, then Repoxygen may provide a way to make it more possible to realize one's overall potential to 'fly.' For many women and others who experience systemic marginalization, the opportunity to surpass self- or other-imposed limits while retaining a sense of one's interdependence can be life-giving. At the same time, learning to accept one's limitations and allowing others to help are also potentially salvific opportunities, particularly from a relational perspective.

Further, the discernment of motive is very complex; to refrain from internalizing dominant social values such as the attainment of wealth and status through winning, or to possess the insight to know when this occurs, is very difficult. Thus, as the sole or most important criterion for justifying the use of genetic modification technologies, including Repoxygen by athletes, the desire to be more authentically human is ethically insufficient.

Although very complex to assess, hope and inspiration are compelling factors in sport and are not limited to elite athletes; recreational athletes and spectators also look to sport for not merely an escape—although that is there too—but to be uplifted through visible assurance that the almost unthinkable can be achieved. Part of this hope is based not only on what one sees but on what one desires to see. For example, the belief that sports' competitions are pure meritocracies hinges on a mistaken perception that there really can be a level playing field. Thus, perhaps one of the most significant critiques against scientific inroads and use of genetic technologies in sport is that it diminishes the mystique and therefore the hope generated by this meritocracy belief. As Caplan explains,

> Strangely, the greatest threat to the future of sport is not necessarily new drugs, gene therapy or better chemistry. The more knowledge we

> gain . . . the greater the threat to our ability to value performance . . . Science does not destroy the possibility of effort but it may diminish our understanding of its role to the point where sport simply devolves into exhibition (Caplan, 2008).

It matters not so much that there never has been a level playing field; the belief that anyone can possibly achieve wonders regardless of background has been captivating and inspiring. This is one of the many ways, as I have discussed elsewhere (Trothen, 2006: 291–305), that sport functions as a popular religion for some people; the yearning to believe in transcendent possibilities that can be achieved in moments of realized eschatology is part of the fuel needed to sustain the work towards a more just world. A danger, of course, is that it will merely serve as fuel to sustain an acceptance of the status quo by providing moments of respite or indulgence of purely self-interest. If the availability of Repoxygen and other genetic modification technologies would threaten the hope needed to enhance global relationships, then that must be weighed in an ethical assessment.[11]

## CONCLUDING REMARKS

Extreme individualism is a predominant Western value that is marketed globally. The preeminence of this value reinforces an unjust global system that systemically marginalizes those groups that do not fit the dominant value system. These groups include all who are understood to be different and therefore 'less' than 'normal.'

Thus, a radically relational ethic, such as that emerging from a Christian theology, can provide a challenging reframing of the issue, particularly when such a theology is generated by a critically aware understanding of systemic power distribution. The model provided by Jesus of Nazareth points to a radical liberation and understanding of salvation that is located in the valuing of people and relationships, particularly those on the margins. This option for the poor celebrates a lack of status, interdependence and justice in the context of right relationship and relational autonomy. In this chapter I have considered only a few of the relevant ethical issues; not discussed in depth are several other issues, including: the value of human fragility in the context of relationship (Parens, 1999), randomness, violence, the internal goods of sport (including fairness), global relationships and nationalism.

My overarching point is that the risks of permitting dominant sociocultural values to go unarticulated and uncritiqued from a relational perspective are growing in correlation with technological developments. Further, deepened discussion of what it means to be human and what it ought to mean to be human, from a relational ethical perspective, is needed.

## NOTES

1. Thank you to Ryan McNally, who served as my highly competent research assistant in the writing of this chapter.
2. There remain many concerns regarding unforeseen side effects of gene therapy. In 1999, 18-year-old Jesse Gelsinger died unexpectedly following a gene transfer directly into his hepatic artery for a rare genetic disorder that blocks the body's ability to break down ammonia. The cause of death was not his liver disorder but the genetic modification which led to multiple organ failure likely as a result of his immune system attacking the injected virus or synthetic gene (Schjerling, 2005: 27–28). Additionally, in January 2003 a second child developed a "leukemia-like" condition from another gene therapy trial to treat X-linked severe combined immunodeficiency disease (e.g., "bubble baby syndrome") (Brownlee, 2004: 280–281).
3. Further, relying on a combination of genetic information and an ensuing commitment to providing the "right" environmental factors such as training, encouragement, etc., assumes genetic and environmental determinisms that, as theologian Ted Peters well argues, fail to take account of a necessary third factor—spirit (Peters, 2003).
4. For me, I have had a longstanding attraction to sport both as a spectator and participant. I often experience sport as having a spiritual component. I also have a longstanding interest in ethics including bioethics and Christian social ethics.
5. WADA held their first interdisciplinary conference on "Genetic Enhancement of Athletic Performance" in 2002 in which ethical issues were considered in addition to legal, policy, and scientific issues (www.wada-ama.org or www.olympic.org).
6. The World Transhumanist Association, founded by Nick Bostrom and David Pierce, recognizes the potential for harm in the developing technologies such as genetic technologies and cyborg implants of additions, and wants to minimize these harms and continue to build towards a posthuman state in which characteristics such as longevity and cognitive functioning are maximized and "equitably distributed." The Institute for Ethics and Emerging Technologies—promoting the ethical use of technology to enhance human capabilities Web site (IEET), homepage http://ieet.org (accessed March, 17, 2010).
7. Some of these experiences will be returned to in the last section of this chapter concerning application.
8. As Gebara explains, "Evil is also a dysfunction between me and myself that leads me to cultivate narcissism and my own interests and to forget that I am in and with others, that I need them if I am to keep on living" (2002, 139).
9. Thus, Nelson's contention that Christians need to move always further along the continuum joining a theology of sexuality to a sexual theology in which all theology—or ways of knowing and thinking about the Holy—is acknowledged clearly as not only mediated by but infused by embodiment and all that embodiment means to us.
10. Ethicist Robert L. Simon points out that one of the potential harms of the availability of genetic technologies or other means of enhancement is the undue pressure if not outright coercion that competitive athletes experience to use whatever their competition uses to give them an "edge." Simon stops short of calling this pressure coercion as there is still a clear element of choice (e.g., "the pressures are self-imposed") and, I would add, pressure not to go against the rules as well (Simon, 2004: 75).

11. Further along the therapy/enhancement continuum is the case of the recreational runner who suffers a muscle or tendon injury and uses IGF-1 technology to heal more rapidly to allow them to resume running more quickly. The only valid arguments against this case that I can see are safety concerns and issues related to resource allocation. Fast, uncomplicated healing from injury would potentially save on health care costs partially since more people will stay active. The main fears regarding cases such as this, which fall more on the therapy end of the continuum, are gradualism and/or repugnance of genetic technologies. Others have argued that we will lose human uniqueness and the capacity to be unpredictable. (For example, see Tennant, 2007: 64.)

## BIBLIOGRAPHY

Anderson, W. French. (1999) Human Gene Therapy, in Tom L. Beachamp and Leroy Walters (Eds.), *Contemporary Issues in Bioethics*, 5th ed., Belmont, CA: Wadsworth Pub. Co., 581–585.

Aschwanden, C. (2000, January 15) Gene Cheats, *New Scientist,* 165: 2221: 24–29.

Associated Press. (2008, February 27) WADA Says It Has Effective Test for HGH, *CBCNews.ca,* retrieved April 30, 2008, from http://www.cbc.ca/news/story/2008/02/27/wada-hgh.html

Brownlee, Christen. (2004, October 30) Gene Doping—Will Athletes Go for the Ultimate High? *Science News,* 166: 18: 280–281.

Campbell, Heidi. (2006, April) On Posthumans, Transhumanism and Cyborgs: Towards a Transhumanist-Christian Conversation, *Modern Believing,* 47: 61–73.

Caplan, A.L. (2008) Does the Biomedical Revolution Spell the End of Sport? *British Journal of Sports Medicine*, 42: 996–997.

Chapman, Audrey. (2001) Religious Perspective on Human Germ Line Modifications, in Ronald Cole Turner (Ed.), *Beyond Cloning,* Harrisburg, PA: Trinity Press International, 64–76.

Cole, R. David. (1998) The Genome and the Human Genome Project, in Ted Peters (Ed.), *Genetics: Issues of Social Justice,* Cleveland, OH: Pilgrim Press, 49–70.

Collins, Francis S. (2002) Human Genetics, in John F. Kilner, C. Christopher Hook, and Diann B. Uustal (Eds.), *Cutting-Edge Bioethics—a Christian Exploration of Technologies and Trends*, Grand Rapids, MI: William B. Eerdmans Publishing Company, 3–17.

Cumming-Long, Grace D. (1993) *Passion & Reason—Womenviews of Christian life,* Louisville, KY: Westminster/John Knox Press.

Dvorsky, George. (2008) Michael Phelps: "Naturally" Transhuman, on the Institute for Ethics and Emerging Technologies Web site, retrieved April 30, 2009, from http://ieet.org/index.php/IEET/print/2575

Eassom, Simon. (2001) Head of Sports Studies at de Montfort University, United Kingdom, interviewed by Amanda Smith, *Sports Factor,* ABC, 12 July 2001, retrieved January 22, 2009, from www.abc.net.au/rn/talks/8.30/sportsf/stories/s435073.htm

Gaudard, A., Varlet, M. E., Bressolle, F., et al. (2003) Drugs for Increasing Oxygen and Their Potential Use in Doping: A Review, *Sports Medicine,* 33: 3: 187–212.

Gebara, Ivone. (2002) *Out of the Depths—Women's Experience of Evil and Salvation,* Minneapolis, MN: Fortress Press.

Hefner, Philip. (1999) Biocultural Evolution and the Created Co-Creator, in Ted Peters (Ed.), *Science and Theology: The New Consonance,* Boulder, CO: Westview Press, 174–188.

Hook, C. Christopher. (2004, January) The Techno Sapiens, in *Christianity Today*, 37–40.

House of Commons, Science and Technology Committee. (2007, February 7) *Human Enhancement Technologies in Sport—Second Report of Session 2006–07*, London.

Johnson, Elizabeth A. (1992) *She Who Is—the Mystery of God in Feminist Theological Discourse*, New York: Crossroad.

Lelwica, Michelle M. (2000) Losing Their Way to Salvation: Women, Weight Loss, and the Salvation Myth of Culture Lite, in Bruce David Forbes and Jeffrey H. Mahan (Eds.), *Religion and Popular Culture in America*, Berkeley: University of California Press, 180–200.

McCrory, P. (2003) Super Athletes or Gene Cheats? *British Journal of Sports Medicine*, 37/3: 193.

Miah, Andy. (2004) *Genetically Modified Athletes: Biomedical Ethics, Gene Doping, and Sport*, New York: Routledge.

Miah, Andy. (2005) From Anti-Doping to a "Performance Policy" Sport Technology, Being Human, and Doing Ethics, *European Journal of Sport Science*, 5(1): 51–57.

Miah, Andy. (2007) Genetics, Bioethics, and Sport, *Sports, Ethics and Philosophy*, 1/2: 146–158.

Moritz, Joshua M. (2007) Natures, Human Nature, Genes and souls: Reclaiming Theological Anthropology through Biological Structuralism, *Dialog*, 46: 263–280.

*Nature—International Weekly Journal of Science* (2009, March 1), retrieved April 3, 2009, from http://www.nature.com/nature/journal/vaop/ncurrent/full/nature07864.html

Nelson, James B. (1987) Reuniting Sexuality and Spirituality, *Christian Century*, 104: 187–190.

Peters, Ted. (2003) *Playing God? Genetic Determinism and Human Freedom*, 2nd ed., New York: Routledge.

Parens, Erik. (1999) The Goodness of Fragility: On the Prospect of Genetic Technologies Aimed at the Enhancement of Human Capacities, in Tom L. Beachamp and LeRoy Walters (Eds.), *Contemporary Issues in Bioethics*, 5th ed., Belmont, CA: Wadsworth Pub. Co., 596–602.

Schjerling, Peter. (2005) The Basics of Gene Doping, in Claudio Tamburrini and Torbjorn Tannsjo (Eds.), *Genetic Technology and Sport—Ethical Questions*, London and New York: Routledge, 19–31.

Simon, Robert L. (2004) *Fair Play—the Ethics of Sport*, 2nd ed., Cambridge, MA: Westview Press.

Smith, Amanda. (2001, July 12) *Sports Factor*, ABC, retrieved April 5, 2009, from www.abc.net.au/rn/talks/8.30/sportsf/stories/s435073.htm

Sutcliffe, Mark. (2008, January 13) Amputee Sprinter Treads Uneven Track, *The Ottawa Citizen*, retrieved January 10, 2009, from http://www2.canada.com

Sweeney, H. Lee. (2004, June 21) Gene Doping, *Scientific American.Com*, retrieved January 5, 2009, from http://www.sciam.com/article.cfm?id=gene-doping

Swift, E.M., and Yaeger, Don. (2001, May 14) Unnatural Selection, *Sports Illustrated*, 94/20: 86–92.

Tennant, Agnieszka. (2007, June) Brave New Salvation—a Vision of a Sinless Future, *Christianity Today*, 64.

Trothen, Tracy J. (2006) Hockey: A Divine Sport?—Canada's National Sport in Relation to Embodiment, Community, and Hope, *Studies in Religion/Sciences Religieuses*, 35/2: 291–305.

Trothen, Tracy J. (2008) Redefining Human, Redefining Sport: The Imago Dei and Genetic Modification Technologies, in Donald Deardorff II and John White

(Eds.), *The Image of God in the Human Body—Essays on Christianity and Sports*, Lampeter, Ceredigion, Wales, UK: The Edwin Mellon Press, Ltd., 217–234.

Trothen, Tracy J. (2009) Holy Acceptable Violence?—Violence in Hockey and Christian Atonement Theories, *The Journal of Religion and Popular Culture*, Special Edition: Religion and Popular Culture in Canada, retrieved from www.usask.ca/relst/jrpc: 42 pages (accessed 2 April, 2009).

Unal, Mehmet, and Unal, Durisehvar Ozer. (2004) Gene Doping in Sports, *Sports Medicine*, 34/6: 35–362.

UltraFuture. (2009, May 19) Transhumanism and the Olympics—May 19, 2009, retrieved May 21, 2009, from http://ultrafuture.com/2008/05/19/transhumanism-and-the-olympics/

Wolbring, Gregor. (2007) NBICS, Other Convergences, Ableism and the Culture of Peace, retrieved April 25, 2009, from http://www.innovationwatch.com/choiceisyours/choiceisyours-2007–04–15.htm

World Anti-Doping Agency (2009) homepage http://www.wada-ama.org/en/About-WADA/Presidents-Welcome-Message (accessed 1 July, 2010).

World Anti-Doping Agency. (2008, June) WADA Gene Doping Symposium Calls for Greater Awareness, Strengthened Action against Potential Gene Transfer Misuse in Sport, retrieved April 25, 2009, from http://www.wada-ama.org/en/newsarticle.ch2?articleId=3115626

World Transhumanist Association. (2002) The Transhumanist FAQ, retrieved May 21, 2009, from http://www.transhumanism.org/faq.html

Zhou, S., Murphy, J. E. Escobedo, J.A., et al. (1998) Adeno-Associated Virus-Mediated Delivery of Erythropoietin, *Gene Therapy*, 5/5: 665–670.

# 4 Living in a Sectarian Maelstrom
## A Christian Professional Football Player's Perspective

*Ian Lawrence*

To paraphrase Samuel Johnson in 1751 (Boswell, 1992), every man intrinsically seeks to establish an identity that discriminates him from other mortals and by which others are persuaded to love him or compelled to fear him. This paper explores the distinctive Christian identity of the professional football player Marvin Andrews within the context of Scottish football. This case study of Andrews is based on a series of interviews with the author. It seeks first to analyze Andrews's personal perceptions as a practicing Christian, and second to provide a historical and social background to the issue of sectarianism.

## INTRODUCTION

'Conventional religion is coming to an end.' This is a claim Geering (1994: 112), along with many others, has consistently claimed since the erosion in church statistics was first highlighted in the late 1960s. In one sense, it is interesting that he was still making the claim most recently in 2003 rather than looking back posthumously on the funeral of conventional religion, as he predicted its demise would come before the end of the century. Are the prophets of doom right, even if the death is being prolonged?

That churchgoing has been in decline in all Western countries, particularly since the 1960s, is beyond dispute (Ward, 2004). Whatever statistics one uses, and however one looks at them, they all point in one direction—down. In Britain, church attendance includes about 18% of the population monthly and 8% weekly, although much of the decline occurred from the late 1960s to the late 1980s and the figures have stabilized somewhat since (Lawrence, 2005). Such statistics certainly raise the question as to whether at some point in the future Britain, as other developed countries, will in fact be a churchless society.

Specifically in Britain, Davie (1994) argues that with increasing modernization, religious belief has become implausible for larger numbers of people, and while there are those who claim that people have stopped 'belonging,' they have still continued to 'believe.' This indicates that believing and belonging have become increasingly separated. While Christian 'belonging' has clearly declined, Christian beliefs nonetheless persist, and in the case of Marvin Andrews they are embodied in a somewhat unconventional public figure.

The impact of celebrity worship in the football-obsessed culture of Scotland cannot be underestimated. The potential for professional players to achieve fame and fortune because of their acts of athletic prowess on the field of play is widely acknowledged by a variety of authors (Boorstin, 1961; Cashmore, 2000; Coakley, 2003). However, Marvin Andrews, as a black Christian, presents a significant challenge to preconceived notions of what constitutes a role model in the context of religious intolerance in the west of Scotland.

Marvin Andrews is from the Caribbean island of Trinidad. To date, his 'football odyssey' has taken him from his birthplace to the heights of a professional football career with one of the world's most famous professional teams, Glasgow Rangers FC. The path from the Caribbean via Raith Rovers, Livingston to Glasgow Rangers and eventually back to finish his career at Raith Rovers is described by Marvin as one long, predestined journey. 'I think I'm in Scotland for a purpose and a reason. I'm a servant of God and I'm here to tell people that he is still alive.' This message of faith and proclamation of the gospel is delivered by Andrews both through his behavior on the pitch and in his role as a deacon at the Zion Praise Centre in Kirkcaldy, where he preaches twice a week. The irony of a practicing and highly committed Christian from a different culture experiencing firsthand the issues of sectarianism was the motivation for my interview and subsequent qualitative analysis.

For two years, Marvin Andrews was a much-admired defender for the Rangers, playing before 50,000 people most Saturdays at Ibrox Stadium. The new Rangers manager then decided to release him, allowing Andrews to return to one of his former teams and in the process be closer to his church in Kirkcaldy, where he could pursue his Christian ministry. Andrews's brand of Pentecostal faith is remarkable in its fixed certainties. In Andrews's belief, 'God is real, God is here.' It is evidently a faith of the purest fundamentalism, of old-world beliefs and certainties that refuse to yield to contemporary jargon such as that proposed by Bailey (2001: 26) '. . . the need is for a model of religion which allows the phenomenon itself sufficient reality to interact with the secular, neither as dictator nor as toady but in the unrelaxed, creative partnership of a dialectical dialogue.' Arguably the opinion of Andrews, having played for a team that is partly defined by its religious origins, presents an 'outsider's' and therefore a valuable perspective. Sports sociologists Nixon and Frey (1996) suggest that historically athletes have rarely explicitly discussed their faith due to fear of being ridiculed by the media. Marvin Andrews is an exception in the context of professional association football, having adopted a pragmatic approach to using the media as a platform upon which to reach an extended audience. His ministerial role within and outside the football arena may be defined as a 'Christian socialist' or 'one who applied the teachings of the Sermon on the Mount to every life' (Woodworth, 1983: 63). He believes that God engages in and cares for daily human affairs, and that this is the reason why we call God 'Father.' This belief is the basis of what Marvin Andrews perceives as his 'social ministry.'

The purpose of this chapter is to discover the personal perceptions of Marvin Andrews and to contextualize some of the social issues and 'life world' of a Christian footballer. Henning, Van Rensburg and Smit (2004) believe that such a description is hardly complete if there is no understanding presented of the social issues that have been researched; and in this case some insight into the sectarian issues within the west of Scotland is required to contextualize the views presented.

## METHODOLOGY

The danger in this type of social research always potentially lurks in interpretive inquiry. The aim is to address any potential bias by presenting the thick description with ample evidence and a coherent convincing argument based on the evidence. The power of interviewing as a means of obtaining data is lodged in the mind of the everyday layperson. In contemporary society, we can relate to what others say about themselves and we can form generalizations about certain categories of experience and of the human condition. We validate our own experience by relating it to the experience of the interviewed person. In this way, informal 'intersubjectivity,' or informal generalization, is established. Getting the person to speak frankly, however, is not easy, and the notion of a 'pure interview' is arguably a fallacy. Holstein and Gubrium (1997: 163) adamantly state, 'The image of the social scientific prospector casts the interview as a search-and-discovery mission, with the interviewer intent on detecting what is already there inside variably cooperative respondents. The challenge lies in extracting information as directly as possible.' The methodology used to facilitate an understanding of Andrews's experience was based upon the qualitative research of Kvale (1996) and Patton (1990). Within their framework, the world from the subject's point of view is unfolded. Interviews for research of this kind differ in important ways from other familiar kinds of interviews or conversations. Unlike conversations in daily life, which are usually reciprocal exchanges, professional interviews involve an interviewer who is in charge of structuring and directing the questioning. The focus of this research was upon an intellectual understanding of Marvin Andrews's faith via open-ended responses that aimed to reveal his levels of emotion toward the context of the study.

The evidence for this study will come from the interview data and also from theory that explicates and explains the data. It is in this articulated interpretation that conclusions will be drawn. The interview embraced aspects of 'autobiography,' 'life history,' and 'personal narrative' (Sparkes, 2002). At the outset, the intention of the interview was to facilitate self-reflection and the 'lived experience' of Marvin Andrews.

## BACKGROUND

In Scotland, religion frequently divides football supporters, especially between the predominantly Catholic-supported Glasgow Celtic and the Protestant-supported Glasgow Rangers. Religion clearly fascinates and is amplified by media attention, the assumption being that both sport and religion are cultural institutions with a global reach and therefore engage an enormous potential audience (Jarvie, 2006). Both institutions are typically characterized by the ecstatic devotion of followers. The role adopted by Andrews as a practicing Christian within football as a 'civil religion' further stimulates debate surrounding the faith he espouses (Magdalinski & Chandler, 2002). He hopes his example as a high-profile football player will potentially serve to support the building of relationships and the role that football has in redemption and as an agent of change.

The study and analysis of sectarianism in Scotland is not a new phenomenon (see Armstrong & R. Giulianotti, 2001; Bradley, 1998; Bairner & Darby, 1999; Bruce, 1998; Bruce, Paterson, Rosie & Glendinning, 2004; *Record of the Summit on Sectarianism, 2005*). Footballing allegiance plays a significant part in the respective social identities for Protestants and Catholics in Scotland and in particular in Glasgow. MacClancy (1996: 182) states that 'sports . . . are vehicles of identity, providing people with a sense of difference and a way of classifying themselves and others, whether latitudinally or hierarchically.' More specifically, Bromberger (1993: 91) argues that 'ultimately [a football match] offers an expressive support for the affirmation of collective identity and local, regional and national antagonisms.' Both of these statements succinctly express the double-sided nature of social identity. Supporting a particular football team not only facilitates a feeling of shared identity with fellow supporters, but it also acts as a means of differentiating oneself from other groups (Jenkins, 1996). In many cases, identification with a particular team indicates what or who one is and, equally important, what or who they are not. It is clearly evident that throughout the world there are a number of teams that operate as '"anchors of meaning" via their role as vehicles through which individuals and groups can strengthen their attachment and identification with a particular community' (Jarvie & Maguire, 1994: 152).

Within most societies there are a variety of means by which social identity can be expressed, yet, for many groups, football can be the sole or at least the primary outlet for such sentiments. This is certainly the case with Glasgow and the issue of perceived religious identity and associated intolerance or bigotry (Bairner, 1997; Bradley, 1994). One of the challenges for Marvin Andrews is to present an alternative identity for both sides of what historically is perceived as a religious schism. 'I'm a servant of the Lord; I'm here to tell people that he is still alive and that we still have the same God.' Within this context, Andrews clearly views his role as that of a 'missionary' through which he can bring communities together:

> Football is like a God in this nation [Scotland], in the whole of Britain. Football is like a God in the whole of Europe. God has put me in the middle of all this. There is no other God but the Lord Jesus Christ. God has created me to prosper, be positive, and be a blessing to other people.

Andrews evidently sees his role within football as one that is not just to play, but also allows him to do the work of the Lord and spread the gospel of the Lord Jesus Christ. 'This is the will of God for me. I play at a high-profile club to let people come to the light and let people know that God can save you.'

The role of 'missionary' within a secular age is one that is clearly embraced by Marvin Andrews. Ironically, many people in his opinion use football to replace a vacuum they feel in their lives (Novak, 1976). In Britain, research by Hay and Hunt (2000) on the spirituality of nonchurchgoers found in 1987 that 48% admitted to a form of religious spiritual experience. In 2000 he found it had increased to 76%. Research by Gill, Hadaway and Marler (1998) demonstrates that in Britain, support for distinctively Christian beliefs appears to be declining. They summarize the data as demonstrating a decline in several traditional Christian beliefs, a confusing pattern of persistence and some slight increase in New Age beliefs. One indicator of this is belief about God. Whereas in 1947 more believed in a personal God than an impersonal God (as Spirit or Life Force), by 1993 the balance had changed so that belief in a personal God was the minority understanding. All of this research indicates that the decline in church belonging cannot primarily be explained by people losing their religious beliefs. Such individuals have not embraced a fundamentally nonreligious stance or lost their religion in the deepest and most fundamental sense. Richard Wright (1953) observed in *The Outsider*, as far back as 1953, that since religion is dead, religion is everywhere. However, this may be confusing the term with the concept of 'spirituality.'

A 2000 survey, carried out for the BBC's *Soul of Britain* series, found that whereas in 1990, 54% of the population surveyed called themselves 'religious,' by 2000 that figure had fallen to 27%, while 31% preferred to call themselves 'spiritual' (Petre & Cobain, 2000: 8). Roof's (1993) research among baby boomers found that 73% preferred to use the language of 'spirituality' rather than 'religion.' The words in this shift signify different realities.

'Religion,' according to these findings, connotes rigid, authoritarian, oppressive institutions; dogmatism and lack of openness to alternative perspectives; and cold formalism or ritualism. 'Spirituality,' by contrast, suggests flexibility and creativity; tolerance and respect for alternative insights from others; room for doubt and searching; and an emphasis upon personal experience. Robert Wuthnow (1994: 53) also tracks this change in Western spirituality since the 1950s. He suggests that a spirituality of 'dwelling' or 'place' has given way to a spirituality of 'seeking' or 'journey.' Spirituality is indicated by a sense of belonging. This sense of community and group identity can be easily identified within distinct sections of a football stadium. Andrews's response is to attempt to integrate and in some cases invent how God could be made more approachable and relevant to supporters' lives in more ways than they had ever imagined. This he believes is an ongoing journey or 'quest,' with the process as important as the destination. Marvin Andrews's perceived role within this environment is to align religion with a quest for fulfillment.

Andrews frequently compares the church 'to a boat or ship afloat on the sea.' Using this analogy, if the ship is leaking on the ocean of contemporary culture of excess and immorality, then the most sensible initial task is to endeavor to stop, or at least slow down, the leaks. This, he preaches, can be achieved by realizing that 'with God nothing is impossible.' Fundamentally, Andrews believes that it is essential to repent for the remission of sins and believe in Jesus Christ as Savior in order to obtain salvation. Those churches, such as his in Kirkcaldy, that have reformed along such Pentecostal theological lines have, to some degree, been clearly successful, if evidence of their increased attendance at worship is an indication.

Football has commonly become regarded as an opiate for the masses in modern-day culture, but in Andrews's opinion it offers no organizing principle or higher cause. The moral and religious decay of values in Scottish society is in Andrews's opinion directly related to individuals forsaking God. He supports this by referring to God's words in the Bible: 'My people have committed two sins: They have forsaken me, the spring of living water and have dug their own cisterns, broken cisterns that cannot hold water' (Jer. 2:13). God in this example is used as a metaphor. According to Andrews, 'only God can provide a constant source of life-giving and pure fulfillment.' The metaphor is challenged by the complex relationship that has historically existed between Scotland's two most successful clubs; characterized not only by their fierce battle for dominance in the domestic game but also by the conflicting religious affiliations of the teams and their supporters (see Murray, 1984, 1998).

Rangers are regarded as exhibiting a Protestant, Unionist and Loyalist identity, whereas Celtic are seen as synonymous symbols of Catholicism, Irish nationalism and Republicanism (Bradley, 1999; Jarvie & Reid, 1999). While these perceptions are strongly substantiated, it is important to recognize that to suggest that all supporters identify with all (or indeed any) of these affiliations would represent a considerable generalization. As Boyle (1994: 91) states, 'while I believe significant political differences do exist between the majority of supporters of Celtic and Rangers, related to religious and historical factors, there can be no simplistic linkage between symbolic sporting displays of allegiance and collective political orientation.' Notwithstanding this, evidence suggests that distinct patterns can be drawn regarding the identities of football supporters in Scotland.

## RELIGIOUS IDENTITY

The 16th century reformation of the Church of Scotland, reinforced by the 1603 Union of the Crowns and the 1707 Treaty of Union, ensured that the once Catholic country of Scotland held a Protestant majority. Murray (1984) and Devine (1991) both feel that the culture of Catholic Scotland was cleansed out and replaced by the austere Calvinism of John Knox. Glasgow in the 1790s was estimated to have 39 Catholic organizations compared to 43 anti-Catholic bodies. Immigration due to the great potato famine increased the number of Irish Catholics in Scotland, but also increased the bitter feelings on the part of Scottish Protestants. Relations between the Protestant and Catholic communities at the end of the 18th century amounted to a virtual state of apartheid. Murray feels this was culturally expressed through football, in the form of Rangers and Celtic. Esplin (2000) concurs with this view, arguing that the most public and durable examples of exclusivity for either community, particularly for the Catholic population, were in football. As Boyle (1994) identifies, historical and religious allegiances are reinforced by the symbols exhibited by supporters at matches. Rangers supporters often display the Union Jack and Celtic supporters the Irish tricolor.

Marvin Andrews believes that both clubs could have maintained their respective religious affiliations without becoming sectarian, but believes that determined individuals on either side allied to significant historical forces ensured that this would not be so. Rangers and Celtic supporters have evidently become polarized in terms of football, politics, religion and culture, an argument that is reinforced by the formation of anti-sectarian campaigns such as 'Nil by Mouth'(Henderson, 2001: 1) and 'Sense over Sectarianism.' Nil by Mouth was Scotland's first organization dedicated to challenging sectarianism. The charity was founded in response to the murder of 15-year-old Mark Scott in 1995. Mark, a Catholic and Celtic supporter, was murdered by Jason Campbell, a Protestant and follower of the Rangers football club.

Despite such campaigns and the findings of Glasgow City Council (2003), several researchers have robustly defended the belief that sectarianism in Scotland is greatly exaggerated (Bruce: 1998). Despite such claims, the Scottish Government provided £100,000 during 2006 to support anti-sectarian project work in schools, promote use of the anti-sectarian education resource, and develop innovative approaches to tackling sectarianism. The Scottish government (2007) also provided £13,500 to support the use of the resource in youth work.

One football club in Andrews's opinion has historically come to represent the Irish Catholics—wearing green and white, waving the Irish tricolor, singing rebel songs from the republic—and the other characterizing the British Protestants—wearing red, white and blue; waving the flags of Great Britain and Northern Ireland; and singing songs from Orange Order and Unionist songbooks. According to Gallagher (1987: 11):

> The enmity and hysteria sometimes on display at Old Firm matches can serve as a timely reminder of just how thin the crust of civilization is. Here, regular battles have been fought between the supporters of a dead Dutch Protestant king and a live continental priest for generations.

This man-made historical hatred has little to do with the fundamental dogma of the Christian religion but is worthy of analysis in order to contextualize the beliefs of Andrews.

## WHAT IS SECTARIANISM?

The singing of sectarian songs contravenes the terms of the Criminal Justice (Scotland) Act of 2003. The offence is defined as acts of 'religious prejudice' the offender evinces toward the victim (if any) of the offence, malice and ill will based on the victim's membership (or presumed membership) of a religious group, or of a social or cultural group with a perceived religious affiliation. 'Religious group' in this context according to the law means a group of persons defined by reference to their (a) religious belief or lack of religious belief, (b) membership of or adherence to a church or religious organization, (c) support for the culture and traditions of a church or religious organization, or (d) participation in activities associated with such a culture or such traditions. In 2003, Glasgow City Council commissioned a survey on sectarianism within the city. The results did not make for comfortable reading. The key findings were that:

- 65% of people surveyed believed there was a serious problem of sectarian violence in Glasgow;
- 71% said that using sectarian language was common;
- 77% said that sectarian jokes were very common;
- 25% believed that sectarian views influenced job decisions;
- more than 50% thought that Orange Walks should be banned;
- the rivalry between Rangers and Celtic was most commonly seen as the way Glasgow's sectarian divide was sustained.

Andrews believes that people use Christianity as an excuse for sectarianism. 'I don't want fans to sing songs attacking the Queen or the Pope. They say it's their religion, but that's an excuse. These sentiments are not in the Bible. I pray God will change people's hearts.' Particularly worrying in Andrews's opinion is the influence parents' singing and chants have on their children who witness those expressing sectarian sentiments: 'You are teaching your kids to hate . . . the kids are the future. The Bible says love your brother as you love yourself and when you hate your brother you commit murder.' The identification that Andrews has with the fans regardless of their loyalties is arguably at the heart of the gospel and the imperative for reconciliation and is supported by St. Paul in Corinthians 1:10 (NIV):

> I appeal to you, brothers, in the name of the Lord Jesus Christ, that all of you agree with one another so that there may be no divisions among you and that you may be perfectly united in mind and thought.

The manner in which Andrews conveys his faith and views may be regarded as crucial to its appeal to those who are nonpracticing Christians. 'I always tell people that I am not here to force my beliefs or religion upon anybody. God has created an entire world and given every human being choices.' This philosophy of 'free will' also extends to teammates who are exposed to Andrews's faith via his actions on the field of play rather than his words, in the belief that 'when the Day of Judgment comes they cannot say that God did not give them the opportunity to be saved or become a Christian.' The presentation of himself as an approachable and humble servant of God is crucial in Andrews's opinion in order to spread the gospel. Andrews exudes impressive conviction that goes beyond the initial skepticism and incongruence of a professional footballer as a preacher in a secular age.

Andrews depicts Jesus as the definite model of Christian conduct, describing Jesus as 'the most religious person.' The emphasis of the humanity of Jesus in his earthly life is the core of Andrews's personal interpretation of 'Christocentricism' of the social gospel and the contemporary classical liberalism. For Andrews, following in Jesus' steps means not just living with a specific moral ideal of what we might become. He consistently emphasizes Jesus as the center of not only Christian behavior but also of Christian worship. The traditional picture of Jesus is clearly represented in Marvin's lectures both in and out of the pulpit where he faithfully, almost literally, adopts the narratives of the four Gospels.

In considering the drift of values and beliefs in British culture from those that have been shaped by centuries of Christian orthodoxy, it is also obvious to Andrews that connecting believing with belonging will be increasingly challenging. This is the main argument of Callum Brown's significant book, *The Death of Christian Britain* (2001: 61), which sees the critical issue as the loss of 'discursive Christianity,' the death of the 'Christian centered culture' from which people found guidance as to how they 'should behave and how they should think about their lives.' It is also obvious that if belonging is in itself less of a cultural value, a focus by the church that is primarily directed at those concerns will mean that its role will be both increasingly diminished and less effective. If, however, the church sees as part of its role the shaping of the values and beliefs of the wider culture and society in which it exists, then it needs to put energy and resources not only into connecting with people's beliefs in order to move them toward belonging but also with connecting in order to help shape those beliefs and values. Unfortunately, the focus of church leadership has seen a preoccupation with these institutional concerns and a neglect of the wider kingdom role of the church as salt, light and leaven in society.

## SINGING SECTARIAN SONGS?

The conscious decision to sing particular songs and chants in preference to others demonstrates a heightened level of awareness and attraction to those songs. Arguably the fan has objectively compared and evaluated the impact and connotations of the song and willingly taken part. The attraction of engaging in such behavior may be a result of the social situation and 'hedonism' or desire for pleasure motives (Funk & James, 2001: 119–150). The influence of role models in this process may be crucial. For example, children may select their favorite football team because of their father's influence. The behavioral norms that accompany attendance at football games is then framed by such 'significant others.' The opportunity for Andrews in this context is to offer himself as a positive role model in the absence of others.

> If I give a young person an autograph and I speak to them for two or three minutes, I can change their life forever. They look up at me as a role model and want to be like me, but I want them to be better than me. Whatever your dreams or goals in life, the Lord Jesus Christ can fulfill them, and that is what I try to portray.

Marvin Andrews arguably encapsulates the Christian belief that regardless of a person's level of fame and spiritual maturity, all in God's eyes are equal (1 John 5:21). The irony of how society upholds a 'caste' system in financial and physical realms is not lost on Andrews; he operates in such realms. However, he perceives his role as a 'spiritual leader' who should not be considered superior, but who helps to maintain a 'faithful walk through the challenges and temptations that confront individuals.' In this context, Marvin presents himself as an instrument of God to accomplish his ends whether they are great or small (Matthew 5:14–16).

The commitment demonstrated by football fans both financially and emotionally toward their teams demonstrates a level of attachment, according to Andrews, that few other sports can equal. Attachment in this context refers to the degree to which physical and psychological features (i.e., attributes and benefits associated with a team) take on internal psychological meaning (Gladden & Funk, 2001). Attachment to the historical and emotionally charged imagery of Catholicism and Protestantism in the west of Scotland may act as triggers for fans of both teams to reduce themselves to outpourings of sectarianism. A multitude of other factors can arguably contribute to reinforcing further the intensity of rivalry and sectarianism observed. Some of these factors may include the behavior of the manager/coach, star players, and other high-profile or status figures associated with the team. Teams inadvertently may foster attachment to religious issues and collectively strengthen attitudes, beliefs and values (Funk & James, 2001). The strength of the psychological connection that fans have for a team is the basis for distinguishing between attraction and attachment. Fans involved in the singing and chanting of sectarian songs clearly demonstrate a form of belief or purpose to their behavior.

What objective observers retain from visiting the respective stadiums of Rangers and Celtic are those moments when the crowd expresses a communal and arguably cathartic and vicarious release of emotion that is either startling in its intensity or plain surprising. Football grounds may therefore provide opportunities to uncover Scottish suppressed ethnic, religious, regional and class tensions. The chants in a football stadium today are no longer proxies for other passions. Football has become a cause in itself.

To facilitate effective Christian morality and to realize social reform in such communities, Andrews believes that the role of the Holy Spirit as absolute needs to be recognized. Andrews connects the Spirit's presence and power with almost every significant challenge, temptation or decision that supporters face. Andrews's thesis seems to contend that the Holy Spirit can work miracles and change people's fixed habits of thought and speech and action in anything. This includes the conversion of the vilest sinners, the elimination of slums, the revitalization of the church, the prohibition of liquor and the reform of society.

Andrews believes that the majority of people who sing sectarian songs are not bigots, but decent people who join in with a hard-core minority of real bigots because they believe it is harmless fun. Taking part in what many naively perceive as a 'bit of a laugh' is in effect practicing and perpetuating the social conditioning of others. Unfortunately, there are people in the crowd who deeply believe in the hate-filled words and, motivated by what they believe is the support of those around them, will later maim or take the life of somebody's son. Many people, Andrews believes, will read about such incidents the following day and shake their heads and say, 'That's terrible. I mean, I sing the songs but I'm not a bigot—my wife/friend etc. is a Catholic/Protestant.' This form of contradiction according to Andrews is a 'form of hatred that is man-made and has nothing to do with religion.'

Whether the perpetrators understand the doctrinal differences between various branches of the Christian faith or even whether they ever put in an appearance at church or chapel is arguably irrelevant. They consider themselves and each other as Catholics or Protestants and divide into opposing camps, which Andrews argues is satisfying the aim of the devil. Sectarianism is in essence focused upon attitudes and prejudices. It is what many people encounter daily in the workplace, in the pub, in the street and of course at football matches. It is real and in Andrews's view continues to have a widespread and corrosive effect on many aspects of Scottish life.

One of Andrews's tenets is that everyone should take responsibility for the language they use and the way they behave. 'Telling a sectarian joke in the pub—or indeed laughing at or just listening to it may seem relatively harmless, but arguably it's the start of a chain, a long chain which can end in violence and even death.' The inherent danger is that the extreme bigots, the ones who perpetrate the violence, imagine that people who laugh at sectarian jokes or sing sectarian songs at football matches must also support more physical expressions of bigotry. According to Andrews, this is how the devil operates, 'he gets into people's heads . . . all of a sudden from nowhere you start to think about it and it becomes action. The Bible says resist the devil and he shall flee from you.'

The most effective way for many football supporters to articulate the elements of their identity is through their behavior at a match. This is due to the fact that not only are similar individuals brought together in the same setting, but the others (i.e., opposition supporters) are also present in close proximity. This provides both groups of supporters with a relatively safe environment in which they can express elements of their identity and behave in a manner that may not be socially acceptable elsewhere. As Bradley (1994: 23) states, 'For Rangers and Celtic fans in particular, games are often viewed as opportunities for para-political expression. Rivalry between the fans of both clubs corresponds in a sense to the much larger religious and colonial rivalries that are centuries old.'

For example, popular songs amongst Rangers supporters include Orange Order anthems such as 'The Billy Boys' and 'The Sash My Father Wore.' As Walker (1991: 63) identifies, 'the tribal folk memory still counts for something, and Orange songs and banners and slogans spell out the claim to an invisible bond between Scotland and Northern Ireland for those who desire, or think it important, to hear it.'

'God Save the Queen' and 'Rule Britannia' are also commonly sung, the latter of which, according to Bradley (1994), probably became common during the 1982 Falklands conflict, a period during which anti-British/pro-Argentinean sentiments were also to be heard at Celtic Park. Furthermore, Rangers *casuals* are titled 'Her Majesty's Service' (Allan, 1989; Giulianotti, 1993). Conversely, Celtic supporters are known to sing Irish 'rebel' songs such as 'The Ballad of Billy Reid' together with chants referring to the political situation in Northern Ireland (e.g., 'Get the Brits, Get the Brits,

Get the Brits out now' and 'Ooh Aah, Up the Ra' [IRA]) and references to IRA icon and hunger striker Bobby Sands (Kuper, 1995). As Bradley (1998: 209) identifies, 'such songs are intrinsic to the nature and identities of both clubs and their respective supporters, as well as to many others in the wider society.' Newspapers such as *The Red Hand* (Loyalist) and *The Captive Voice* (Republican) have also traditionally sold well at Ibrox and Celtic Park, respectively, while members of paramilitary organizations have often publicly sported Celtic and Rangers jerseys to emphasize their allegiances to their respective causes. However, it is important to understand that some supporters neither understand nor agree with the sentiments they are expressing or do not fully appreciate the consequences of their actions.

After the IRA bomb at Enniskillen in 1987, the *Glasgow Herald* noted 'the tacit support for the IRA that you can read off virtually any wall in Glasgow and which you can hear chanted from the terraces of Celtic Park, or wherever Celtic players take the field' (Bradley, 1994: 13). The following year the *Sunday Mirror* claimed that during the Scottish Cup Final, 'Celtic supporters waved tricolor flags and sang choruses of Irish rebel songs, and there were chants of anti-British slogans from sections of the crowd' (Bradley, 1994: 41). In 1996 a 'Provos on Tour' flag was displayed by Celtic fans in Hamburg (Murray, 1984), while the Celtic fanzine *Tiocfaidh Ar La* is explicitly pro-IRA (Moorhouse, 1994). Such events have led contributors to Rangers fanzine *Follow Follow* regularly to refer to Celtic as 'the athletic wing of the IRA' (Murray, 1984: 147).

Heroes traditionally entertain their audience and in order to do this must imitate the tastes of their audience to keep their attention (Silk, Slack & Amis, 2007). Andrews is the exception to this. Andrews advocates religion to be used for brotherhood and social cohesion. In allowing himself to be accessible to the media, he offers a guide to moral values. The context of professional football provides society with an opportunity to entertain and provide diversion from societal demands. It clearly invokes excitement and emotional commitment from individuals whether as a spectator or participant. Durkheim's 1915 classic study of religion explored the functional relationship between the sacred and the profane elements in society (Thompson, 1982). The extraordinary prominence given to the role of football in modern Scottish society may make it akin to the sacred, but it also highlights the role of the profane. The conviction with which Marvin Andrews espouses his faith clearly provides spiritual support in the face of the often racist and vitriolic sectarian abuse he receives.

> Fans always have things to say. Some are clearly under the influence of alcohol which means that tomorrow they won't remember a word they have said. But, I know that even when they have sobered up for some of them the hatred is there. But for me it doesn't matter whether you are a Celtic or a Rangers supporter. Possibly one of the most beautiful sights that you can ever see is one where two children are playing

> football together in a park; one kid wearing a Celtic shirt and one with a Rangers shirt. I hope this is how it will become one day between fans of both teams in Glasgow.

'Faith,' according to Christian tradition, is the 'gift of God'; it is not given to all, and thus it is impossible for all people to share the perspective (Dawes, 2003). Andrews, while acknowledging this dogma, seeks to demonstrate through his personal commitment to God that nobody has a valid excuse for not knowing the truth since God has made God's self known to all through creation. His philosophical line of reasoning is founded upon the work of St. Paul: 'For since the creation of the world, God's invisible qualities—his eternal power and divine nature—have been clearly seen, being understood from what has been made, so that men are without excuse' (Rom. 1:18–21, NIV). Both Catholics and Protestants are part of the Christian faith. In some schools there are pupils who still perceive Catholics and Protestants to be of different faiths rather than two denominations of the same faith. Andrews's opinion is that Catholics and Protestants are different yet the same, 'The sad thing about sectarianism between Protestants and Catholics is that they belong to the same Christian faith.'

Sectarianism is a profoundly complex and controversial issue within contemporary Scottish society. The potential of charismatic individuals such as Marvin Andrews to sow 'seeds of hope' in such historically and religiously entrenched communities is clear, however. In Andrews's opinion, it can be summarized as a matter of 'faith.' He paraphrases St. Luke when he states, 'What is impossible with men is possible with God' (Luke 18: 27). The notion of tolerance and justice is fundamentally at the heart of Marvin Andrews's faith. The acceptance of different people, ideas and values is essential. Andrews refers to St. Luke in support of his views: 'treat others as you want them to treat you' (Luke 6:31).

Despite the obvious challenges inherently facing any practicing Christian, Marvin Andrews believes that his high-profile role in Scottish professional football is a demonstration of the awareness that 'for evil to flourish good men only need do nothing' (Hastings & Selbie, 2003: 127). For Andrews, this social goal is possible through the transformation of each individual. For such a transformation he has consistently emphasized the definite role of the Christian community (the church) for this vision. Andrews strongly believes that the church is the best institution to carry out social service.

Andrews seeks the social ideal of a good Christian community, which is possible through the individual following in Jesus' steps with the practice of philanthropy and with the communal disciplines and works. Since Andrews believes that each individual can be best nurtured through communal disciplines in the church, such as participating in public services, conferences and prayer meetings, Andrews's ministry continuously demonstrates that these Christian forms of worship and fellowship are the driving forces for an individual's following in Jesus' steps.

## CONCLUSION

In Andrews's belief, selfishness is the best known sin in the world, and does not improve on acquaintance. It is the source of wars, cruelty, injustice, greed and lust. It fills jails, asylums, poor houses and cemeteries. It sins against the unborn and condemns them to lifelong pain and poverty. Andrews defines 'the greatest world problem' as 'human selfishness,' which causes all kinds of social problems. Because all the social sins and issues are rooted in individual problems, Sheldon insists that the church must begin with the 'cure' of an individual mind. 'The Church is an organization that stands for character building to change people's minds' (in Woodworth, 1983: 53).

Based on this definition, Andrews continues to fight against the contemporary social evils, including violence, cruelty, gambling, secular amusements, gossip, drug abuse and tobacco. The church in Sheldon's view must relate to the culture in a double movement. To summarize Marvin Andrews's beliefs, not only must the church be shaped by the culture as it seeks to incarnate the Christian message into relevant forms, but it must also seek to shape the culture by the gospel values that transcend it. It must be both faithful to its 'context' and faithful to its 'text.'

As our fragmented society seeks to redefine common values and beliefs without which it cannot function, Andrews argues that the church can play a significant public role. Countries such as Scotland may have to accept that the church is no longer at the centre of society and must learn to function and speak from the margins, as one voice among many. Marvin Andrews sincerely believes in his goal of a Christian form of idealism:

> It is perfectly possible and it is ideal, but life without ideals is not worth living. The world will never know an ideal of business, politics, journalism, church life, recreation, education, and brotherhood until people everywhere, of all tongues and climates begin to walk in His steps.

In Marvin Andrews's opinion, the most important principle by which he conducts himself both on and off the pitch is not the attainment of the 'perfect life' but the sincere motivation to apply the question of 'what would Jesus do?' to our daily lives. In echoing the work of many social gospel proponents, Andrews presents a strong view on the importance of the church in citizenship and politics with this question. Andrews strongly insists, 'If Jesus was on earth today,' he would provide many social programs in church to transform the society. Andrews believes not only that the church has 'a mission *in* the world' but also that the church has 'a mission *to* the world.'

## BIBLIOGRAPHY

Allan, J. (1989) Bloody Casuals: Diary of a Football Hooligan, Glasgow: Famedram.

Armstrong, G., and Giulianotti, R. (2001) *Fear and Loathing in World Football*, Oxford: Berg.

Bailey, E. (2001) *The Secular Faith Controversy: Religion in Three Dimensions*, London: Continuum.

Bairner, A. (1997) Up to Their Knees?: Football, Sectarianism, Masculinity and Protestant Working-class Identity, in *Who Are 'The People'? Unionism, Protestantism, and Loyalism in Northern Ireland*, P. Shirlow & M. McGovern (Eds.), London: Pluto Press, 95–113.

Bairner, A., and Darby, P. (1999) Divided Sport in a Divided Society: Northern Ireland in John, in *Sport in Divided Societies*, John Sugden and Alan Bairner (Eds.), Aachen: Meyer & Meyer, 51–72.

Boorstin, D. (1961) *The Image: A Guide to Pseudo-Events in America*, New York: Random House.

Boswell, J. (1992) *The Life of Samuel Johnson*, New York: Random House.

Boyle, R. (1994) "We are Celtic Supporters . . .": Questions of Football and Identity in Modern Scotland, in *Game without Frontiers: Football, Identity, and Modernity*, Richard Giulianotti and John Williams (Eds.), Aldershot: Arena, 73–98.

Bradley, J. (1994) *Ethnicity: The Irish in Scotland—Football, Politics and Identity*, Caledonian, Papers in the Social Sciences, Social and Public Policy Series no.1: Glasgow Caledonian University.

Bradley, J. (1998) "We Shall Not Be Moved!": Mere Sport, Mere Songs—A Tale of Scottish Football, in *Fanatics! Power, Identity and Fandom in Football*, Adam Brown (Ed.), London: Routledge, 203–218.

Bradley, J. (1999) British and Irish Sport: The Garrison Game and the G.A.A. in Scotland, in *Sports Historian*, 19/1: 81–96.

Bradley, J. (2004) (Ed.) *Celtic Minded: Essays on Religion, Politics, Society, Identity, and Football*, Glendaruel: Argyll Publishing.

Bromberger, C. (1993) Fireworks and the Ass, in *The Passion and the Fashion*, Steve Redhead (Ed.), Aldershot: Avebury, 89–103.

Brown, C.G. (2001) *The Death of Christian Britain*, London: Routledge.

Bruce, S. (1998) Sectarianism in Scotland: A Contemporary Assessment and Explanation, in *Scottish Government Yearbook*, Edinburgh: Scottish Executive Publications, 150–168.

Bruce, S., Paterson, I., Rosie, M., and Glendinning, T. (2004) *Sectarianism in Scotland*, Edinburgh: University Press.

Cashmore, E. (2000) *Making Sense of Sports*. 3rd ed., London: Routledge.

Coakley, J.J. (2003) *Sport in Society: Issues and Controversies*, Boston: McGraw-Hill.

Criminal Justice Act (Elizabeth II: Queen's Printer of Acts of Parliament), Edinburgh: Scottish Executive Publications, 2003, Chapter 44.

Davie, G. (1994) *Religion in Britain Since 1945: Believing without Belonging*, Oxford: Blackwell.

Dawes, G.W. (2003) Religious Studies, Faith, and Presumption of Naturalism, in *Journal of Religion & Society*, 5 (ISSN: 1522–5658), retrieved: April 23, 2004 from http://moses.creighton.edu/JRS/2003/2003–8.html

Devine, T. (1991) *Irish Immigrants and Scottish Society in the Nineteenth and Twentieth Century*, Edinburgh: John Donald.

Durkheim, E. (1915) *The Elementary Forms of the Religious Life*, London: Allen & Unwin.

Esplin, R. (2000) *Down the Copland Road*, Argyle: Argyll Publishing.

Funk, D.C., and James, J. (2001) The Psychological Continuum Model: A Conceptual Framework for Understanding an Individual's Psychological Connection to Sport, in *Sports Management Review*, 4/2: 119–150.

Gallagher, T. (1987) *Glasgow: The Uneasy Peace: Religious Tension in Modern Scotland*, Manchester: Manchester University Press.

Geering, L. (1994) *Tomorrow's God: How We Create Our Worlds*, Wellington: Bridget Williams Books Ltd.

Gill, R., Hadaway, C.K. and Marler, P.L. (1998) Is Religious Belief Declining in Britain? in *Journal for the Scientific Study of Religion,* 37/3: 507–516.

Giulianotti, R. (1993) Soccer Casuals as Cultural Intermediaries, in *The Passion and the Fashion*, S. Redhead (Ed.), Aldershot: Avebury, 155–203.

Gladden, J.M., and Funk, D.C. (2001) Understanding Brand Loyalty in Professional Sport: Examining the Link between Brand Association and Brand Loyalty, in *International Journal of Sports Marketing & Sponsorship,* 3 (ISSN: 1464–6668), 67–94.

Glasgow City Council. (2003) *Sectarianism in Glasgow: Final Report*, Edinburgh: NFO Social Research.

Hastings, J., and Selbie, J.A. (2003) *Encyclopedia of Religion and Ethics*, part 21, Montana: Kessinger Publishing.

Hay, D., and Hunt, K. (2000) *Understanding the Spirituality of People Who Don't Go to Church, Daily Telegraph* Newspaper, May 28.

Henderson, C. (2001) *Nil by Mouth Newsletter,* 1. Summer, 1–15.

Henning, E., Van Rensburg, W.A.J. and Smit, B. (2004) *Finding Your Way in Qualitative Research*, Pretoria: Van Schaick Publishers.

Holstein, J.A., and Gubrium, J.F. (1997) Narrative Practice and the Coherence of Personal Stories, *Sociological Quarterly,* 39/1: 163–187.

Jarvie, G. (2006) *Sport, Culture, and Society: An Introduction*, London: Routledge.

Jarvie, G., and Maguire, J. (1994) *Sport and Leisure in Social Thought*, London: Routledge.

Jarvie, G., and Reid, I. (1999) Sport, Nationalism and Culture in Scotland, *Sports Historian,* 19/1: 97–124.

Jenkins, R. (1996) *Social Identity*, London: Routledge.

Kuper, S. (1995) *Football against the Enemy*, London: Phoenix Press.

Kvale, S. (1996) *Inter Views: An Introduction to Qualitative Research Interviewing*, Thousand Oaks, CA: Sage.

Lawrence, I. (2005) The Emergence of "Sport and Spirituality" in Popular Culture, *Sport Journal,* 8/2, Spring, retrieved June 15, 2006 from http://www.thesportjournal.org/article/emergence-sport-and-spirituality-popular-culture

MacClancy, J. (1996) Nationalism at Play: The Basques of Vizcaya and Athletic Club Bilbao, in *Sport, Identity, and Ethnicity*, Jeremy MacClancy (Ed.), Oxford: Berg, 181–199.

Magdalinski, T., and Chandler, T. (2002) (Eds.), *With God on Their Side: Sport in the Service of Religion*, London: Routledge.

Moorhouse, H. (1994) From Zines Like These—Tradition and Identity in Scottish Football, in *Ninety Minute Patriots?: Scottish Sport in the Making of the Nation*, Grant Jarvie and Graham Walker (Eds.), Leicester: Leicester University Press, 173–194.

Murray, B. (1984) *The Old Firm: Sectarianism, Sport, and Society in Scotland,* Edinburgh: John Donald.

Murray, B. (1998) *The Old Firm in the New Age: Celtic and Rangers Since the Souness Revolution*, Edinburgh: Mainstream.

Nixon, H.L., and Frey, J.H. (1996) *A Sociology of Sport*, San Francisco: Wadsworth.

Novak, M. (1976) *The Joy of Sports: The Consecration of the American Spirit*, New York: Basic Books.

Patton, M.Q. (1990) *Qualitative Evaluation and Research Methods*, 2nd ed., Newbury Park, CA: Sage.

Petre, J., and Cobain, I. (2000) Survey Charts the Soul of Britain, in the *Daily Telegraph* Newspaper, London, May 28, 8.

*Record of the Summit on Sectarianism.* (2005) Edinburgh: Scottish Executive Publications.

Roof, W.C. (1993) *A Generation of Seekers*, San Francisco: HarperCollins.
Scottish Government. (2007) Action Plan Update on Education, retrieved from http://www.scotland.gov.uk/Publications/2007/02/15092146/2/Q/Zoom/100
Silk. M., Slack, T., and Amis, J. (2007) Bread, Butter, and Gravy: An Institutional Approach to Televised Sport Production, *Sport in Society*, 3/1: 1–21.
Sparkes, A. (2002) *Telling Tales in Sport and Physical Activity*, Leeds: Human Kinetics.
Thompson, K. (1982) *Emile Durkheim*, London: Tavistock Publications.
Walker, G. (1991) The Protestant Irish in Scotland, in *Irish Immigrants and Scottish Society in the Nineteenth and Twentieth Century*, Tom Devine (Ed.), Edinburgh: John Donald, 44–66.
Ward, S. (2004) Is New Zealand's Future Churchless? *Stimulus*, 12/2, May, 2.
Woodworth, R.L. (1983) *The Life and Writings of Charles M. Sheldon with Special Reforms to His Relations with the Press*, unpublished PhD dissertation, Carbondale: South Illinois University.
Wright, R. (1953) *The Outsider*, New York: Harper & Rowe.
Wuthnow, R. (1994) *God and Mammon in America*. New York: Free Press.

# Part II

# Psychological and Spiritual Dimensions of Sport

# Part II Introduction

*Mark Nesti*

## INTRODUCTION

This part of the book deals with the relationship between psychology and spirituality in sport. Recent years have seen a growth of interest in the psychological aspects of competitive sport, and the benefits of exercise and physical activity for mental health. The academic discipline of sports psychology is now well established. In the UK alone, there are at least 60 universities that offer courses or modules in sports psychology. Despite this, the topic of spirituality has very rarely been considered at the British Association of Sport and Exercise Sciences (BASES) annual conferences, or at similar gatherings in North America. It seems that sports psychologists are as reluctant as their colleagues in the parent discipline of psychology to acknowledge the concept of spirituality, and its possible link to the mind. This prejudice is all the more difficult to understand, given that the term "psyche" is usually translated to mean soul.

The chapters that follow either state explicitly, or at least hint, that the roots of much modern psychology preclude any possibility of spirituality being accepted as a legitimate topic for study, because sports psychology has tended to follow the materialist, deterministic and positivist paradigm of mainstream psychology. This has governed our dealings with other paradigms such as Freudian psychoanalysis, behaviorism, and cognitive and trait approaches to the discipline.

In Chapter 5, Nick Watson investigates the important issue of identity in sport. He argues that despite being studied in sports psychology in relation to career development, injury and retirement, there are very few examples of where this topic has been considered in relation to spirituality and religious belief. Watson suggests that the work of Erikson could be used by sport psychology researchers to expand their notions of identity to include reference to transcendence and religion. He discusses how this would help broaden work in this area and develop a more empirical (i.e., real) approach to an understanding of sports identity.

Since the 1960s, humanistic psychologists have been at the forefront of those who were prepared to discuss peak experiences, mystical states and religious belief and practices. Within this movement, a small number of psychologists have turned their attention to investigate personally significant, subjectively measured emotional states, which are sometimes encountered in sport performances. Variously described as peak experiences, optimal states and flow, these and other closely related terms have been reported by athletes, often during their best performances.

In Chapter 6, Fr. Pat Kelly draws on Csikszentmihalyi's concept of flow to describe how sport can encompass notions of play and the experience of joy. Linking this to ideas contained in Ignatian spiritual exercises, Fr. Kelly suggests that sport performers can find meaning in sport despite the negative experiences that can exist in this most human of enterprises. Kelly presents a convincing case for the capacity of sport to develop our spiritual lives, when we engage fully in the task.

The language used to describe these experiences sounds uncannily close to descriptions of spiritual moments in other kinds of activities beyond sport, and this shared vocabulary has provided an impetus to some of the studies mentioned in this part, which also discusses ways in which terms such as 'courage', 'spontaneity' and 'sacrifice' are evidence of a spiritual dimension within sport.

In Chapter 7, Mark Nesti addresses such issues. His account uses aspects of existential theory to interrogate how spirit may be encountered in Premiership football. These concepts and others, such as team spirit, selflessness and joy, have been recognized by humanistic psychologists, and especially existential psychologists, as important psychological categories.

Sports psychologists open to these ideas are extending their work by asking questions about the role of prayer and religious ritual in competitive sport (cp. Hoffman in Chapter 2). This is guided by a recognition that for many sports performers across the world, religious belief and personal faith are central to their identity as individuals and as athletes. Interest in this logically follows from within those perspectives in sports psychology which advocate a study of the person first, and the athlete second. Related to this, the discipline has at last turned some attention towards an examination of sources of meaning that athletes draw upon to sustain their motivation and performances in sport. It seems that, for some participants in sport, their spiritual and religious beliefs are a central part of who they are. The chapters in this part aim to highlight this empirical fact.

Beyond academic study and specific research strands within sports psychology, the real world of sport has long since found a place for spirituality. Evidence of this is seen every week in newspapers, and can be heard on TV channels when athletes, coaches and commentators describe exceptional performances as being due to great team spirit, courage or spirited individuals. Sports psychologists who work with these groups frequently stress that these terms used by sport practitioners do not simply refer to motivation, confidence or mental toughness. Although they generally value these attributes in their athletes, coaches, managers and sports fans remain convinced that spirit, whether at team or individual level, is ultimately the most important psychological quality to possess. Due to this, the issues discussed in these chapters may cause more difficulty for academic sports psychologists than for those untrained in the discipline. This has often been the case in the history of new ideas, where those in the establishment are rarely in the vanguard! However, it may be that, without a substantial shift in focus towards research methods that can accommodate the personal dimension in sport, little will be achieved. It may also be that there needs to be a repositioning of the paradigm towards a recognition that psychology cannot proceed as a second-rate natural science, but that it must take its place as a valued and useful human science.

It is noteworthy that the sports psychologists who have contributed to this part draw, for the most part, on their own experiences as sports participants, and from their work with athletes. It is to be hoped that the result of these kind of data, and of such experiences gained in the field, will be the removal of some of the barriers and the opening of new opportunities for the study of sport, psychology and spirituality.

# 5 Identity in Sport

## A Psychological and Theological Analysis

*Nick Watson*

*Sport, as many commentators have noted, is the new religion. It has superseded Christianity in many cultural theorists' eyes as the social practice par excellence that initiates persons into rules and norms of virtuous and vicious behaviours which orientate us more broadly in the world.*

Mike McNamee[1]

*Fourth in the Olympics hurt, but retirement is like a death in the family . . . I struggled for three months . . . I'd walk around and just start filling up. I'd wake up lost. I didn't know what to do. My emotions were so intense I felt I'd lost a member of the family. I'd lost a major part of my life, something was dead. Everything I'd lived for was over.*

British Olympic Decathlete, Dean Macey,
on retiring from sport. (Slot, 2008, p. 98)

## INTRODUCTION

Sports philosophers, such as Howard Slusher (1967), Scott Kretchmar (1998) and Heather Reid (2002), have argued that we need to think more philosophically about the *meaning* of sport participation and competition. Kretchmar has recently suggested that in studying sport 'to do ethics *in vacuo,*' without some sort of metaphysical (i.e., religious) basis, is a questionable endeavor. He sees athletes as 'meaning-seeking, story-telling creatures' who can encounter real drama, experience excellence and self-discovery in healthy sporting contests. In relation, a small number of sport psychologists have also challenged the current dominance within their discipline of positivistic research and cognitive-behavioral consultancy *techniques* advocating the need for more holistic, philosophical (Corlett, 1996a, 1996b; Martens, 1987; Ravizza, 2002), existential (Dale, 1996, 2000; Nesti, 2004) and spiritual and religious approaches (Berger, Pargman & Weinberg, 2002; Salter, 1997; Schinke & Hanrahan, 2009; Watson & Nesti, 2005).[2] The dominant schools of mainstream 20th-century psychology (the parent discipline of sport psychology)—experimental, behaviorist, cognitivist and clinical—have also adopted mainly secular theories of human identity based on scientific and positivist philosophy. There are, however, some notable psychologists in the past 70 years who accommodated existential and spiritual ideas in their work, and thus provided a valuable resource for understanding the complexities of human identity in life and sport.

Surprisingly, largely absent from most sports psychology research, with some exceptions (Begel, 2000b; Brewer, Van Raalte & Linder, 1993; Gray & Polman, 2004), is the foundational clinical and interdisciplinary work on human development and identity of Erik H. Erikson (1902–1994). The curious omission of such *foundational* work on identity within the sports psychology literature is not the case in theology, with major figures such as Wolfhart Pannenberg's drawing heavily on Erikson in his chapter on *The Problem of Identity* (1985). Erikson's (1968) well-used eight-stage *Human Life Cycle* (inc. stages of identity crises) model of human development has led some to herald him as a prophet of the 'age of identity' in which we now live (Hoover, 2004: 1). Alongside the anthropological work of Margaret Mead (1937) and the remarkable sociohistorical study of Charles Taylor, *Sources of Self: The Making of Modern Identity* (1989), it is Erikson (1959: 114) who showed any student of identity that 'an individual life cycle (psychological) cannot be adequately understood apart from the social context in which it comes to fruition' and that 'individual and society are intricately woven, dynamically in continual change.'[3]

This will be an important part of my study of identity in sport, for as Phil Night, founder and chairperson of Nike, states, sports arguably 'define the culture of the world' (cited in Smart, 2005: 1). Although Erikson was always reasonably open to the value of various religious and spiritual paths and non-empirical concepts, such as love and wisdom (Hoare, 2000), it was not until the end of his career that Erikson reflected more on spirituality and transcendence, in what has been called by his wife the 'ninth-stage' of his Life-Cycle Model (Erikson, 1997a, 1997b). Following Erikson, some other well-known 20th-century psychologists were also open to spiritual and religious notions *broadly conceived*. Abraham Maslow (1962), the founder of humanistic psychology, advocated the need for spiritual growth (an oxymoronic concept in humanism?), as have many others in this school and in sport psychology (Ravizza, 1984, 2002). The existential psychiatrist Victor Frankl, author of the best-selling book *Man's Search for Meaning* (1959)—surely a prophetic title for the times in which we live—even talked of God (*logos*, trans. Word; see John 1:1–2), fully articulated in his *quasi*-religious understanding of identity and means of soul care, logotherapy (Frankl, 1986: xii). In his own words:

> . . . logotherapy sees in religion an important ingredient in human existence; religion, that is, in the widest possible sense of the word, namely, religion as an expression of "man's search for *ultimate* meaning." Yet

> logotherapy—by its very name a meaning centered psychotherapy—views even man's orientation toward the *ultimate* meaning as a *human* phenomenon rather than divine.

The recent shifts toward spiritual and religious concepts, such as love, creativity, faith and wisdom, within the disciplines of sport philosophy and sport psychology, positive psychology (Seligman & Csikszentmihalyi, 2000) and in the works of Erikson, Maslow and Frankl, are then encouraging, and make a significant contribution to my thinking in terms of understanding the complexities of athletic identity. This said, the foundational source of identity (ontologically and epistemologically)[4] throughout this body of work is, as Frankl (1986: xii) states, '. . . a *human* phenomenon rather than divine,' and thus puts the *self* at the centre of the framework of meaning (humanism and naturalism), rather than God (supernaturalism). I will argue that this is *diametrically opposed* to a Christian theological perspective of identity as described in the Bible,[5] in which humans are called to deny them*selves* and live *in* Christ (Matt. 16:24–27)[6]. This is *not* as burdensome a thing as it may sound to some but rather something that, as C.S. Lewis[7] notes, actually leads humans to freedom of heart, peace and becoming 'more truly themselves . . . it is when I turn to Christ, when I give up myself to His personality, that I first begin to have a personality of my own.'

In hopefully adding something new to the valuable past psychological (Brewer, Van Raalte & Petitpas, 2000), psychiatric and clinical (Begel & Burton, 2000; Beisser, 1967; Gardner & Moore, 2006), sociological (Harris & Parker, 2009; Parker, 1995; Roderick, 2006) and pedagogical (Macdonald & Kirk, 1999) work on athletic identity and related research on self-worth and dispositional neurotic perfectionism in sport (Hall, 2008; Hill et al., 2008) that is based on a secular and humanistic worldview, this approach provides a significantly different understanding of personhood and how we understand ourselves and others in competitive sport.[8] Its core premise is that humans' identity, that is, their feeling, thinking, attitudes and behavior, should be grounded in, and flow from, the heart of a loving Father God. As Paul states in the Bible (Acts 17:28), when addressing the Athenian philosophers, 'for in him we live and move and have our being. . . .'

This study is also needed due to longitudinal sports ethics research that has suggested that athletes in Christian and secular American schools show very little difference, if any, in moral reasoning and that Christian athletes had a tendency to compartmentalize their faith and exclude it from competitive sport (Beller et al., 1996; Stoll & Beller, 2008).[9] Why is this so? Can Christian athletes simply follow the strict moral code of the Bible and feel, think and act in the heat of competition and in relationships, in a Christ-like manner? I will argue not, due to the foundational biblical principle that the state of the 'heart' of the believer, their *disposition*—the depth of relationship and intimacy with God through Jesus Christ—is the source of all right and wrong, feeling, thinking and acting.

> Above all else guard your heart, for it is the wellspring of life
>
> (Proverbs 4:23)

> The mouth speaks out of the overflow of the heart
>
> (Matthew 12:34)

My anthropological start point is predicated on the biblical position that *all* humans are made in the image of God—*imago Dei* (Gen. 1:27)—and comprise soul, body and spirit (1Thessalonians 5:23).[10] This division of self is useful in analyzing identity in sport. However, throughout this chapter, I wish to combat the Platonic-Cartesian mind-body dualism entrenched in Western thought by referring to the soul, body and spirit holistically as the *heart*, a Hebrew and Pauline perspective (Jeeves, 1997; Pannenberg, 1985).[11] This view maintains that the human being is thoroughly integrated, though with different aspects.

Consistent with this idea that the Christian faith can be described as a *personal* and *intimate* relationship with God in the 'heart' of the human believer versus a dry rule-governed legalistic and judgmental religion (arguably an idol and huge defense mechanism in the modern world),[12] and that the word 'heart' is spoken of hundreds of times in the Bible, it is necessary to provide some explanation of this term. In a little-known and arguably neglected book, *Biblical Psychology* (1962/1936: 97–105), Oswald Chambers provides some clarity on the spiritual nature of the human heart, which he calls the 'radiator of the personal life'—the source of human identity and moral reasoning:

> The use of the Bible term 'heart' is best understood by simply saying 'me'. The heart is not merely the seat of the affections, it is the centre of everything. The heart is the central altar, and the body is the outer court. What we offer on the altar of the heart will tell ultimately through the extremities of the body . . . the centre from which God's working and the devil's working, the centre from which everything works which moulds the human mechanism . . . Our Lord undertakes to fill the whole region of the heart with light and holiness . . . (2 Corinthians. 4: 6) . . . Do I realize that I need it done? Or do I think I can realize myself? That is the great phrase today, and it is growing in popularity—'I must realize myself'.

'I must realize *myself*'? Indeed, Chambers's reflections from the early 20th century are, I would argue, prophetic for the age in which we live. The cultural ethos of 'self-realization,' or what has been called 'selfism' by psychologist Paul Vitz (1994), is so encultured in the West that I agree with those who have argued that pride of the heart 'is now synonymous with virtue' in the institutions of media, sport and religion (Higgs & Braswell, 2004: 372). To be sure, this view of identity and self-worth that has no objective foundation, as it is relative to each person, is so deeply woven into the fabric of society that it is, as the 19th-century writer Kierkegaard (1989/1849) states, the worst form of despair, a 'fictitious health.' Why? Because it is, as Kierkegaard called it, the disposition of the 'automatic cultural man' an *unconscious* denial of the reality of life built on *self*, instead of the source of our being, a holy loving God. This idea is not new and supports the maxim 'read an old book for a new idea'!

The Nobel Prize–winning, atheistic existential philosophers and playwrights of the 1950s, Jean-Paul Sartre (1956) and Albert Camus, amongst others, brilliantly showed the meaningless and absurdity of life without belief in a supernatural God. Ironically, this was only a rehash of ideas clearly articulated in the biblical books of Ecclesiastes and Job thousands of years before and has provided theists with a logically 'watertight' case, when arguing the need for belief in God to provide purpose and meaning in life. Focusing these ideas back on issues of identity in sport and other domains of life, such as work—a major source of meaning, especially for men—John Eldridge (2001: 90, 150) painfully and truthfully deconstructs any models of identity built on self-realization and the West's idea of worldly success:

> The world [the Western system] offers man a false sense of power and a false sense of security . . . the world cheers the vain search on . . . Be brutally honest now—where does your own sense of power come from? Is it . . . how well [you] play sport? . . . Is it how many people attend your Church? Is it *knowledge*—that you have an expertise and that makes others come to you, bow to you? Is it your position, degree, or title? A white coat, a Ph.D., a podium [?] . . . what happens inside you when I suggest you give it up? . . . what you would think of yourself if tomorrow you lost everything that the world has rewarded you for?

Elsewhere, I have reflected on Eldridge's words, suggesting that 'for those embedded in the post-modern world of sport, which is constructed from socio-cultural norms and reinforced and manipulated by the mass media, Eldridge's words may be a little too piercing and thus quickly dispatched to the caverns of the mind, and consequently they will continue to 'travel with the carnival''[13] (Watson & White, 2007: 78). The 'carnival' is what Ernest Becker (1973: 82), in his magnificent presentation of Kierkegaard's psychoanalysis (a Freudian term), calls the 'social hero system,' wherein modern humans 'successfully . . . play . . . the standardized hero-game' of their age to protect themselves from the existential *angst* of the realities of the human condition—absurdity and meaninglessness, without belief in a supernatural God.

As articulated in the writings of St. Augustine, Kierkegaard, Dostoyevsky, Oswald Chambers, G.K. Chesterton and C.S. Lewis and of course the fountain of all their musings, the Bible, the insidiousness of pride and narcissism in the West's cultural value system has resulted in widespread cultural and social fragmentation. This is, in part, a consequence of the liberalization of ethics and the 'human potential' movement (e.g., Esalen Institute) in America.[14] The titles of notable books such as *The Culture of Narcissism: Life in an Age of Diminishing Expectations* (Lasch, 1980), *Psychology as Religion: The Cult of Self-Worship* (Vitz, 1994) and Ernest Becker's award-winning *The Denial of Death* (1973) also accurately convey our current situation. Nonetheless, liberal-humanist and postmodern voices that dominate academic sports studies (e.g., sociology, philosophy, psychology, pedagogy) and other disciplines at times seem oblivious to the evidence all around them that the 19th- and 20th-century utopian 'myths of progress'[15] have been unable to prevent, and have often contributed to, what David Blankenhorn (1995) and many others in theology (Marx, 2003;[16] McClung, 2005; Nouwen, 1979; Prince, 2008; Stibbe, 1999; Vitz, 1999) and leisure studies (Coakley, 2006; Kay, 2006a, 2006b) have accurately called a *Fatherless Generation*.

Blankenhorn has convincingly demonstrated, using a range of historical and empirical data, that the postmodern liberalism and nihilism that characterize much of modern culture has resulted in the breakdown of the family, the most vital and *foundational social unit*. In particular, the related problem of fatherlessness and its *unavoidable* affect on the identity of those who have grown up not knowing the love, care and protection of their natural father[17] (and Heavenly Father) pervades all areas of culture, including sport. A principal aim of this chapter is to suggest that the foundational answer to this problem lies in individuals, communities and nations coming into a knowledge and personal revelation of the love of a Father God. To achieve any clear understanding of individual human identity from this perspective, I must also examine the dominant characteristics (identity) of the society and culture in which individual identity is formed—what Margaret Mead (1937), the well-known anthropologist, called the process of 'enculturation.'

After providing a rationale for the need of this study, my first task is to analyze the conceptual nature of sports competition and its role in understanding 'athletic identity,' which has been defined as 'the degree to which an individual identifies with the athlete role' (Brewer, Van Raalte and Linder, 1993: 237). This will allow for a theological and psychological analysis of identity in sport, focusing on pride, humility and idolatry. Pride and humility are the two states of heart that I see as fundamental in understanding both positive and negative aspects of identity in sport. I will then provide extended *Concluding Remarks* due to the embryonic nature of the study of identity in sport from a Christian perspective and some suggestions for future empirical research and scholarship and a range of resources to assist in this process.

## IDENTITY AND COMPETITION IN SPORT

In his book *Winning: The Psychology of Competition* (1980: 4), Stuart Walker makes a number of points about athletic competition, which are important when examining issues of identity in sport:

> Most competitors think of themselves as being primarily motivated to develop, demonstrate, and enjoy competence. Many, however, are also concerned with the demonstration of power, courage, and aggressiveness. They use competition to overcome feelings of dependence, helplessness, and loss of individuality. Others are more concerned with being approved, appreciated, and admired. They use competition to overcome feelings of being separated, abandoned, and unloved. Competition permits the demonstration of individual significance, which gratifies desire for both assertiveness and approval. The key word is "demonstration." Competitors perform in public; they assert themselves in the presence of others—of their competitors at the very least.

Walker's psychological thesis holds *some* weight; however, as Newman (1989) notes, Walker overstates his point as to how competitions are *primarily* activated, that is, winning is the *only* goal of the athlete. This thesis is far too simplistic and I would agree with Simon (1991: 33), who notes that competition in sport is ethically defensible and that the 'meeting of the demands athletes place upon their talents often involves beauty, courage, dedication, and passion.' Nonetheless, the intense emotion and passion often present in the delicately balanced dialectic of competitive sport, Hyland (1988: 177) suggests, also carries the risk that 'such intensity will devolve into alienation and violence.' This is closely tied to athletes' (and coaches', parents' etc.) *need* for recognition, love and demonstrating power and significance, which is conveyed by Walker and is arguably *one* mainstay of modern competitive sport.

A psychoanalytical perspective of these needs in competitive sport, Kohn (1992: 106) suggests, would basically run something like: winning = coach's approval = parental acceptance (in child/youth sport) = acceptance of self (self-worth).[18] In extending Kohn's social-psychological analysis to include the spiritual, this unhealthy 'disordering of our affections,' as church father St. Augustine (354–430) put it, may lead to perversion and corruption of the activity in which 'the athlete may delude himself into thinking that his own quest for wealth and fame, or even a championship, will make him happy' (Hamilton, 2003: 7). In other words, for athletes and coaches of this mind-set it would seem that 'sport *is* life' (Reid, 2002: 106) and to lose, or be unable to play for whatever the reason, can have catastrophic consequences for the emotional and psychological balance of an individual; that is, their identity.

England Rugby Union World Cup star Johnny Wilkinson has recently confessed the underlying reason for the 'near destruction of his career—an obsessive quest for perfection' (Jackson, 2006: 50). This is something that is acutely conveyed in the title of his recent biography, *Tackling Life: Striving for Perfection* (2008). In light of the 'win-at-all-costs' ethic, reflect on Wilkinson's very honest and illustrative comments about his injuries, the meaning of rugby for him and how this has impacted upon his psychological well-being and understanding of *life itself*:

> The truth is that I was wracked with anxiety, almost constantly. I wanted it [to achieve] so badly that I was beating myself up. It was the same whether I played for Newcastle, England or the Lions. Before the game it was nerves. After the game it was a harsh post-mortem—why did I miss that tackle? Why did I miss that conversion? . . . All the intensity and attrition brought with it intense fatigue. That resulted in injuries which, in turn, have resulted in a lot of pain and anguish . . . You hear yourself saying only good things will come of this, that there's a reason for it and you've saved yourself for two years of being battered but none of it is really true . . . I would have given anything to have played consistently . . . There have been times when it's been hugely painful. I've been incredibly depressed, demoralised, even bitter . . . I feel as if I've let myself down then, because it's all about setting benchmarks as a person and there have been times when I've failed to reach these marks. It has made me lose my way in so far as all my life I've done nothing but think and play rugby. When it's taken away from you for as long as it has been, it makes you unsure over what you're supposed to do with your life. (Jackson, 2006: 80).

Interestingly, Wilkinson's emotional rollercoaster, following a catalogue of injuries since his moment of glory with that famous dropkick in the dying seconds of the 2003 Rugby World Cup Final (Sydney), has led *Times* journalist Souster (2009: 84), to suggest that he has now undergone an almost '. . . spiritual change.' Arguably, Wilkinson has experienced what the Jewish philosopher Martin Buber called a 'shudder of identity' (Agassi, 1999), that is, one of the primary sources of meaning in *life* has been removed and he is searching his soul for purpose and meaning. Ruben (cited in Kohn, 1992: 111) captures something of this in stating that for 'many strong competitors, upon reaching the summit of their aspirations . . . the discovery, ultimately, that "making it" is often a hollow gain, is one of the most traumatic events that the successful can experience.' Along with many others, Wilkinson has encountered the existential angst, fear and sense of worthlessness that often accompanies the loss of a significant 'life project'

(Sartre, 1956) like sport, what cultural anthropologist Ernest Becker (1973: 3) aptly describes as the 'dread of insignificance.' This anxiety and sense of worthlessness is likely to be more intense for professional full-time athletes (Null, 2008) such as Wilkinson, in comparison to amateurs due to the greater time, significance, meaning and ultimately sense of identity invested in sport, a 'life project.'

Sad stories of retired athletes, for example, British soccer players from the 1980s and early 1990s, in particular, sliding into alcoholism and suffering from serious relationship problems (e.g., divorce), illustrates the potentially catastrophic identity issues that can ensue when sport, the 'life project,' is lost (e.g., Jupitus, 2008; Roderick, 2006).[19] The poignant and yet often failed and embarrassing 'comebacks' of professional athletes at the end of their careers is another example of how sport can become an 'unhealthy obsession.' The 'old pro' is unable to let go of their sporting life in an anxious quest to hold onto a major source of their identity in *life*.

These fears of loss and failure are very often *hidden* behind psychological defenses, what Christian psychologists have aptly called 'fig-leaves,'[20] such as a mask of competence, outward success and sense of 'having it all together,' the very ethos of the Western world. This is most often an *unconscious* response and stems from *foundational* low self-worth.

Evidence of this existential angst in elite and youth sport performers has been shown in research on dispositional neurotic perfectionism (Hall, 2008) and 'fear of failure' (Sager, Lavallee & Spray, 2009), psychiatric writings on the mental health of athletes (Begel, 1992; Burton, 2000) and theological (Hamilton, 2002) and philosophical (McNamee, 2008)[21] reflection on shame in sport, with athletes suffering from feelings of narcissism, guilt, shame, negative mood and resultant decrements in performance.

For an athlete in competitive sports, the feeling associated with moving teams, athletic retirement (Kerr & Dacyshyn 2000; Lavallee & Wylleman, 2000), career-ending injuries (Udry et al., 1997) and defeat can be great and is often the precursor to feelings of loss and neurotic anxiety[22] and in some cases what consultant sport psychiatrist Robert Burton (2000) classifies as post-traumatic stress disorder (PSTD). Indeed, for some athletes this loss of identity and self-worth associated with these *perceived* traumatic occurrences in sport has resulted in clinical depression and occasionally suicide attempts (Oglivie, 1987; Smith & Milliner, 1994), as was sometimes the case in ancient Greek athletics (Higgs & Braswell, 2004).

Although this is not a simple correlation, since many other factors determine an athlete's sense of identity, such as sex, personality, race and ethnicity, education, culture, family background and past experience (Brewer, Van Raalte & Petitpas, 2000), the physical body, the individual's name[23] and group membership (Pannenberg, 1985: 225), nevertheless playing and winning equals 'being,' and losing equates to 'non-being.' 'Non-being threatens man's self-affirmation,' suggests theologian Paul Tillich (1952: 41). In the athletic arena this may lead to a sense of unworthiness and insecurity in the athlete when they lose, or fail to come up to the often unrealistic and unhealthy expectations of pushy coaches, parents and even nations.[24]

Though by definition these losses are simply a temporal evaluation, ask any athlete or coach and, if honest, they will admit that at times they allow their performance to define their being and so for them a *loss* is tantamount to defeat or failure (symbolic death) as a person (Reid, 2002). This is what sport psychologists call the 'hero-to-zero' syndrome. In discussing the loss and sorrow of losing in competitive sport, Higgs and Braswell (2004: 75) use 'the term "pseudo-sorrow" to express the emotional state of losers' and state that 'real sorrow lives in hospitals and in funeral homes and indeed ordinary homes without number.' While of course there is very real suffering in sport that can be a mix of physical, mental and spiritual (Howe, 2004; Loland, Skirstad & Waddington, 2005; Nesti, 2007b), this again conveys how sport has become for many in the West an idol[25] that is intimately tied to the identity and self-worth of athletes and fans. I am not suggesting that athletes should not passionately[26] care about sport and become emotionally involved. This is in part what makes sport participation and competition so exciting, fulfilling and healthy.

In support of Hochstetler, Hopsicker and Kretchmar (2008) and Twietmeyer's (2008) holistic conception of sport, neither do I advocate a dualistic worldview in which 'real sorrow' only exists in 'real life' outside of sport. I hold firmly to a biblical, Pauline and ultimately Jewish anthropology—mind, body and spirit are viewed as *one* (*nephesh*)—supporting the notion that our experience of suffering, loss, joy and sorrow is valid in all of life's diverse situations and messiness (Johnson, 1998). However, if 'post-match blues' slide into prolonged self-pity, moods and depression that affect the athlete and are *projected* on to others, then arguably sport has become an idol. The destructive consequences of the 'win-at-all-costs' ethic of modern sport (especially on individual identity) has been examined in more detail elsewhere (Watson & White, 2007) and is also prevalent in organized child and youth sport that reflects trends in professional adult sport.

A wealth of studies and writings exist that have documented the negative and worrying trends in elite child and youth sport development strategies and grassroots sport policy, which are linked to the cultural ethos of winning-at-all-costs.[27] I would argue the most comprehensive analysis of this endemic problem is Paulo David's important book *Human Rights in Youth Sport: A Critical Review of Children's Rights in Competitive Sports* (2005), which covers areas such as overtraining, eating disorders, physical and mental burnout, elite youth sport programs and the negative effect of parental pressure and expectations.[28]

Instead of viewing competition as a healthy test or mutual striving toward excellence, the etymological root of the term (Hyland, 1988), or as a *playful* form of developmental recreation, it has become to some degree a questioning of the athlete's or child's/youth's very existence and their source of self-worth. This has been clearly articulated by religious studies scholar Michael Grimshaw (2000: 87), in his analysis of the idolatrous nature of modern sport, in which he argues a 'pagan mythology of fallible gods' has evolved. To be sure, for many participants and spectators modern sport is a religion in the ritualistic and functional sense (see Prebish, 1993),[29] with many similarities evident between the practice and rituals of modern sport and religion.

For the elite athlete, winning in sport is then frequently inflated to a form of immortality (Schmitt & Leonard, 1986) and thus idolatry, resulting in the individual seeking to justify the meaning of their existence through their sport participation. The complex and differing motivations *of heart* to succeed, in the 1924 Olympic Games, shown by Harold Abrahams and Eric Liddle, is beautifully portrayed in the award-winning film *Chariots of Fire*, and is a good example of this. [30] As Cashmore (2008: 162) has noted in his sociohistorical analysis of the film, Abrahams's '. . . individualistic, self-interested approach to competition . . . is . . . entirely congruent with the 'win-at-all-costs' mentality that was to become prevalent in [modern] sport.' From a Christian perspective, glorification of the *self* in any human endeavor, as was arguably *one* motivation of Harold Abrahams in this film, is rooted in the sin of pride, the 'complete anti-God state of heart,' according to C.S. Lewis (1997/1952: 100).

## THE ROLE OF PRIDE AND HUMILITY IN SPORTING IDENTITY

> Pride is *essentially* competitive above all other vices
>
> C.S. Lewis

> Learn from me for I am gentle and humble in heart
>
> Jesus of Nazareth

Sporting tales, as those described earlier, illustrate how the ego of the athlete can predominate in a quest to win and ultimately to appear and feel superior or even godlike,[31] which, when you consider Harold Abrahams's words and the boasts of modern athletes together with the explicit *worship* of modern sports stars in the media and their institutionalization in halls of fame, I would argue is not an exaggeration for *some*. Drawing on excerpts from Schneider's theology of personhood and his criticisms of Sartre's atheism, Pannenberg (1985: 234) articulates this clearly:

> To the extent that human beings try to gain their wholeness and strive to be "in and for themselves," they are always a "desire to be God"

> . . . Thus the striving for the self-realization that is directed toward the wholeness of one's being is in fact to be understood as an expression of sin, of the will "to be like God".

From a psychological standpoint, this can be understood as the athlete, coach, sporting parent (vicariously) needing to attain 'self-actualization' (Maslow, 1962) through worldly success, adulation and affirmation in competition and their career. Van Kaam (1975: 177, 195), in his incisive assessment of modern psychology and modern culture, points to this, in suggesting that 'an overemphasis on introspective attitudes has seriously hindered the spiritual growth of western man . . . we are ego-centered, when we should be God-centered.' In support of Van Kaam and the reflections of the theologian Pannenberg, psychologist Paul Vitz (1994: 91) concludes in his trenchant critique of humanistic and atheistic-existential psychology—the work of Jung, Rogers, Fromm and Maslow—that the 'relentless and single-minded search for and glorification of the self . . . is at direct cross-purposes with the Christian injunction to lose the self.'[32] Lose the *self* in an age of success?

By modern *worldly standards* of success, *Jesus Christ was the greatest failure in human history*, something that was clearly prophesied in the writings of the Old Testament prophet Isaiah[33] seven hundred years before his birth. To be sure, the Christian story does not portray Jesus as a 'self-actualizer'! No, the Christian narrative records that he '. . . made himself nothing, taking the very nature of a servant, being made in human likeness. And being found in appearance as a man, he humbled himself and became obedient to death on a cross!' (Philippians 2:7–8). The gospels (trans. Greek, *good news*) in the New Testament, which are both prophetic and historical documents,[34] state that from the time Jesus 'set his face to go to Jerusalem' and after his wrestling with his calling and destiny in the garden of Gethsemane, the words of Isaiah the prophet began to be fulfilled:[35]

> 'He was despised and rejected by men, a man of sorrows, and familiar with suffering . . . he was despised and we esteemed him not . . . surely he took up our infirmities and carried our sorrows . . . he was pierced for our transgressions, he was crushed for our iniquities; the punishment that brought us peace was upon him, and by his wounds we are healed . . . he was oppressed and afflicted yet he did not open his mouth; he was led like a lamb to the slaughter . . . Yet it was the Lord's will to crush him and cause him to suffer . . . the Lord makes his life a guilt offering . . . after the suffering of his soul he will see the light of life. . . .'
>
> (Isaiah 53)

Why did Jesus have to tread the path that theologian Timothy Savage (1996: 188) notes is a 'strange' and 'alien' glory anticipated by . . . Isaiah, a light revealed in the darkness of death, a splendour manifested in the most appalling object of antiquity—a cross'? Indeed, the blood-soaked cross paradoxically speaks of reconciliation, light and love, as personified in Jesus himself being described as the 'light of the world' in the prologue to John's gospel. The purpose of Jesus Christ's sacrifice, as described in Christian thought, was to reconcile his Father's creatures (humans) back into an intimate relationship with himself: *at-one-ment*. Theologians call this the *atonement* and contend that all three dimensions of the Trinity, the Father, Son and Holy Spirit, are involved in the process (McGrath, 2001)[36] and that it is the path to eternal life, deep joy and a 'peace . . . which transcends all understanding' (Philippians 4:7a; Isaiah. 26:3) regardless of earth's circumstances. This is clearly described in an oft-cited bible verse

> For God so loved the world that he gave his one and only son, that whoever believes in him shall not perish but have eternal life
>
> (John 3:16)

Commenting on the meaning of the atonement for individual identity, the priest-psychologist Adrian Van Kaam (1975: 143) notes that 'an infinite love tenderly called me forth out of nowhere and nothingness; an unspeakable Love emptied itself to redeem the identity that I lost sight of in sinfulness; an enlightening Love keeps calling me back to what I am.' Herein lies the paradox[37] of the Christian faith, articulated by C.S. Lewis in that 'the more we let God take us over, the more truly ourselves we become—because he made . . . it is when I turn to Christ, when I give up myself to His personality, that I first begin to have a personality of my own,'[38] in all domains of life, including sport.

Following this central biblical theme of surrender to Christ—'If anyone is in Christ, he is a new creation' (2 Corinthians 5:17)—it is then the *relationship in the heart* of the Christian believer with a Father God, through the third person of the Trinity, the Holy Spirit,[39] that Christians believe 'guards' their 'hearts and minds in Christ Jesus' (Philippians 4:7b). Coherent with the Christian anthropology laid out in my introduction, the *heart* is then understood as the seat of all wrong or right feeling, thinking and behaving, and thus is the foundational source of human identity in all of life's activities, including sport. Considering that the Psalmist (51:17) states that it is 'a broken and contrite heart . . .' that allows for an intimate relationship with God, how does this fit with a modern understanding of Christianity in the West, and conceptions of identity in sport?

The Reverend Mark Townsend's words in his recent thought-provoking book *The Gospel of Falling Down: The Beauty of Failure in an Age of Success* (2007: 44–45)[40], conveys a realistic picture of the god-man who walked the earth two thousand years ago and the religion he expressed:

> Failure, rather than success, is at the heart of the life of Jesus and his message. He came to liberate us from the "gospel of success". It is not in "climbing the ladder of perfection" [i.e., maladaptive perfectionism] that we meet God, but in falling from it. And it is then that we discover the most beautiful spiritual gold . . . The Gospel is not about *success* . . . To make the Gospel into a means of being successful is to seriously miss the point. We live in a success-dominated world, and much of the (especially Western) Church has become a success-dominated religion. What is the central symbolic image for the Christian faith? It's a cross of wood, with a figure of a man nailed to it—a naked, bleeding man. A man so wounded, so humiliated, so crushed that one can barely imagine . . .

Therefore, as Clements (1994) and Savage (1996) have articulated, it is *through* a journey of weakness (*not* in character), brokenness, vulnerability and sacrificial love that Jesus went to the cross, and it is believed by Christians, resurrected by his Father—the event on which the Christian story stands or falls. Interestingly, then, consultant sport psychiatrist Dr. Daniel Begel (2000a: xiv–xvi), who has worked with amateur and professional American sports teams, elucidates how thoughts of 'weakness and vulnerability' in modern sport are often *diametrically opposed* to the identity of the modern athlete:

> If there is any character trait that is anathema to an athlete it is that of weakness. Being unable to handle one's feelings, and confessing that inability to another human being in intimate conversation, is not usually concordant with an athlete's sense of mastery . . . the role of professional athlete may increase the risk of suffering a specific narcissistic vulnerability, and retirement from sports at any level carries with it an increased risk of clinical depression, especially if the retirement is forced by injury, or waning abilities . . .

Not to be misinterpreted at this juncture in my argument, achievement and excellence, strength of character and body and success in sport are *not* at all antithetical to the Christian way of life. But it can be dangerous, because of the proud and self-reliant ethos of Western culture that dominates big-business professional sport, which is often, but certainly not always, characterized by individualism, vainglory and ultimately pride of the heart (Lasch, 1980; Watson & White, 2007). Pride of the heart is what C.S. Lewis (1997/1952) and professor of pastoral psychology Donald Capps (1987: 46–52) call 'the great sin' and is the root of most other sins which are arguably prevalent in modern sport, such as greed, vanity and self-glorification.

Both Lewis and Capps are, however, balanced in their reflections on pride, emphasizing that there are positive and negative forms of pride. For example, in sport, having a sense of one's own self-worth and dignity in performance as an athlete or coach, taking pleasure in being praised by parents, coaches, fans and teammates and satisfaction in one's sporting achievements are all examples of pride in a positive sense. This said, it has been argued, and I agree, that pride 'is now synonymous with virtue' in the institutions of sport, religion and the media (Higgs & Braswell, 2004: 372). According to Christian scripture, 'life projects,' like sport, can then easily become idols that blind people to deeper spiritual truths about 'who they are'—their identity—and what is *ultimately* important in life.

C.S. Lewis unwittingly provided a sound theoretical basis for analyzing identity in sport from a Christian theological perspective (Watson & White, 2007). If pride, as Lewis (1997/1952: 101) suggests, 'is *essentially* competitive above all other vices,' how does this specifically relate to understanding identity in sport? The findings of Stevenson's (1997) qualitative investigation of the culture of elite sport and the moral dilemmas this raises for Christian athletes, shed some light on this. One participant comments, 'It's weird. I just couldn't let go of not winning. If we lost, I just couldn't let it go for a week—it would, like, boil inside me.' Another participant states, 'I think there's times when . . . as an athlete, when we're excelling to become our best . . . [that] we lose sight of everything [else] around us.'

Stevenson concludes that 'these athletes struggled with the overwhelming priority placed on winning in the contemporary sport culture' that 'led to a number of consequences with which they were uncomfortable' (244–245). Clearly, organized child and youth sports are also a major vehicle for this cultural ethos and its subsequent problems. 'In childhood, the discovery of athletic talent may determine a person's role within the family and identity within society in significant, if not always salutary, ways,' suggests sport psychiatrist Begel (2000a). It seems that the centrifugal forces that act upon and within the microcosm of sport are difficult to step outside of.

Thomas á Kempis (1380–1471), in his well-known devotional work *The Imitation of Christ* (1952: 50), advises that 'no man can live in the public eye without risk to his soul.' Christian teaching suggests that the 'weapons' and source of 'power' with which humans (modern athletes) can combat their prideful human nature that will cause them to desire recognition, seek *vain*-praise and glory and act in a manner that will possibly lead to the alienation of others (opponents and family etc.) are love and humility from surrendering to God. As Capps (1987: 50) has observed, 'pride is also a form of *isolation* . . . and personal bondage . . . because it is a form of self-love in which we deny our need for community with others.' Humility is the virtue directly opposite the sin of pride that leads to alienation and isolation, which Lewis (1997/1952: 100) contends is the 'complete anti-god state of mind' and which had its genesis in the fall from grace of some of God's angelic realm and humanity. From this point in world history, in every dimension of life including sport, Murray (1982: 118) suggests that 'pride and humility are the two master powers—the two kingdoms at war' in our hearts, which will determine our feelings, thoughts and actions in the heat of sporting competition.[41]

In this fallen, messy and broken world, what theologians call the state of the 'already, not yet,'[42] this will be a process of struggling and wrestling with issues of the heart, whether a believer or not, due to *common grace*[43] afforded to all humans, and the paradoxical and mysterious nature of human existence, as acknowledged by Paul in his second letter to the Corinthians (5:2–4 and 17). Empirical research on moral reasoning in Christian and non-Christian athlete college populations (Stoll & Beller, 2008) seems to provide evidence of this. It is argued that *self*-control is not the master Christian virtue as some have suggested (Baumeister & Exline, 2000). But rather that all 'Christians must yield actively to God. Yielding is the master virtue, which produces control by the "new self". Attempting to achieve moral control is . . . a battle . . . a Christian view of self-control finds the self to be *inadequate* to win the struggle for virtue' (Worthington & Berry, 2005: 157), as the apostle Paul found out in his life of dependence and surrendering his heart to God (Romans 7:7–25).

Surrendering the heart to God, according to Andrew Murray (1982), is when 'true humility comes . . . in the light of God, we . . . have consented to part with and cast away self—to let God be all. The soul that has done this and can say "I have lost myself in finding You," no longer compares [the root of pride and alienation] itself with others' (Murray, 1982: 59–60). Belief in this worldview then transforms Sartre's (1956) 'life projects' such as sport, family, work and all forms of recreation into *gifts* from God (James 1:17) to provide his creatures with meaning, enjoyment and health, well-being and even enhanced sport performance (this is *not* the aim of Christianity!).[44] But as gifts they do not provide 'ultimate meaning' and the primary source of our identity, as the painful biblical story of Job (1:6–22) and modern stories of alienation, abuse and depression in sport show.

## CONCLUDING REFLECTIONS

> . . . Christian psychology is not the study of human nature Christianised, but the endeavour to understand the wonder and the mystery of "Christ in you, the hope of glory"
>
> Oswald Chambers (1922)

> God made me for a purpose but he also made me fast and when I run I feel his pleasure
>
> Eric Liddell, *Chariots of Fire*

The aim of this chapter was to provide a psychological and theological analysis of identity in sport while also acknowledging the importance of social, cultural and historical forces in identity formation. Following others, I have argued that as a 'moulder and reflection of 20th century attitudes towards human nature' (Johnson, 1997: 12), modern psychology (and sport psychology) that is largely characterized by individualism, humanism, positivism and a relativist epistemology is diametrically opposed to Christian psychology (especially anthropology and ontology). Nonetheless, I also heartily support Dallas Willard (2000: 256), who wisely notes that 'psychological and theological understanding of the spiritual life must go hand in hand. Neither of them is complete without the other.' Therefore, in any comprehensive study of identity in sport, both empirical and theoretical research in sport psychology, on areas such as 'athletic identity' (e.g., Athletic Identity Measurement Scale) motivational theory, human development models (e.g., Erikson), forms of psychological abnormality and mechanisms of the brain must be synthesized with sound theology and biblical anthropology.

In particular, I would emphasize the accuracy of the anthropological starting point when studying identity in sport from a Christian perspective, in that 'the image of God in the New Testament reflects a theological and philosophical struggle with some of the most important questions of human existence. Who are we as humans, and to whom do we ultimately belong?' (Krause, 2005: 360). In trying to answer these questions in sport, scholars should carefully examine both Hebrew and Christian anthropology (e.g., Chambers, 1957; John Paul II, 1997; Macquarrie, 1982; McFadyen, 1990; Pannenberg, 1985)[45] when deciding how they should respond to the tenets of modern psychology, so that, as Johnson (1997) in pointing to the bible stresses, they are not taken '. . . captive through hollow and deceptive philosophy, which depends on human tradition and the basic principles of this world rather than Christ' (Colossians 2:8)—humanism, secularism, nihilism and selfishness. For those wishing to examine issues of identity in sport from a Christian standpoint, there are a number of useful nonsport sources in the psycho-theological literature and writings on the 'Fatherhood of God,' which I have argued is central to understanding Christian identity in sport.[46]

Although previous writings specifically on athletic identity in the sports literature are sparse, the excellent work of scholar Ashley Null (2004, 2008), sport psychologists Mark Nesti (2007a, 2007b, 2007c) and Derek de la Peña (2004), reflections from the Vatican's office for 'Church and Sport' on chaplaincy in sport (Libreria Editrice Vaticana, 2008) and analyses of idolatry in sport (Gibson, 2008; Moltmann, 1989; Watson & White, 2007; White, 2008) should all be of use in grasping the psychological and theological complexities of identity in the sports realm. Returning to the work of Erikson (1959: 114), let us also remember when analyzing athletic identity, the 'social context in which it (identity) comes to fruition' is vitally important. While not allowing 'sociology to displace theology' (e.g.,

Feuerbach, Marx, Durkheim et al.) and understanding that theologizing 'does not take place in a vacuum,' Campbell (2008: 11, 2) warns that 'it is important to review our understanding of *historic Christian identity* in its social, cultural and theological dimension, and reflect upon this in the light of new evidence.' Therefore, it is also crucial to draw on key mainstream sociological works such as that of Erving Goffman, *The Presentation of Self in Everyday Life* (1990/1959), and Anthony Giddens's (1991) specific sociological analyses of the sport-religion interface (e.g., Coakley, 2007; Jarvie, 2006; Magdalinski & Chandler, 2002), recent important work on social identity formation in sport contexts (Harris & Parker, 2009) and the ever-increasing corpus of writings on the cultural and sociological (e.g., Coakley and Dunning, 2002; Elias & Dunning, 1986) and sociohistorical (e.g., Guttman, 1978) dimensions of sport.

Nonetheless, since the evolution of modern atheistic sociology in the 19th century, the foundation of the discipline of sports sociology in the 1960s and the advent of so-called postmodernism, Cobb (2005: 185) argues that 'we find ourselves casting about for new moorings upon which to secure our identities.' In short, the majority of modern sociology (and psychology) I would argue stands on 'epistemological and ontological sand,' in which identity construction is like 'shopping for a self' (Lyon, 2000). A 'false myth,' which according to C.S. Lewis, was brilliantly deconstructed by the philosopher (epistemologist) Michael Polanyi, in what many view as a 'paradigmatic' but often neglected book, *Personal Knowledge: Towards a Post-Critical Philosophy* (1958). A depressing reality, when considering the logically watertight philosophy of the avowed atheist Bertrand Russell, in which he concludes that 'unless you assume a God, the question of life's purpose is meaningless.'[47] The Christian view of life's meaning, the created world and society and culture, is, however, far removed from this honest but bleak *human-centered* outlook and shows how societal structures and culture can be a means of God's grace and love to His creatures.

Although there is an ever-increasing literature on the *Theology of Culture* (e.g., Cobb, 2005; Lynch, 2005; Percy, 2005) that is helpful for Christian scholars in sport seeking to grasp social and cultural dynamics in sport studies, it is the seminal book of H. Richard Niebuhr, *Christ and Culture* (1951), which is arguably a key starting point for those wishing to explore how Christians relate to culture and how identity can be positively or negatively formed within it. Michael Wittmer (2008) has adapted Niebuhr's five-point typology to examine modern sport and thus has provided an excellent foundation for others. Scholars should also not overlook Karl Barth's theology as a source of much wisdom (Metzger, 2003), in keeping theological (and psychological) study of identity Christocentric—Barth's great contribution to the 20th-century theological enterprise. These psychological, theological and sociological analyses suggested earlier should be helpful for those wishing to critically explore a multitude of unanswered questions concerning personal and social identity in sport from a Christian standpoint.

Following the mapping of the human genome at the turn of the 20th century and the valuable but primarily humanistic analyses of genetic enhancement in sport (e.g., Miah, 2004), theological analyses are crucial in assessing the wider implications of being able to tamper with the makeup (anthropology and legal issues)[48] of human beings (e.g., Trothen, 2008). Exploration of how states of heart, such as pride and humility, impact upon moral reasoning (Worthington & Berry, 2005) and relationships (e.g., Marshall, 1992; Mason, 1999; Quoist, 1965) in sport is another important area to explore, for as C.S. Lewis (1997/1952: 102) has suggested, 'pride has been the chief cause of misery in every nation and every family since the world began . . . pride means enmity—it *is* enmity.' A prideful heart that seeks personal glory, gain and self-worth primarily in sporting success will often alienate and disregard others, leading to the damage and breakdown of relationships (e.g., Hellstedt, 2000). The role of shame and guilt in this process, which often leads to *striving* for personal glory and self-worth in sport and to the alienation of others, is a related area for further enquiry (see Hamilton, 2002; Tournier, 1962; Twitchell, 1997).

Research on how identity may impact upon sports leadership models from a Christian worldview is also needed. The concept of *Servant Leadership* described in Rieke, Hammermeister and Chase's (2008) empirical study of basketball coaches, a qualitative investigation by Macdonald and Kirk (1999) on Christian identity in health and physical education teachers (see also Schroeder & Scribner, 2006) and the legendary reflections of 'Coach Wooden' (e.g., Wooden, 2005)[49] all provide a foundation for this and pave the way for related topics such as the influence of prayer[50] and gender on identity formation and maintenance and leadership.

The recent scholarship of Deardorff and Deardorff (2008) on Christian 'masculine and feminine templates' and Farooq and Parker's (2009) research on Islamic masculinity, within the confines of sporting subculture, also open up an important line of enquiry on athletic identity. Investigating Judeo-Christian counseling models for sport psychologists, coaches and chaplains, perhaps based on Martin Buber's concept of *I and Thou* (see Agassi, 1999; Buber, 1958/1923; Nesti, 2004; Progen & DeSensi, 1984; Watson, 2006; Watson & Nesti, 2005), is another topic to explore, as arguably that the foundational identity of the counselor or practitioner can have a significant impact upon the effectiveness of the therapeutic/practitioner relationship. According to the teaching of the Bible, the Christian believer is expected to live *supernaturally*, in faith and dependence on God, in all domains of life, including sport; thus, the use of spiritual gifts[51] underpinned by the *foundational* fruits of the spirit[52]—love and humility—should also be an area for further enquiry. The testimony of Scottish professional footballer Marvin Andrews, allegedly having his ruptured anterior cruciate ligament miraculously healed though faith in God and prayer, as reported in the *Times* (Slot, 2005), and Ian Lawrence's (2009)[53] fascinating qualitative study in which he interviewed Andrews are examples of this.

To develop past thought-provoking work on identity in disability sport (e.g., Smith & Sparkes, 2008; Sparkes & Smith, 2002) from a theological stance, researchers could begin to examine existential meaning and spirituality in athletes with physical and intellectual disabilities. What does physical movement through sporting activities mean, if anything, for those with profound intellectual disabilities? How does participation in sport impact on the identity of those with physical disabilities and how, if at all, could this have spiritual meaning? How do individuals in a society bound to a dominant worldview of competition, physical competence (e.g., able-bodied Olympics), rationality and intellectualism respond to the broken minds of those with profound intellectual disabilities that can't be fully 'understood,' 'fixed' or 'cured'?

Commenting on the theme of my last question, Graeme Watts (2008: 8–9) draws on the provocative suggestion of Wolf Wolfensberger (2001) that people with an intellectual disability may have actually been chosen by God to be the prophets of our age—an age in which many seek to win at all costs, to appear competent to 'have it all together.' Watts observes that Wolfensberger may be making this case with more than a touch of hyperbole but argues that in promoting values opposite to those so tightly held as 'normal,' it is perhaps the obviously limited capacity of those with an intellectual disability which acts as a reminder that to be human also includes those who are dependent and fall short of generally held ideals. In this context I would also agree with Stanley Hauerwas's (1986: 176) assertion that those with profound disabilities often '. . . remind us of the limits of our power, and we do not like those who remind us,' something that has perhaps significantly affected the church's limited theological reflection on disability. Further study in this area may help 'self-reliant' Westerners to consider life's purpose, which of course includes the meaning and purpose in sports and accurate conceptions of humility.

Some sections of the church have historically had a *false* view of humility, in which God-given gifts, talents and desires of the heart have been deemphasized and shunned '. . . under the guise of *devotion to Christ*' (Johnson, 2006: 38). Following Bill Johnson, I would argue this is not an accurate portrayal of Christian life, in which creativity, joy and excellence should, where possible, be sought in all domains of life, including sport. I also wholeheartedly support some of the conclusions of Barry Smart (2005: 198–199), in his comprehensive analysis of *The Sport Star . . . Sporting Celebrity*: 'the achievements of high profile professional sporting figures possess a quality that is increasingly rare in a world made cynical (corruption in sport) . . . the excitement and emotion aroused by the uncertainty of sporting encounters . . . the pleasure derived, and frequently collectively shared . . . as a spectator or viewer.' In this vein, through analyzing Karl Barth's work on the famous composer Wolfgang Amadaeus Mozart and his appreciation of Mozart's playful creativity and expression of his musical gift *in* the world, Metzger (2003: 197)[54] reminds us that the Christian God delights in his creatures being . . .

> . . . creative within human culture . . . to give glory to God by simply being . . . by *simply* working or playing, one glorifies God . . . God is glorified in the very imaginative and enterprising acts of human creation and recreation. Before God, there is room for free play.

Beginning with the seminal work of Dutch historian Johan Huizinga (1950) and followed by reflections from theologians (e.g., Johnston, 1983; Moltmann, 1972; Pannenberg, 1985: 323–339) and sport philosophers (e.g., Kretchmar's Chapter 8, this volume), this playful, aesthetic and creative dimension of life that is often seen in sport has been well-documented. It seems to most readily manifest itself in fun 'pickup games' and when sport competition is played in the spirit of a 'mutual stringing together for excellence,' the etymological root meaning of the term 'competition' (Hyland, 1978, 1988). In the modern era, the men's 2008 Wimbledon Tennis final (and the 2009 Australian Open final) between Roger Federer and Rafael Nadal was perhaps an example of this. The TV commentator and ex-British number one tennis player Andrew Castle said of this exciting and passionate dual between two men at the height of excellence in the field that it was not solely a demonstration of great tennis but an advert for the value and beauty of sport *itself*—it had a transcendent dimension (my paraphrase). There seemed to be a deep mutual respect between the Spaniard (Nadal) and the Swiss (Federer) and a form of humility that ironically is often only witnessed in those at the very peak of their field, in this case sport because, from a humanist's standpoint, they are secure (if with a degree of *fragility*, perhaps)[55] in who they are and confident in *their* abilities, their *selves*.

Sport itself could then be argued to possess a spiritual dimension, in that it seems to provide opportunity akin to what the sociologist of religion Peter Berger (1970: 52) called 'signals of transcendence . . . within the human condition.' Indeed, the great 19th-century Russian novelist Dostoyevsky (1967/1927: 259)[56] was not ignorant to the fact that 'the universal and everlasting craving of humanity' is 'to find someone to worship' and in the sporting realm it is perhaps these 'moments of transcendence' and aesthetic beauty[57] (amongst many other 'earthy' things), and the sporting demigods who provide them, that fit the bill. There is, however, a real danger in this *quasi*-transcendent understanding of life and sport, as poetically described by C.S. Lewis:

> The books or the music [and sporting moments] in which we thought the beauty was located will betray us if we trust to them; it was not *in* them, it only came *through* them, and what came through them was longing. These things—the beauty, the memory of our own past—are

> good images of what we really desire; but if they are mistaken for the thing itself they turn into dumb idols, breaking the hearts of their worshippers. For they are not the thing in itself; they are only the scent of a flower we have not found, the echo of a tune we have not heard, news from another country we have never visited . . . Our lifelong nostalgia, our longing to be reunited with something in the universe from which we now feel cut off . . . is no mere neurotic fancy, but the truest index of our real situation.[58]

Our 'real' situation? In his analysis of the idol-pride interface in the human heart, in both Augustine's autobiography, *Confessions*, and his most well-known theological work, *The City of God*, Reno (2006: 176) concludes that '. . . we wrap our love of worldly things in this false tinsel of divinity and propose them to ourselves as idols worthy of worship. This strategy of self-deception allows us to pursue the finite goods of creaturely life as if they were images of the divine.' Similarly, when describing humans' often unconscious yearning for eternity, Van Kaam (1975: 138) suggests this leads to seeking '. . . something lasting amidst the transitoriness of countless self-expressions.'

It is argued that sport could just be one such 'transitory self-expression' among many others, *if* it is an idolatrous quest and thus may lead to self-deception as to the deeper spiritual meaning of life. As C.S. Lewis contends earlier, if a human being takes a 'life-project' like sport, which Christians believe is a gift from God, but mistake it '. . . for the thing itself they turn into dumb idols, breaking the hearts of their worshippers.' History shows that human beings begin to consider and commit to religious faith for a whole range of reasons;[59] nonetheless, it is quite often only when there is, as the Jewish philosopher Martin Buber (Agassi, 1999) called it, a 'shudder of identity,' when the pride and self-sufficiency of the human heart (*not* character) has been 'weakened,' or what Wolfensburger (1983: 98) calls 'gentled', through an athlete's life—retirement, career-ending injury, or failure—that the deep religious-existential question might be asked: who am I without *my* abilities, *my* source of self-worth, *my* importance and status in the media, sporting subculture and world?

This said, I do not want to propose a *false dichotomy* in this broken and messy world and, I emphasize again, personal excellence, aesthetic beauty, creativity and human achievement should be sought in all walks of life, including sport. Nelson Mandela,[60] in his inaugural presidential speech, conveys something of this:

> Our deepest fear is not that we are inadequate. Our deepest fear is that we are powerful beyond measure. It is our light, not our darkness, that most frightens us. We ask ourselves, who am I to be brilliant . . . talented . . .? Actually, who are you *not* to be? You are a child of God. Your playing small doesn't serve the world. There is nothing

> enlightening about shrinking so that other people won't feel insecure around you [false humility]. We were born to manifest the glory of God that is within us. It's not just in some of us; it's in everyone. And as we let our own light shine, we unconsciously give other people permission to do the same. As we are liberated from our own fear, our presence automatically liberates others.

To be sure, such inspirational words resonate deep into all our hearts, but I challenge the reader to consider where this *inspiration* and *motivation* comes from. The Catholic priest-psychologist Adrian Van Kaam, I would argue, was writing prophetically in 1975 when he observed that 'we are on the rebirth of the awareness of human need for the transcendent . . .' (181). The following two quotes I then believe can *both* be true, if we '. . . seek first his kingdom and his righteousness' (Matthew 6:33). A recent newspaper advertisement for *Gillette*[61] that features three of the sporting world's demigods, Tiger Woods (until recently), Roger Federer and Thierry Henry, encourages the reader to

> 'Show the world how phenomenal you can be.'

In the gospels, the founder and cornerstone of Christianity, Jesus of Nazareth, a humble carpenter and who Christians believe to be the son of God, encourages the reader to consider where this talent came from and what *ultimately* matters . . .

> If anyone would come after me, he must deny himself and take up his cross and follow me. For whoever loses his life for me will find it. What good will it be for a man if he gains the whole world, yet forfeits his soul?
>
> Matthew 16:24–26

## ACKNOWLEDGMENTS

I would like to thank Professor Drew Gibson (Union Theological College, Belfast, NI), Professor Scott Kretchmar (Penn State University, USA) and Professor Andrew Parker (University of Gloucester, UK) for their most insightful comments on my first draft. I would also like to thank Dr. Chris Bell and Kath Watson for their invaluable help in proofreading this work.

## NOTES

1. Cited in the foreword of Steenbergen, Knop and Elling (2001: 11)
2. Sports psychology is arguably 'hanging onto the coat tails' of its parent discipline in terms of introducing and accepting spiritual and religious psychologies (see Watson & Nesti, 2005). The existence of a division in the American

Psychological Association (APA) for spiritual and religious issues and a section for transpersonal psychology in the British Psychological Association (BPS) and academic textbooks (e.g., Miller and Delaney, 2005; Shafranske, 1996) published by the APA and others on Christian psychology (Vitz, 1994, 1999, 1998), indicate the growing acceptance and need for this area of study in sport. It is important to note that the use of cognitive-behavioral consultancy techniques (mental skills training), such as imagery, thought-stopping, goal-setting and relaxation methods, are foundational to the theory and practice of the discipline of sport psychology and thus are invaluable in many consultancy situations where performance enhancement is the only goal. However, it is the *lack* of consultancy approaches that allow for deeper existential and religious concerns to be addressed (e.g., identity boundary situations, such as retirement from sport and career-ending injuries) and the exploration of the *meaning of sport* (and life) for the athlete that I would argue is a major omission from the discipline.

3. Within the interdisciplinary literature on 'identity,' three schools of thought (that are often in heated debate) exist—constructionists, essentialists and individualists—and all hold some value in understanding the complexities of identity. Social constructivism is particularly helpful in understanding how social forces can shape individual identity in sport, especially in relation to the desires of those in institutions of power. See Hoover (2004, Ch. 1) for an overview of the three different schools of thought and Taylor's (1989) classic work for a comprehensive historical, sociological, philosophical and psychological account of identity formation.
4. Ontology is a philosophical term that relates to questions of *being* and as Zizioulas (1991: 33) notes is '. . . specific to the problem of identity.'
5. This is certainly not to say that the existing body of empirical research and theory should not be scoured for every insight on human nature in trying to understand athletic identity in the world of sport. Sport psychologist Mark Nesti (2007a, 2007b, 2007c) provides a good example of this, in his Catholic-based accounts of applied work with athletes, which also draws on the work of Frankl and others that have provided unique insight into life's journey. The way in which Donald Capps (1987), professor of pastoral psychology, has overlaid Erikson's Life Cycle theory with biblical narratives and the beatitudes in an attempt to more fully understand the development of Christian identity is another good example of drawing on humanistic models, while maintaining theological and doctrinal rigor.
6. All Biblical citations, unless otherwise stated, are from NIV (International Bible Society, 2002).
7. Cited in Warren (2002: 80).
8. Other examples of recent research on sport identity in sport psychology in able-bodied sport are Yannick and Brewer (2007), Visek et al., (2008), Grove, Fish and Eklund (2004), Black and Smith (2007) and Warriner and Lavalle (2008) and in disability sport, Smith and Sparkes (2008) and Sparkes and Smith (2002). And in sociology, Cassidy, Jones and Potrac (2008) and Yiannakis and Melnik (2001).
9. Further evidence of this is provided by the Josephson Institute, *Centre for Youth Ethics*—Character Counts projects: http://charactercounts.org/programs/reportcard/.
10. For detailed accounts of the etymology and usage of terms such as the soul (Hebrew trans. *Nephesh* and Greek trans. *Psyche*), see Jeeves (1997: 108–111). The terms 'soul' and 'mind' are often used interchangeably to collectively describe the will, intellect and emotions, which in modern psychology is commonly understood as *personality* and in Christian anthropology and

psychology as *personhood* (see McFadyen, 1990; Pannenberg, 1985). The *body* is viewed as the 'temple [vehicle] of the Holy Spirit' (1 Cor. 3:16) and as such should not be subjugated to a lesser importance (as in Platonic-Cartesian mind-body dualism) than the other component parts, soul and spirit (i.e., holism). *Spirit* can have two meanings. First, as an 'animating' principle which creates and *gives* life (Gen. 2:7). Second, as the Spirit of God that came upon His prophets and people in Old Testament times (e.g., 1 Sam. 10:10; Num. 11:25; 2 Kings. 2:9) and as the Holy Spirit that came in *a new way* at Pentecost (Acts. 2:1–41) and which *can* redeem and guide human beings (Rom. 8:1–17; 10:9–13).

11. *The New Bible Dictionary* (1982, cited in Jeeves, 1997: 110) describes the heart: "it was essentially the whole man, with all his attributes, physical, intellectual and psychological, of which Hebrew thought and spoke, and the heart was conceived of as the governing centre of all these . . . character, personality, will, mind are modern terms which all reflect something of the meaning of the 'heart' in biblical usage . . . mind is perhaps the closest modern term to the biblical usage of the heart." For the purposes of my analysis, the term 'heart' will be used to describe the whole person (physical, intellectual and psychological); it is important to note, however, that some scriptures suggest that the heart was principally the 'inner-life' of the human being and does not include the body (Ezekiel 44:7, 9). Paul also used various terms ambiguously. For example, heart—*kardia*—is used 52 times in the epistles and means character, emotional states, seat of intellectual activity and volition. Flesh (*sarx*) is used 91 times and ranges over a number of meanings from our physical nature to a 'seat of sin.' In most places, it seems that *sarx* is used to represent the whole (sinful) person . . . not just the physical or sensuous part. Body (*soma*—89 times in the Pauline letters) likewise has a holistic meaning to it and is used more regularly to mean the entire person—along with four or five other meanings.
12. An idol can be defined as any idea, person or object that is worshipped (prioritized) in the place of God (Exodus. 20:4). Idols may include money, religion, human relationships, sports, music, sex, etc. Arguably, dry, rule-governed and legalistic religion (in *both* Protestant and Catholic Christian forms and other religions) is a major idol of the modern world, in which believers (and non) may worship what C.S. Lewis (1997/1952; see pp. 102–103) called an 'imaginary God.' Isaiah 29:13–14 conveys this type of religion: 'The Lord says, "These people come near to me with their mouth and honor me with their lips, but their hearts are far from me. Their worship of me is made up of rules taught by men." ' This is also spoken by Jesus to the Pharisees: Matthew 15:8–9. Manning (1990) and Yancey (1997) provide two excellent corrective responses to modern legalistic Christianity and religion, by providing a biblical view of God as a gracious and loving, but also holy, Father. For an excellent analysis of how legalistic religion and other idols (sport included) can act as 'massive defense mechanisms' to authentically experiencing God through Christ, see Johnson and Burroughs (2000: 187) and Kierkegaard (1989/1849).
13. This term was cited in Middleton and Walsh (1995: 61).
14. Taylor (1989) heavily critiques this in his analysis of modern identity and it is something that is personified in the writings of Murphy and White (1995) and George Leonard (1974) on the spiritual and mystical dimensions of sport, which I have critiqued elsewhere (Watson, 2007a).
15. The 'myths of progress' that Middleton and Walsh (1995) refer to come from the disciplines of anthropology (Feuerbach), psychology (Freud et al.), sociology (Marx and Durkheim et al.) and biology (Darwin and Dawkins). Following

the completion of the 'Genome project' in 2000, genetic determinism has arguably become the latest mythic utopia for some. Undisputedly, some of these ideas have in varying ways led to *very positive* scientific, technological and *some* social advancements that we should be most thankful for. However, the point is that the proponents and followers of these utopias have often slid into idolatry, seeing them as *all-encompassing* explanations (metanarratives) for social and cultural existence and in turn ignoring God's guidance for how humanity should live. The history of the 20th century *and the state of the modern world* clearly shows the folly in this view, which we are warned about in the Bible (1 Cor. 1:18–31, 2). Some of this footnote is also cited in Watson and White (2007: 219).

16. The social work and ministry of Joe Ehrmann, ex-NFL footballer, through his award-winning book (Marx, 2003) and nationally renowned organization, *Building Men and Women for Others* (see http://www.buildingmenandwomen.org/2007/default.asp ), is an excellent initiative in America that is trying to address the issue of fatherlessness through the vehicle of sport.
17. I in *no way* devalue the mutually essential and irreplaceable role of the mother in a child's development but as Blankenhorn (1995) argues, it is the loss of fatherhood in society that is at the root of many social ills and identity issues. Neither do I suggest in anyway that loving single parents (most often women) cannot bring up a healthy and balanced child, often in very difficult circumstances that frequently stem from the *sins of men*—often sins of omission (e.g., abdicating responsibility). But that the absence of a parent through death, emotional detachment, abandonment, neglect, divorce etc. will *unavoidably* impact upon the identity and self-worth of the child and the thinking and behavior of the adult that they will become in all realms of life, including sport. According to the Christian story, this is, however, nothing that cannot be healed through the love of a supernatural God, who can do *all things*, and through the care and love of others (often the vehicle for God's love).
18. In supporting his thesis, Kohn cites the research of Jenifer Levin, who interviewed competitive junior swimmers and found that the 'love and approval of a significant parental figure' was a major motivation to compete. For those wanting to further examine competition and winning from a specifically social-psychological angle, see Chapter 5 of Kohn's book and Watson and White (2007).
19. Sport sociologist Martin Roderick (2006), an ex-professional footballer himself (thus an 'insider'), has undertaken an excellent qualitative study (using symbolic interactionism) of 47 current and retired British professional footballers that touches on many issues of identity that are addressed in this chapter. This book is based on his Ph.D.
20. Some theologians use the 'rule of first mention' when exploring the foundations of a biblical concept or aspect of human nature. Here, this points toward the fall of humanity (Gen. 3:7) when Adam and Eve's 'eyes were opened' and they needed 'fig leaves' to hide their nakedness as the point at which shame and guilt entered the world, as beautifully conveyed in Milton's *Paradise Lost*.

    This is described in the incisive and seminal work on psychological defense mechanisms of Kierkegaard (1989/1849) and more recently by Johnson and Burroughs (2000) and Becker (1973), who argued that there is a widespread 'denial of death' (and thus need for belief in a salvific God) in the Western psyche.
21. See Chapters 7, 8 and 10 of McNamee's book, which examines aspects of shame, humility and envy in sport from a mainly philosophical (esp. Greek) perspective.

22. Existential sport psychologist Mark Nesti (2004, 2007a), who has done applied work in a number of British Premier League Football clubs, makes the important point that 'normal anxiety' in sport (and life) is a healthy emotion that if 'worked through' appropriately can lead to a stronger sense of self, increased 'psychological hardiness' and performance enhancement. Conversely, 'neurotic anxiety' in sport *may* lead to mental health problems and/or performance decrements due to less potential for experiencing health, well-being and optimal psychological states—*flow-states* (Jackson & Csikszentmihalyi, 1999).
23. In ancient culture the name of a person carried significant meaning and parents often thought very carefully when naming their child, especially in Hebrew culture. For example, the etymological root of the name 'Jesus' is 'Yahweh/God saves(!),' which conveys his earthly mission, as the God-man.
24. Consider the clear nationalistic fervor evident in the 1936 Berlin Olympics amongst many others in the 20th century. Indeed, scholars have suggested that there are many similarities, if not in context, between the 2008 Beijing Olympics and the Nazi Olympics of 1936. To be sure, communist China's recent exponential economic and political growth on the world stage has been seen by many as their quest to become the next superpower (Close, Askew and Xin, 2007). The power and political weight of modern sport is reflected in the 20th-century trend of world superpowers topping the Olympic gold-medal tables. The 2008 Chinese Olympic squad did not disappoint! But the long-term physical and psychological cost of brutal training regimes and unhealthy expectations from country, parents and coaches (see Beamish & Ritchie, 2006; Hoberman, 1992; Hong, 2006) will for many pay back with interest. Athletes and coaches, like all human beings, must do something with these unrealistic pressures and the perceived threat to their personhood in sport. So, what is forged in *some* is a dysfunctional and potentially destructive, codependent relationship with sport, with winning as the primary goal. Identity issues flow from this worldview.
25. John White (2008) has provided an in-depth analysis of idolatry in sport from a Christian theological perspective and this is also a major theme addressed in Watson and White (2007).
26. For an interesting and informative account of *passion* in sport in relation to identity issues, see Vallerand and Miquelon (2007).
27. For historical documentation of this development in America, see Berryman (1975).
28. For further documentation of problems in youth sport: overtraining and physical and psychological burnout in adult, youth and child sport (Smith, Lemyre & Raedeke, 2007); eating disorders, such as anorexia nervosa and bulimia, especially in 'aesthetic sports' (Burton, 2000); emotional developmental issues in the identity-forming process of childhood and adolescent sport (Begel, 2000b, 2000c); damaging child and youth athlete training programs and state-sponsored performance-enhancing drug policies in 1960–70s Communist Eastern bloc countries (Hoberman, 1992); abusive Chinese elite sport youth academies in the run-up to the 2008 Beijing Olympics (BBC, 2005; Hong, 2006; Reason & Craig, 2008); negative consequences of excessive pressure and expectations to perform from parents and coaches (Burton, 2000; Hellstedt, 2000; Murphy, 1999; Norton et al., 2000).
29. In support of the trenchant critique of Higgs and Braswell (2004), I argue that sport is *not* by definition formally a religion. However, worldviews function from the heart (Proverbs 4:23) and thus any activity like sport can be used as a vehicle for trying to answer these most fundamental existential questions and which often gives rise to idolatry.

30. Harold Abrahams, in commenting on the importance of winning the 100m final, notes that 'I'm twenty-four and I've never known [contentment]. I'm forever in pursuit and I don't even know what it is I am chasing. Aubrey, old chap—I'm scared. In one hour's time, I'll be out there again. I'll raise my eyes and look down that corridor—four feet wide with ten lonely seconds to justify my whole existence. But will I?' In stark contrast, Eric Liddell, a Scottish rugby player and member of the Chinese missionary service and Abrahams's competitor, comments on the meaning of the Olympic race in the oft-cited words 'God made me for a purpose but he also made me fast and when I run I feel his pleasure' (see Keddie, 2007). Liddell's life was not *principally* justified by whether he won the race, or even competed, as shown in his refusal to compete in the 100m Olympic sprint race due to its scheduling on the Sabbath, but rather first by his identity in a Father God (Rom.8:15–17) shown by the pleasure (rather than striving) he experienced when he *surrendered* his running into the hands of his God. The themes in this footnote on the *Chariots of Fire* are taken from White and Watson (2006) and are also described by Rick Warren (2002: 69–76) in his chapter, *What makes God Smile*? (Ch. 9).
31. Feeling godlike is a dimension of Maslow's (1962) 19-point typology of the *Peak Experience*, which is based on humanistic psychology. It has been suggested by Ravizza (1984, 2002) and others (Murphy & White, 1995) that peak experiences in sport can have a mystical or spiritual dimension. Although acknowledging the very positive nature of these experiences in sport, both in terms of enjoyment and enhanced performance, both Higgs and Braswell (2004) and Watson (2007a) have strongly questioned the Christian theological authenticity of these mind-states, in terms of their supernatural origin and impact on understanding identity in sport.
32. For a comparative analysis of 'identity' from a humanistic and Christian perspective that draws on the ideas of Augustine, Kierkegaard, Merton, Pascal and Rahner etc., see Morea (1997).
33. Isaiah 9:1–7; 52:13–15; 53:1–12.
34. The first-century Jewish historian Josephus documents some of what occurred in the gospels (Jewish history) in his work, in particular in his book *Antiquities of the Jews* (c. 94).
35. For those wishing to more fully understand the redemptive story of Christianity, see the Hollywood movie, directed by Mel Gibson, *The Passion of the Christ*.
36. See chapter 10 and 13 of McGrath (2001). The doctrine of atonement explains how following the separation of God the Father (creator) from humans (creatures) at the fall of humanity (Genesis 3), in which humans in their *pride*, *wilfully chose* to disobey God's will for their lives, God the Father mercifully sent his Son, the second person of the Trinity, the 'sacrificial lamb,' to *atone* for the sins of humanity. This, it is argued in Christian thought, was so that God the Father could come back into a relationship with his creatures (humans)—*at-one-ment*—and offer eternal life, deep joy and a 'peace . . . which transcends all understanding' (Philippians 4:7a).
37. Following the European enlightenment and the rise of science, the rationalistic Western mind-set often finds it difficult to accept paradox in life (e.g., love and suffering or dying to self to *gain self in* Christ), as shown in the Platonic dualistic anthropology/theology (versus Hebrew and Pauline) of much of the American Protestant Church, which in turn significantly impacts upon their approach to sport (see Watson, 2007b and 1 Corinthians 1:22). Conversely, the Middle Eastern (e.g., Hebrew-Jewish) people historically have been much more comfortable with the paradoxes of life.
38. Cited in Warren (2002: 80).

39. The Bible records that the Holy Spirit was sent to the earth after Jesus' 'ascension' to His Father (it is stated that he conquered death through the cross and *resurrection*) as described in Acts 1 and 2. Following the coming of the Holy Spirit (often called Jesus Spirit, as it is the same thing in essence), it is the Holy Spirit that is the relational source between God and Christians (e.g., communication in prayer is *through* the Holy Spirit that lives in the Christian believer; see Romans 8:11).
40. The first half of this quote is taken from the back cover of Townsend's book. While I heartily support the general theme of this book, there are some elements of it that I would question in terms of orthodox Christian doctrine, which the author himself acknowledges. For another similar account of 'Strength through Weakness' and brokenness in Christian living, see Clements (1994).
41. I am sure that this all seems too simple, neat and unrealistic for some readers, due to the *fact* that *some* non-Christians are generally 'nicer' in terms of how they relate to others and may cope better with adversity and suffering in sport. Christian identity is not 'first' predicated on how 'nice' a person is, but rather *belief* and *faith* in Jesus Christ (John. 6:29; Romans. 10:9). The biblical story of the repentant thief that was crucified next to Jesus (Luke. 23:40–43) clearly demonstrates this. Importantly, however, after making the *conscious decision* to believe and follow Christ, a person *should* actively seek to become more 'Christ-like' in their life-journey, hopefully exhibiting the fruits of the spirit (Galatians. 5:22–25; 1 Corinthians. 13:4–7) *and* operating powerfully in the gifts of the Holy Spirit as *given* to each individual (1 Corinthians. 12:14). *Both* these are hallmarks (esp. humility and love) of Christian maturity. For an accessible overview of this point, see Chapter 11, *Nice People or New Men*, of Lewis's *Mere Christianity* (1997/1952) and McClung (2005).
42. For example, see Morphew (1991): the state of the 'already, not yet' in kingdom theology relates to the paradoxical idea that the kingdom of God has already come in the first coming of Jesus Christ in his life, death and resurrection (it is inaugurated) but it is also *not yet* in that the kingdom of God won't be fully realized (consummated) until Christ's second coming (see the book of Revelation, 21, 22).
43. The protestant theological concept (strongly Calvinistic) idea of *Common Grace*, which is different to *Saving Grace* (salvation through belief in the work of Christ), is an idea that God gave all humans (believers or not) grace for the common good of all mankind (so they could operate relationally in society and develop). The scholar Louis Berkhof (1996: 434) suggests common grace '. . . curbs the destructive power of sin, maintains in a measure the moral order of the universe, thus making an orderly life possible, distributes in varying degrees gifts and talents among men, promotes the development of science and art, and showers untold blessings upon the children of men.'
44. Hubbard's (1998) book provides a number of testimonies of athletes who, after coming into a relationship with God, found a deep peace (a centeredness) that subsequently led to enhanced performance and enjoyment (and, I would argue, ability get into flow states/being-in-the-zone), due to reduced anxiety of failure and others' expectations, etc.
45. See also Schwobel and Gunton (1991), Lints, Horton and Talbot (2006), Towner (2005), Krause (2005), Jeeves (1997), Kaplan and Schwartz (1997) and a special edition of the *Journal of Psychology and Christianity* (1998, Vol. 26, No. 1).
46. See *Journal of Psychology and Theology*, the *Journal of Psychology and Christianity* (that has published work on prayer in sport contexts), the *Journal of Psychology and Judaism* and the recent text of Miller and Delaney (2005).

The work of psychologists Paul Vitz (1994, 1998, 1999) and Vitz and Felch (2006), Peter Morea (1997) and Donald Capps (1987, using Erikson), the prophetic insights on human nature of Oswald Chambers (1922, 1962/1936), the reflections of Catholic priest-psychologist Adrian Van Kaam (1975) and the writings of Swiss psychiatrist Paul Tournier (e.g., 1957; Collins, 1973) should all be of assistance in forming a sound understanding of Christian psychology. As I have argued, the doctrine of the 'Fatherhood of God' is also central to understanding Christian identity in sport; thus the writings of Floyd McClung (2005), Mark Stibbe (1999) and Christopher Wright (2007) will be useful in synthesizing psychological and theological ideas.

47. Cited in Warren (2002: 17).
48. The potential socio-legal issues that may arise from genetic enhancement in sport may well be a line for future research. Although not related directly to theology or genetics in sport, Parker's (2009) work provides a starting point for examining issues of identity in sport from a legal angle. The recent book by Hundley and Billings (2009), which examines identity in sports media, could also be helpful in analyzing how 'super-athletes/celebrities' identity is formed and portrayed—*hyperreality*?
49. For the official site of John Wooden, see http://www.coachwooden.com/.
50. Simply defined, prayer is talking to and listening to God. There is a growing body of research and writings on the use and value of prayer in sport in ways that relate to athletic identity issues, i.e., to provide deeper meaning to sport participation, as a coping strategy to reduce neurotic anxiety etc. Notable sports psychology, sports science and sport sociology journals have published empirical research (Czech & Bullet, 2007; Lee, 2006; Park, 2000; Vernacchia et al., 2000) and reviews of literature and essays (Watson & Czech, 2005; Watson & Nesti, 2005) that have identified the use of, and value of, prayer in sporting contexts and sport psychology consultancy. This is in addition to empirical research published in religious psychology journals (Czech et al., 2004; Murray et al., 2005) and one article on the ethics of using prayer in organized sport (Kreider, 2003).
51. The spiritual gifts, as described in 1 Corinthians 12, are wisdom, faith, healing, prophecy, tongues, miracles etc.
52. The fruits of the spirit listed in Galatians 5:22–23 are love, joy, peace, patience, kindness, goodness, faithfulness, gentleness and self-control. Why I make the point that the fruits of the spirit are *foundational* to the powerful and authentic use of the spiritual gifts (1 Corinthians 12) is because the gifts of the spirit can be elevated to be seen as more important than the fruits, or they can be misused and abused by individuals whose Christian character (in humility, love and wisdom) is lacking. The key thing is that the fruits of the spirit and the gifts of the spirit should operate in harmony, as they did in the life of Jesus (see Johnson, 2009).
53. This article is reprinted in this book.
54. Van Kaam (1975: 145), in discussing our 'spiritual calling' in Christ, suggests 'a person like Mozart could find out that musical self-expression is so much a part of the incarnation of his life call that the refusal to express himself musically in any way at any time could be an infidelity to his identity.' Null (2008) has done an excellent job of analyzing 'life-calling', for elite/professional sportspersons.
55. It is interesting to consider that ironically the dynamic between Federer and Nadal may also have been shaped by an intense 'fragility' of their identities, in that when one reaches the elite level it is precisely the fear of being beaten, that is, being knocked off the precipice of sporting domination, that demands a sense of humility (or caution?) with an opponent.

56. Cited in Metzger (2003: 188).
57. See Dubay (1999) for an excellent analysis of how beauty in the world, in both creation and human endeavors, points to God. The recent work of Hans Ulrich Gumbrecht (2006) on athletic beauty is also a good source for examining this topic.
58. This quote from Lewis's book *Transposition and Other Addresses* (Ch. 2) was cited in Kilby (1968: 22–23).
59. Some people inherit religious faith from their parents and then often make a 'personal' commitment as they move through adolescence into adulthood; others have powerful 'Damascus road' religious experiences like the apostle Paul; others through study and reasoning come to accept faith and make a willful commitment (e.g., C.S. Lewis); some are deeply influenced by others around them (the testimony of their lives) who already have faith and then begin to ask questions and read and prayer; others cry out to God in times of need when they are brought 'to the end of them*selves*' (often in a life crisis, when a human being begins to ask questions of meaning). A key thing to note here is that, regardless of the journey a person takes to faith and in turn making a commitment to follow Christ (see Romans 10:8–10), it is *only* by the leading/beckoning of the Holy Spirit that the Father draws a human being back to Himself (i.e., to make a commitment).
60. Cited in Mason (1999).
61. See *Gillette Mens Razors & Blades Range—Gillette Fusion Roger, Thierry And Tiger,* available: http://www.visit4info.com/advert/Gillette-Fusion-Roger-Thierry-And-Tiger-Gillette-Mens-Razors-Blades-Range/55260.

## BIBLIOGRAPHY

Á Kempis, T. (1952) *The Imitation of Christ* (trans. Leo Sherley-Price), London: Penguin Books.

Agassi, J.B. (1999) (Ed.) *Martin Buber on Psychology and Psychotherapy: Essays, Letters, and Dialogue*, New York: Syracuse University Press.

Baumeister, R.F., and Exline, J.J. (2000) Self-Control, Morality and Human Strength, *Journal of Social and Clinical Psychology*, 19: 29–42.

BBC (2005) Pinsent Shocked by China Training: Olympic Legend Sir Matthew Pinsent Has Been Left Stunned by the Treatment of Young Gymnasts in Beijing, BBC Sport Online, Retrieved November 6, 2008, from http://news.bbc.co.uk/sport1/low/other_sports/gymnastics/4445506.stm

Beamish, R., and Ritchie, I. (2006) *Fastest, Highest, Strongest: A Critique of High-Performance Sport*, London: Routledge.

Becker, E. (1973) *The Denial of Death*, New York: The Free Press.

Begel, D. (1992) An Overview of Sport Psychiatry, *American Journal of Psychiatry*, 149: 606–614.

Begel, D. (2000a) Introduction: The Origins and Aims of Sport Psychiatry, in D. Begel and R.W. Burton (Eds.), *Sport Psychiatry: Theory and Practice*, New York: W.W. Norton and Company, xiii–xx.

Begel, D. (2000b) The Psychologic Development of the Athlete, in D. Begel and R.W. Burton (Eds.), *Sport Psychiatry: Theory and Practice*, New York: W.W. Norton and Company, 3–21.

Begel, D. (2000c) The Dilemma of Youth Sports, in D. Begel and R.W. Burton (Eds.), *Sport Psychiatry: Theory and Practice*, New York: W.W. Norton and Company, 93–109.

Begel, D., and Burton, R.W. (Eds.) (2000) *Sport Psychiatry: Theory and Practice*, New York: W.W. Norton and Company.

Beisser, A. (1967) *The Madness in Sports*, New York: Appleton-Century-Crofts.

Beller, J.M., Stoll, S.K., Burwell, B., and Cole, J. (1996) The Relationship of Competition and a Christian Liberal Arts Education on Moral Reasoning of College Student Athletes, *Research on Christian Higher Education*, 3: 99–114.

Berger, B.G., Pargman, D., and Weinberg, R. (2002). Personal Meaning in Exercise, in B.G. Berger, D. Pargman, and R. Weinberg (Eds.), *Foundations of Exercise Psychology*, Morgantown, WV: Fitness Information Technology, 223–243.

Berger, P. (1970) *A Rumour of Angels*, Garden City, NY: Doubleday.

Berkhof, L. (1996) *Systematic Theology* (preface by Richard A. Muller), Grand Rapids, MI: Wm. B Eerdmans Publishing.

Berryman, J. (1975) From the Cradle to the Playing Field: America's Emphasis upon Highly Organized Competitive Sports for Preadolescent Boys, *Journal of Sport History*, 2, Fall: 112–131.

Black, J.M., and Smith, A.L. (2007) An Examination of Coakley's Perspective on Identity, Control and Burnout among Adolescent Athletes, *International Journal of Sport Psychology*, 38, 4: 417–436.

Blankenhorn, D. (1995) *Fatherless America: Confronting our Most Urgent Social Problem*, New York: Harper Perennial.

Brewer, B.W., Van Raalte, J.L., and Linder, D.E. (1993) Athletic Identity: Hercules' Muscles or Achilles Heel? *Academic Athletic Journal*, 24: 237–254.

Brewer, B.W., Van Raalte, J.L., and Petitpas, A.J. (2000) Self-Identity Issues in Sport Career Transistions, in D. Lavallee and P. Wylleman (Eds.), *Career Transitions in Sport: International Perspectives*, Morgantown, WV: Fitness Information Technology, 29–43.

Buber, M. (1958/1923) *I and Thou* (W. Kaufmann, Trans.), New York: Charles Scribner's Sons.

Burton, R.W. (2000) Mental Illness in Athletes, in D. Begel, and R.W. Burton (Eds.), *Sport Psychiatry: Theory and Practice*, New York: W.W. Norton and Company, 61–81.

Campbell, W.S. (2008) *Paul and the Creation of Christian Identity*, London: T and T Clark.

Capps, D. (1987) *Deadly Sins and Saving Virtues*, Philadelphia: Fortress Press.

Cashmore, E. (2008) *Chariots of Fire*: Bigotry, Manhood and Moral Certitude in an Age of Individualism, *Sport and Society*, 11, 2/3: 159–173.

Cassidy, T., Jones, R., and Potrac, P. (2008, 2nd ed.), Understanding Athletes' Identities, in T. Cassidy, R. Jones, and P. Potrac (Eds.), *Understanding Sports Coaching: The Social, Cultural and Pedagogical Foundations of Coaching Practice*, London: Routledge, 106–118.

Chambers, O. (1922) The Psychology of Redemption, in D. McCasland (Ed.), *The Complete Works of Oswald Chambers*, Grand Rapids, MI: Discovery House Publishers, 1059–1104.

Chambers, O. (1957) Our Portrait in Genesis, in D. McCasland (Ed.), *The Complete Works of Oswald Chambers*, Grand Rapids, MI: Discovery House Publishers, 957–981..

Chambers, O. (1962/1936) *Biblical Psychology*, London: Oswald Chambers Publications Association and Marshall Morgan Scott.

Clements, R. (1994) *The Strength of Weakness: How God Uses Our Flaws to Achieve His Goals*, Fearn, Tain, Ross-shire, Scotland: Christian Focus Publications.

Close, P., Askew, D., and Xin, X. (2007) *The Beijing Olympiad: The Political Economy of a Sporting Mega-Event*, London: Routledge.

Coakley, J. (2006) The Good Father: Parental Expectations and Youth Sports, *Leisure Studies*, 25, 2: 153–163.

Coakley, J.J. (2007) Sport and Religion: Is It a Promising Combination? in J.J. Coakley, *Sport in Society: Issues and Controversies* (9th ed.), Maidenhead, UK: McGraw-Hill Education, 528–563.

Coakley, J., and Dunning, E. (Eds.) (2002) *Handbook of Sports Studies*, London: Sage Publications.

Cobb, K. (2005) *The Blackwell Guide to Theology and Popular Culture*, Oxford, UK: Blackwell Publishing.

Collins, C.R. (1973) *The Christian Psychology of Paul Tournier*, Grand Rapids, MI: Baker Book House.

Corlett, J. (1996a) Sophistry, Socrates, and Sport Psychology, *The Sport Psychologist*, 10: 84–94.

Corlett, J. (1996b) Virtues Lost: Courage in Sport, *Journal of the Philosophy of Sport*, 23: 45–57.

Czech, D., and Bullet, E. (2007) An Exploratory Description of Christian Athletes' Perceptions of Prayer in Sport: A Mixed Methodology Pilot Study, *International Journal of Sports Science and Coaching*, 2, 1: 49–56.

Czech, D.R., Wrisberg, C., Fisher, L., Thompson, C., and Hayes, G. (2004). The-Experience of Christian Prayer in Sport—an Existential Phenomenological Investigation, *Journal of Psychology and Christianity*, 2: 1–19.

Dale, G. (1996) Existential Phenomenology: Emphasizing the Experience of the Athlete in Sport Psychology Research, *The Sport Psychologist*, 10: 158–171.

Dale, G. (2000) Distractions and Coping Strategies of Elite Decathletes During Their Most Memorable Performance, *The Sport Psychologist*, 14: 17–41.

David, P. (2005) *Human Rights in Youth Sport: A Critical Review of Children's Rights in Competitive Sport*, London: Routledge.

Deardorff, D.L., and Deardorff, J.D. (2008) Escaping the Gender Trap: Sport and the Equality of Christ, in Deardorff, D, II., and White, J. (Eds.), *The Image of God in the Human Body: Essays on Christianity and Sports*, Lampeter, Wales: The Edwin Mellen Press, 195–216.

Dostoyevsky, F. (1967/1927) *The Brothers Karamazov* (Vol. 1, trans. Constance Garnett with an Introduction by Edward Garnett), London: J.M. Dent and Sons.

Dubay, T. (1999) *The Evidential Power of Beauty: Science and Theology Meet*, San Francisco: Ignatius Press.

Eldridge, J. (2001) *Wild at Heart: Discovering the Secret of a Man's Soul*, Nashville, TN: Thomas Nelson, Inc.

Elias, N., and Dunning, E. (1986) *Quest for Excitement*, Oxford: Blackwell.

Erikson, E.H. (1959) *Identity and the Life Cycle*, Psychological Issues, Monograph No.1, New York: International Universities Press.

Erikson, E.H. (1968) The Human Life Cycle, in S. Schlein (Ed.), *A Way of Looking at Things: Selected Papers from 1930 to 1980 of Erik H. Erikson*, New York: W.W. Norton and Company, 595–610.

Erikson, J. (1997a) The Ninth Stage, in E.H. Erikson (Ed.), *The Life Cycle Completed*, New York: WW. Norton, 105–115.

Erikson, J. (1997b) Gerotranscendence, in E.H. Erikson (Ed.), *The Life Cycle Completed*, New York: WW. Norton, 123–129.

Farooq, S., and Parker, A. (2009) Sport Social Identity and Islam, in A. Parker and J. Harris (Eds.), *Sport and Social Identities*, Basingstoke, UK: Palgrave Press, pp. 109–131.

Frankl, V.E. (1959) *Man's Search for Meaning: An Introduction to Logotherapy* (preface by Gordon W. Allport), Boston: Beacon Press.

Frankl, V.E. (1986) *The Doctor and the Soul: From Psychotherapy to Logotherapy*, New York: Vintage Book.

Gardner, F., and Moore, Z. (2006) *Clinical Sport Psychology* (see Chapter 10, Career Termination), Champaign, IL: Human Kinetics.

Gibson, D. (2008) Latest Score: Liverpool 20, Manchester Unites 10, *Ministry Today*, Issue 44. Retrieved 2008 from http://www.ministrytoday.org.uk/article.php?id=638

Giddens, A. (1991) *Modernity and Self Identity: Self and Society in Late Modern Age*, Cambridge: Polity Press.

Goffman, E. (1990/1959) *The Presentation of Self in Everyday Life*, London: Penguin.

Gray, J., and Polman, R. (2004) Craft-Idiocy, Erikson & Footballing Identities, paper presented at the 3rd International Biennial SELF Research Conference, Berlin, abstract available online: self.uws.edu.au/Conferences/2004_Gray_Polman.pdf

Grimshaw, M. (2000) I Can't Believe My Eyes: The Religious Aesthetics of Sport as Postmodern Salvific Moments, *Implicit Religion*, 3, 2: 87–99.

Grove, R.J., Fish, M., and Eklund, R.C. (2004) Changes in Athletic Identity Following Team Selection: Self-Protection Versus Self-Enhancement, *Journal of Applied Sport Psychology*, 16: 75–81.

Gumbrecht, H.U. (2006) *In Praise of Athletic Beauty*, Boston, MA, USA: Belknap Press.

Guttman, A. (1978) *From Ritual to Record: The Nature of Modern Sports*, New York: Columbia University Press.

Hall, H.K. (2008) Perfectionism: A Hallmark Quality of World Class Performers, or a Psychological Impediment to Athletic Development, in D. Hackfort and G. Tenenbaum (Eds.), *Essential Processes for Attaining Peak Performance*, Oxford, UK: Meyer and Meyer Sport Ltd., 178–211.

Hamilton, M.J. (2002) Shamelessness and Its Effects on Contemporary Sport, paper presented at the 30th International Association of Philosophy of Sport Conference, Penn State University, PA, October 23–27.

Hamilton, M. (2003) Disordering of Affections: An Augustinian Critique of Our Relationship to Sport, paper presented at the 31st International Association of Philosophy of Sport Conference, University of Gloucestershire, Cheltenham, UK, September 18–21.

Harris, J., and Parker, A. (Eds.) (2009) *Sport and Social Identities*, Basingstoke, UK: Palgrave Press.

Hauerwas, S. (1986) *Suffering Presence*, Notre Dame: University of Notre Dame.

Hellstedt, J.C. (2000) Family Systems-Based Treatment of the Athlete Family, in D. Begel and R.W. Burton (Eds.), *Sport Psychiatry: Theory and Practice*, New York: W.W. Norton and Company, 206–248.

Higgs, R.J., and Braswell, M.C. (2004) *An Unholy Alliance: The Sacred and Modern Sports*, Macon, GA: Mercer University Press.

Hill, A.O., Hall, H.K., Appleton, P.R., and Kozub, S.A. (2008) Perfectionism and Burnout in Junior Elite Soccer Players: The Mediating Influence of Unconditional Self-Acceptance, *Psychology of Sport and Exercise*, 9: 630–644.

Hoare, C.H. (2000) Ethical Self, Spiritual Self: Wisdom and Integrity in the Writings of Erik H. Erikson, in M.E. Miller and S.R. Cook-Greuter (Eds.), *Creativity, Spirituality, and Transcendence: Paths to Integrity and Wisdom in the Mature Self*, Stamford, CT: Ablex Publishing Corporation, 75–98.

Hoberman, J. (1992) *Mortal Engines: The Science of Performance and the Dehumanization of Sport*, Caldwell, NJ: Blackburn Press.

Hochstetler, D., Hopsicker, P., and Kretchmar, S.R., (2008) The Ambiguity of Embodiment and Sport: Overcoming Theological Dichotomies, in D. Deardoff and J. White (Eds.), *A Christian Theology of Sport*, 61–77

Hong, F. (2006) Innocence Lost: Child Athletes in China, in R. Giulianotti and D. McArdle (Eds.), *Sport, Civil Liberties and Human Rights*, London: Routledge, 46–62.

Hoover, K. (Ed.) (2004) *The Future of Identity: Centennial Reflections on the Legacy of Erik Erikson*, Oxford: Lexington Books.

Howe, P.D. (2004) *Sport, Professionalism and Pain*, London: Routledge.

Hubbard, S. (1998) *Faith in Sports: Athletes and Their Religion on and off the Field*, New York: Doubleday.

Huizinga, J. (1950) *Homo Ludens: A Study of the Play Element in Culture*, Boston: Beacon.

Hundley, H.L., and Billings A.C. (2009) *Examining Identity in Sports Media*, London: Sage Publications, Inc.

Hyland, D. (1978) Competition and Friendship, *Journal of the Philosophy of Sport*, 5, Fall: 27–37.

Hyland, D.A. (1988) Opponents, Contestants, and Competitors: The Dialectic of Sport, in W.J. Morgan and K.V. Meier (Eds.), *Philosophic Inquiry in Sport* (2nd ed.), Champaign, IL: Human Kinetics, 177–182.

Jackson, P. (2006) My Rugby Obsession Has Left Me in Agony, *Daily Mail*, March 7, 80.

Jackson, S., and Csikszentmihalyi, M. (1999) *Flow in Sports*, Champaign, IL: Human Kinetics.

Jarvie, G. (2006) Sport and Religion, in *Sport, Culture and Society: An Introduction*, London: Routledge, 253–266.

Jeeves, M.A (1997) Human Nature: Biblical and Psychological Portraits, in M.A. Jeeves, *Human Nature and the Millennium: Reflections on the Integration of Psychology and Christianity*, Grand Rapids, MI: Bake Books, 98–126.

John Paul II. (1997) *The Theology of the Body: Human Love in the Divine Plan* (foreword by John S. Grabowski), Boston: Pauline Books and Media.

Johnson, B. (2006) *Dreaming with God: Secrets of Redesigning Your World through God's Creative Flow* (foreword by James W. Goll), Shippensburg, PA: Destiny Image Publishers Inc.

Johnson, B. (2009) *Release the Power of Jesus*, Shippensburg, PA: Destiny Image Publishers Inc.

Johnson, E.L. (1997) Christ, the Lord of Psychology, *Journal of Psychology and Theology*, 25, 1: 11–27.

Johnson, E.L. (1998) Whatever Happened to the Human Soul? A Brief Christian Genealogy of a Psychological Term, *Journal of Psychology and Theology*, 26, 1: 16–28.

Johnson, E.L., and Burroughs, C.S. (2000) Protecting One's Soul: A Christian Inquiry into Defensive Activity, *Journal of Psychology and Theology*, 28, 3: 175–189.

Johnston, R.K. (1983) *The Christian at Play*, Grand Rapids, MI: William B. Eerdmans Publishing Company.

Jupitus, P. (2008) Unbearable Pain of an Icon Becoming Ordinary Again: Life after Football Was Hard Enough for Kenny Sansom, Even without Alcoholism, *The Times* (The Game), July 14, 10.

Kaplan, K.J., and Schwartz, M.B. (1997) Religion, Psychotherapy and the Body-Soul Relationship, *Journal of Psychology and Judaism*, 21, 3: 165–176.

Kay, T. (2006a) Editorial: Fathering through Leisure (special ed.), *Leisure Studies*, 25, 2: 125–131.

Kay, T. (2006b) Where's Dad? Fatherhood in Leisure Studies, *Leisure Studies*, 25, 2: 133–152.

Keddie, J.W. (2007) *Running the Race: Eric Liddell, Olympic Champion and Missionary* (foreword, Lord Sebastian Coe), Darlington, UK: Evangelical Press.

Kerr, G., and Dacyshyn, A. (2000) Retirement experiences of elite, female gymnasts, *Journal of Applied Sport Psychology*, 12,2, 115–133.

Kierkegaard, S. (1989/1849) *The Sickness unto Death: A Christian Exposition of Edification and Awakening* (Alastair Hannay, Trans.), London: Penguin Books.

Kilby, C.S. (Ed.) (1968) *A Mind Awake: An Anthology of C.S. Lewis*, New York: Harcourt Brace and Company.

Kohn, A. (1992) *No Contest: The Case against Competition* (Rev. ed.), New York: Houghton Mifflin.

Krause, D. (2005) Keeping It Real: The Image of God in the New Testament, *Interpretation: A Journal of Bible and Theology*, 59, 4: 358–368.

Kreider, A.J. (2003) Prayers for Assistance as Unsporting Behavior, *Journal of the Philosophy of Sport*, *XXX*: 17–25.

Kretchmar, S.R. (1998) Soft Metaphysics: A Precursor to Good Sports Ethics, in M. McNamee and J. Parry (Eds.), *Ethics and Sport*, London: Routledge, 19–34.

Lasch, C. (1980) *The Culture of Narcissism: Life in an Age of Diminishing Expectations*, London: Abacus.

Lavallee, D., and Wylleman, P. (Eds.) (2000) *Career Transitions in Sport: International Perspectives,* Morgantown, WV: Fitness Information Technology.

Lawrence, I. (2009) Living in a Sectarian Maelstrom: A Christian Professional Football Player's Perspective, *International Journal of Religion and Sport*, Chapter 4 .

Lee, J.W. (2006) Prayer in American Scholastic Sport, *Sociology of Sport Online*, 6, 1. Retrieved 2007 from http://physed.otago.ac.nz/sosol/v6il/v6il_2.html

Leonard, G. (1974) *The Ultimate Athlete*: *Re-visioning Sports, Physical Education, and the Body,* New York: Avon.

Lewis, C.S. (1997/1952) *Mere Christianity,* New York: HarperCollins.

Liberia Editrice Vaticana (2008) *Sport*: *An Educational and Pastoral Challenge* (a series of studies edited by the Pontifical Council for the Laity), Citta del Vaticano, Italy: Liberia Editrice Vaticana.

Lints, R., Horton, M.S., and Talbot, M.R. (2006) *Personal Identity in Theological Perspective*, Grand Rapids, MI: William B. Eerdmans Publishing Company.

Loland, S., Skirstad, B., and Waddington, I. (2005) *Pain and Injury in Sport: Social and Ethical Analysis*, London: Routledge.

Lopiano, D.A. and Zotos, C. (1992) Modern Athletics: The Pressure to Perform, in K.D. Brownell., J. Rodin and J.H. Wilmore (Eds.), *Eating, Body Weight, and Performance in Athletes*, Philadelphia: Lea and Febinger, 275–292.

Lynch, G. (2005) *Understanding Theology and Popular Culture*, Oxford, UK: Blackwell Publishing.

Lyon, D. (2000) *Jesus in Disneyland*: *Religion in Postmodern Times*, Cambridge, UK: Polity Press.

Macdonald, D., and Kirk, D. (1999) Pedagogy, the Body and Christian Identity, *Sport, Education and Society*, 2, 4: 131–142.

Macquarrie, J. (1982) *In Search of Humanity*: *A Theological and Philosophical Perspective*, London: SCM Press Ltd.

Magdalinski. T., and Chandler, T.J.L. (2002) (Eds.) *With God on Their Side*: *Sport in the Service of Religion*, London: Routledge.

Manning, B. (1990) *The Ragamuffin Gospel*: *Embracing the Unconditional Love of God*, Milton Keynes, UK: Authentic Lifestyle.

Marshall, T. (1992) *Right Relationships*: *How to Create Them How to Restore Them*, UK: Sovereign World.

Mason, M. (1999) *Practicing the Presence of People*: *How We Learn to Love*, Colorado Springs, CO, USA: WaterBrook.

Martens, R. (1987) Science, Knowledge, and Sport Psychology, *The Sport Psychologist*, 1: 29–55.

Marx, J. (2003) *Seasons of Life*: *A Football Star, a Boy, a Journey to Manhood*, London: Simon & Schuster.

Maslow, A. (1962) *Toward a Psychology of Being*, Princeton, NJ: Van Nostrand.
McClung, F. (2005) *The Father Heart of God*, Eastbourne, UK: Kingsway Publications.
McFadyen, A. (1990) *The Call to Personhood: A Christian Theory of the Individual in Social Relationships*, Cambridge, UK: Cambridge University Press.
McGrath, A. (2001) *Christian Theology: An Introduction* (3rd ed.), Oxford: Blackwell Publishing.
McNamee, M. (2008) *Sports, Virtues and Vices: Morality Plays*, London: Routledge.
McNamee, M. (2001) Foreword, in J. Steenbergen, P. De Knop and A.H.F. Elling (Eds.), *Values and Norms in Sport: Critical Reflections on the Position and Meanings of Sport in Society*, Oxford, UK: Meyer and Meyer Sport, 11–13.
Mead, M. (Ed.) (1937) *Cooperation and Competition among Primitive Peoples*, New York: McGraw-Hill.
Metzger, P.L. (2003) *The Word of Christ and the World of Culture: Sacred and Secular through the Theology of Karl Barth* (foreword by Colin Gunton), Cambridge, UK: William B. Eerdmans Publishing Company.
Miah, A. (2004) *Genetically Modified Athletes: Biomedical Ethics, Gene Doping and Sport*, London: Routledge.
Middleton, J.R., and Walsh, B.J. (1995) *Truth Is Stranger Than It Used to Be: Biblical Faith in a Postmodern Age*, London: SPCK.
Miller, W.R., and Delaney, H.D. (Eds.) (2005) *Judeo-Christian Perspectives on Psychology: Human Nature, Motivation, and Change*, Washington, DC: American Psychological Association.
Moltmann, J. (1989) Olympia between Politics and Religion, in Gregory and John Coleman Baum, *Sport*, Edinburgh: T and T Clark, 101–109.
Moltmann, J. (1972) *Theology of Play*, New York: Harper.
Morea, P. (1997) *In Search of Personality: Christianity and Modern Psychology*, London: SCM Press.
Morphew, D. (1991) *Breakthrough: Discovering the Kingdom*, Cape Town, South Africa: Vineyard International Publishing.
Murphy, M., and White, R.A. (1995) *In the Zone: Transcendent Experience in Sports*, London: Penguin.
Murphy, S. (1999) *The Cheers and the Tears: A Healthy Alternative to the Dark Side of Youth Sports Today*, San Francisco: Jossey-Bass.
Murray, A. (1982) *Humility*, New Kensington, PA: Whitaker House.
Murray, M.A., Joyner, A.B., Burke, K.L., Wilson, M.J., and Zwald, A.D. (2005) The Relationship between Prayer and Team Cohesion in Collegiate Softball Teams, *Journal of Psychology and Christianity*, 24, 3: 233–239.
Nesti, M. (2004) *Existential Psychology and Sport: Implications for Research and Practice*, London: Routledge.
Nesti, M. (2007a) The Spirit of Sport: An Existential Psychology Perspective, in J. Parry, S. Robinson, N.J. Watson and M.S. Nesti (Eds.), *Sport and Spirituality: An Introduction*, London: Routledge, 119–134.
Nesti, M. (2007b) Suffering, Sacrifice, Sport Psychology and the Spirit, in J. Parry, S. Robinson, N.J. Watson and M.S. Nesti (Eds.), *Sport and Spirituality: An Introduction*, London: Routledge, 151–169.
Nesti, M. (2007c), Persons and Players: A Psychological Perspective, in J. Parry, S. Robinson, N.J. Watson and M.S. Nesti (Eds.), *Sport and Spirituality: An Introduction*, London: Routledge, 135–150.
Newman, J. (1989) *Competition in Religious Life*, Waterloo, Ontario, Canada: Wilfrid Laurier University Press.
Niebuhr, R. (1951) *Christ and Culture*, New York: Harper and Brothers.

Norton, P.J., Burns, J.A., Hope, D.A., and Bauer, B.K. (2000) Generalization of Social Anxiety to Sporting and Athletic Situations: Gender, Sports Involvement and Parental Pressure, *Depression and Anxiety*, 12, 4: 193–202.

Nouwen, H.J.M. (1979) *The Wounded Healer: In our Woundedness, We Can Become a Source of Life for Others*, New York: Image Books, Doubleday.

Null, A. (2004) *Real Joy: Freedom to Be Your Best*, Ulm, Germany: Ebner and Spiegel.

Null, A. (2008) "Finding the Right Place": Professional Sport as a Christian Vocation, in D. Deardorff, II, and J. White (Eds.), *The Image of God in the Human Body: Essays on Christianity and Sports*, Lampeter, Wales: The Edwin Mellen Press, 315–366.

Ogilvie, B.C. (1987) Counseling for Sports Career Termination, in J.R. May and M.J. Asken (Eds.), *Sport Psychology: The Psychological Health of the Athlete*, New York: PMA, 213–230.

Pannenberg, W. (1985) *Anthropology in Theological Perspective*, Philadelphia: Westminster Press.

Park, J. (2000) Coping Strategies by Korean National Athletes, *The Sport Psychologist*, 14: 63–80

Parker, A. (1995) Great Expectations: Grimness and Glamour? The Football Apprentice in the 1990s, *Sport in History*, 15, 1: 107–126.

Parker, A. (2009) Sport, Celebrity and Identity: A Socio-Legal Analysis, in A. Parker and J. Harris (Eds.), *Sport and Social Identities*, Basingstoke, UK: Palgrave Press, 202–227.

Peña, D. (2004) *Scripture and Sport Psychology: Mental-Techniques for the Christian Athlete*, New York: iUniverse, Inc.

Percy, M. (2005) *Engaging with Contemporary Culture: Christianity, Theology and the Concrete Church: Explorations in Practical, Pastoral and Empirical Theology*, Aldershot, UK: Ashgate Publishing Limited.

Polanyi, M. (1958) *Personal Knowledge: Towards a Post-Critical Philosophy*, Chicago: University of Chicago Press.

Pope John Paul II. (2004) Rights Cannot Be Only the Prerogative of the Healthy, *Zenit News Agency*, August 1.

Prebish, C.S. (1993) Religion and Sport: Convergence or Identity?, in C.S. Prebish (Ed.), *Religion and Sport: The Meeting of Scared and Profane*, Westport, CT: Greenwood Press, 45–76.

Prince, D. (2008) *Husbands and Fathers: Rediscover the Creator's Purpose for Men*, Lancaster and London: Sovereign World.

Progen, J.L., and DeSensi, J.T. (1984) The Value of Theoretical Frameworks for Exploring the Subjective Dimension of Sport, *Quest*, 36, 1: 80–88.

Quoist, M. (1965) *The Christian Response*, Dublin: Gill and Macmillan Ltd.

Ravizza, K. (1984) Qualities of the Peak Experience in Sport, in J. Silva and R. Weinberg (Eds.), *Psychological Foundations of Sport*, Champaign, IL: Human Kinetics, 452–461.

Ravizza, K. (2002) A Philosophical Construct: A Framework for Performance Enhancement, *International Journal of Sport Psychology*, 33: 4–18.

Reason, M., and Craig, O. (2008) Beijing Olympics: The Games Are Not Child's Play, *The Telegraph*, retrieved November 6, 2008, from http://www.telegraph.co.uk/sport/othersports/olympics/2571096/Beijing-Olympics-The-Games-are-not-childs-play.html

Reid, H.L. (2002) *The Philosophical Athlete*, Durham, NC: Carolina Academic Press.

Reno, R.R. (2006) Pride and Idolatry, *Interpretation: A Journal of Bible and Theology*, 60, 2: 166–181.

Rieke, M., Hammermeister, J., and Chase, M. (2008) Servant Leadership in Sport: A New Paradigm for Effective Coaching Behaviour, *International Journal of Sports Science and Coaching*, 3, 2: 227–239.

Roderick, M. (2006) *The Work of Professional Football: A Labour of Love?* London: Routledge.

Sager, S.S., Lavallee, D., and Spray, C.M. (2009) Coping with the Effects of Fear of Failure: A Preliminary Investigation of Young Elite Athletes, *Journal of Clinical Sports Psychology*, 3: 73–98.

Salter, D. (1997). Measure, Analyse and Stagnate: Towards a Radical Psychology of Sport, in R.J. Butler (Ed.), *Sports Psychology in Performance*, Oxford: Reed Educational and Professional Publishing Ltd., 248–260.

Sartre, J.-P. (1956) *Being and Nothingness* (Trans. Hazel E. Barnes), New York: The Philosophical Library, Inc.

Savage, T.B. (1996) *Power through Weakness: Paul's Understanding of the Christian Ministry in 2 Corinthians* (Society for New Testament Studies Monograph Series 86), Cambridge: Cambridge University Press.

Schinke, R.J., and Hanrahan, S.J. (Eds.) (2009) *Cultural Sport Psychology*, Champaign, IL; Human Kinetics.

Schmitt, R.L., and Leonard, W.M, II. (1986) Immortalizing the Self through Sport, *American Journal of Sociology*, 91, 5: 1088–1111.

Schroeder, P.J., and Scribner, J.P. (2006) To Honor and Glorify God: The Role of Religion in One Intercollegiate Athletics Culture, *Sport, Education and Society*, 11, 1: 39–54.

Schwobel, C., and Gunton, C.E. (1991) *Persons, Divine and Human*, Edinburgh: T and T Clark.

Seligman, M.E.P., and Csikszentmihalyi, M. (2000). Positive Psychology: An Introduction, *American Psychologist*, 55, 1: 5–14.

Shafranske, E.P. (Ed.) (1996) *Religion and the Clinical Practice of Psychology*, Washington, DC: American Psychological Association.

Simon, R.L. (1991) The Ethics of Competition, in R.L. Simon (Ed.), *Fair Play: Sports, Values and Society*, Oxford: Westview Press, 13–36.

Slot, O. (2005) Why Marvin Andrews Believes He Is Walking Proof that Miracles Happen, *The Times* (Times-online), retrieved 2009 from: http://www.timesonline.co.uk/tol/sport/football/article571995.ece

Slot, O. (2008) Fourth in the Olympics Hurt, but Retirement Is Like a Death in the Family, *The Times* (Sport), December 19, 98–99.

Slusher, H. (1967) *Man, Sport and Existence: A Critical Analysis*, Philadelphia: Lea and Febinger.

Smart, B. (2005) *The Sport Star: Modern Sport and the Cultural Economy of Sporting Celebrity*, London: Sage Publications Ltd.

Smith, A.L., Lemyre, P.N., and Raedeke, T.D. (Eds.) (2007) Athlete Burnout: Special Issue, *International Journal of Sport Psychology*, 38, 4: all pages of special edition.

Smith, A.M., and Milliner, E.K. (1994) Injured Athletes and the Risk of Suicide, *Journal of Athletic Training*, 29: 337–341.

Smith, B., and Sparkes, A.C. (2008) Changing Bodies, Changing Narratives and the Consequences of Tellability: A Case Study of Becoming Disabled through Sport, *Sociology of Health and Illness*, 30, 2: 217–236.

Souster, M. (2009) Wounded Hero Finally Set to Take His Leave in Pursuit of Fresh Challenge, *The Times* (Sport), March 13, 84.

Sparkes, A.C., and Smith, B. (2002) Sport, Spinal Cord Injury, Embodies Masculinities, and the Dilemmas of Narrative Identity, *Men and Masculinities*, 4, 3: 258–285.

Stevenson, C.L. (1997) Christian Athletes and the Culture of Elite Sport: Dilemmas and Solutions, *Sociology of Sport Journal*, 14: 241–262.

Stibbe, M. (1999) *From Orphans to Heirs: Celebrating Our Spiritual Adoption*, Oxford, UK: The Bible Reading Fellowship.

Stoll, S.K., and Beller, J.M. (2008) Moral Reasoning in Athletic Populations: A 20 Year Review, *Centre for Ethics*, University of Idaho, retrieved November 11, 2008, from http://www.educ.uidaho.edu/center_for_ethics/research_fact_sheet.htm

Taylor, C. (1989) *Sources of Self: The Making of Modern Identity*, Cambridge, MA: Harvard University Press.

Tillich, P. (1952) *The Courage to Be*, New Haven, CT: Yale University Press.

Tournier, P. (1957) *The Meaning of Persons*, Harper & Row Publishers, Inc.

Tournier, P. (1962) *Guilt and Grace: A Psychological Study*, San Francisco, CA, USA: Harper & Row Publishers, Inc.

Towner, W.S. (2005) Clones of God: Genesis 1: 26–28 and the Image of God in the Hebrew Bible, *Interpretation: A Journal of Bible and Theology*, 59, 4: 341–356.

Townsend, M. (2007) *The Gospel of Falling Down: The Beauty of Failure in an Age of Success*, Winchester, UK: O Books.

Trothen, T.J. (2008) *Redefining Human, Redefining Sport: The Imago Dei and Genetic Modification Technologies*, in D. Deardorff, II, and J. White (Eds.), *The Image of God in the Human Body: Essays on Christianity and Sports*, Lampeter, Wales: The Edwin Mellen Press, 217–234.

Twietmeyer, G. (2008) A Theology of Inferiority: Is Christianity the Source of Kinesiology's Second-Class Status in the Academy? *Quest*, 60: 452–466.

Twitchell, J.B. (1997) *For Shame*, New York: St. Martin's Griffin.

Udry, E., Gould, D., Bridges, D., and Beck, L. (1997) Down but Not Out: Athlete Responses to Season-Ending Ski Injuries, *Journal of Sport and Exercise Psychology*, 3: 229–248.

Vallerand, R.J., and Miquelon, P. (2007) Passion for Sport for Athletes, in S. Jowett and D. Lavallee (Eds.), *Social Psychology in Sport*, Champaign, IL: Human Kinetics, 249–263.

Van Kaam, A.L. (1975) *In Search of Spiritual Identity*, Denville, NJ: Dimension Books.

Vernacchia, R.A., McGuire, R.T., Reardon, J.P., and Templin, D.P. (2000) Psychosocial Characteristics of Olympic Track and Field Athletes, *International Journal of Sport Psychology*, 31: 5–23.

Visek, A.J., Hurst, J.R., Maxwell, J.P., and Watson, J.C., II. (2008) A Cross-Cultural Psychometric Evaluation of the Athletic Identity Measurement Scale, *Journal of Applied Sport Psychology*, 20: 473–480.

Vitz, P.C. (1994) *Psychology as Religion: The Cult of Self-Worship*, Grand Rapids, MI: Williams Eerdmans Publishing.

Vitz, P.C. (1998) *Sigmund Freud's Christian Unconscious*, Grand Rapids, MI: Wm. B. Eerdmans Publishing Co.

Vitz, P.C. (1999) *Faith of the Fatherless: The Psychology of Atheism*, Dallas: Spence Publishing Company.

Vitz, P.C., and Felch, S.M. (Eds.) (2006) *The Self: Beyond the Postmodern Crisis*, Wilmington, DE: Intercollegiate Studies Institute.

Walker, A. (1996) *Telling the Story: Gospel, Mission and Culture*, London: SPCK.

Walker, S.H. (1980) *Winning: The Psychology of Competition*, New York; W.W. Norton.

Warren, R. (2002) *The Purpose Driven Life: What on Earth Am I Here For?* Grand Rapids, MI: Zondervan.

Warriner, K., and Lavalle, D. (2008) The Retirement Experiences of Elite Female Gymnasts: Self Identity and the Physical Self, *Journal of Applied Sport Psychology*, 20, 3: 301–317.

Watson, N.J. (2006) Martin Buber's *I and Thou*: Implications for Christian Psychotherapy, *Journal of Psychology and Christianity*, 25, 1: 35–44.

Watson, N.J. (2007a) Nature and Transcendence: The Mystical and Sublime in Extreme Sports, in J. Parry, S. Robinson, N.J. Watson and M.S. Nesti (Eds.), *Sport and Spirituality: An Introduction*, London: Routledge, 222–223.

Watson, N.J. (2007b) Muscular Christianity in the Modern Age: "Winning for Christ" or "Playing for Glory"?, in J. Parry, S. Robinson, N.J. Watson and M.S. Nesti (Eds.), *Sport and Spirituality: An Introduction*, London: Routledge, 80–94.

Watson, N.J., & Czech, D. (2005). The use of Prayer in Sport: Implications for Sport Psychology Consulting, *Athletic Insight: The Online Journal of Sport Psychology*, 17, 4, available from http://www.athleticinsight.com/Vol7Iss4/PrayerinSports.htm

Watson, N.J., and Nesti, M. (2005) The Role of Spirituality in Sport Psychology Consulting: An Analysis and Integrative Review of Literature, *Journal of Applied Sport Psychology*, 17: 228–239.

Watson, N.J., and White, J. (2007) "Winning at All Costs" in Modern Sport: Reflections on Pride and Humility in the Writings of C.S. Lewis, in J. Parry, S. Robinson, N.J. Watson and M.S. Nesti (Eds.), *Sport and Spirituality: An Introduction*, London: Routledge, 61–79

Watts, G. (2008) Spirituality in the Context of Profound Intellectual Disability, paper read at the Conference on Spirituality, Human Development & Well-being, University of Western Sydney, July 24–25.

White, J. (2008). Idols in the Stadium: Sport as an "Idol Factory," in D. Deardorff, II and J. White (Eds.), *The Image of God in the Human Body: Essays on Christianity and Sports*, Lampeter, Wales: The Edwin Mellen Press, 127–172.

White, J., and Watson, N.J. (2006) Exegeting Homo Sportivus, *World of Sports*, 22: 1–2.

Wilkinson, J. (2008) *Tackling Life: Striving for Perfection*, London, UK: Headline.

Willard, D. (2000) Spiritual Formation in Christ: A Perspective on What Is and How It Might Be Done, *Journal of Psychology and Theology*, 28, 4: 254–258.

Wittmer, M. (2008) *A Christian Perspective of Sport*, in D. Deardorff, II, and J. White (Eds.), *The Image of God in the Human Body: Essays on Christianity and Sports*, Lampeter, Wales: The Edwin Mellen Press, 43–59.

Wolfensberger, W. (1983) The Most Urgent Issues Facing Us as Christians Concerned with Handicapped Persons Today, in W. Gaventa and C. Coulter (Eds.), *The Theological Voice of Wolf Wolfensberger*, Binghamton, NY: The Haworth Pastoral Press, 91–102.

Wolfensberger, W. (2001) The Prophetic Voice and the Presence of Mentally Retarded People in the World Today, in W. Gaventa and C. Coulter (Eds.), *The Theological Voice of Wolf Wolfensberger*, Binghamton, NY: The Haworth Pastoral Press, 11–48.

Wooden, J. (2005) *Wooden on Leadership* (with Steve Jamison), Maidenhead, UK: McGraw-Hill.

Worthington, E.L. Jr., and Berry, J.W. (2005) Virtues, Vices, and Character Development, in W.R. Miller and H.D. Delaney (Eds.), *Judeo-Christian Perspectives on Psychology: Human Nature, Motivation, and Change*, Washington, DC: American Psychological Association, 145–164.

Wright, C.J.H. (2007) *Knowing God the Father through the Old Testament*, Downers Grove, IL: IVP Academic.

Yancey, P. (1997) *What's So Amazing about Grace*? Grand Rapids, MI: Zondervan.

Yannick, S., and Brewer, B.W. (2007) Perceived Determinants of Identification with the Athlete Role among Elite Competitors, Journal of Applied Sport Psychology, 19, 1: 67–79.

Yiannakis, A., and Melnik, M.J. (Eds.) (2001) The Construction and Confirmation of Identity in Sport Subcultures, in Contemporary Issues in Sociology of Sport, Champaign, IL: Human Kinetics, 399–411.

Zizioulas, J.D. (1991) On Being a Person: Towards an Ontology of Personhood, in C. Schwobel and C.E. Gunton (Eds.), Persons, Divine and Human, Edinburgh: T and T Clark, 33–46.

# 6 Sport Psychology and Spirit in Professional Football

*Mark Nesti*

## INTRODUCTION

The first thought that springs to mind on seeing spirituality and football in the same sentence is usually one of incomprehension, or disbelief. Football, especially at the most elevated levels of performance, appears to be an intensely physical activity and one where utilitarian attitudes to the body are the norm. Although recent research literature (Thelwell et al., 2005) and accounts of professional practice (Nesti & Littlewood, 2009) highlight a growing recognition of the importance attached to psychological factors in top-level professional football, few would argue that it provides an ideal vehicle to encounter spiritual experiences.

Special moments and extraordinary emotional states have been reported by participants from many different sports, which often seem to share some of the qualities attributed to spiritual experiences. For example, sky divers and skiers and endurance athletes (Cooper, 1998) have described moments of optimal performance, peak experiences and flow in language that, according to Watson and Nesti (2005), shares much with accounts of spiritual experiences from outside of sport. Although some writers suggest that sport cannot produce moments of spirituality since it is merely a psychophysical activity (Watson, 2007), others claim that reference to altered mental states, flow experiences and similar terms provides evidence that sport is the new religion and is infused with the spiritual (Prebish, 1993).

Other objections to the possibility of discovering a spiritual dimension in professional football relate to its status as a team sport. The idea has grown up that spirituality is something personal and that it can not apply to the group. This perspective finds support in various strands of Protestant theology, where the individual alone has a personal spiritual relationship with God without the need of church, sacraments or the invocation of priests. Catholic theological tradition, in contrast, states that the church (as a community of believers) and a personal relationship with God (at an individual level) are both equally necessary to encounter the spiritual. This corresponds with the ideas of existential psychologists (Caruso, 1964) and personalist philosophers (Marcel, 1948), who explain that the person is a synthesis of the individual and community. According to this perspective, the development of the person requires that there must be an individual, a world and a relationship between the two (Kingston, 1961). Such a view could be used to support the idea that team spirit is not just the sum total of individual spirituality, but *also* includes the team as a singular spiritual entity in its own right.

Nevertheless, none of these discussions so far will satisfy the skeptic who refuses to accept that such an increasingly materialistic, phenomenally wealthy and celebrity-driven activity such as Premier League football can be an arena for spiritual experiences.

This chapter challenges such a narrow and restricted view of both football and many of the ideas surrounding spirituality. Drawing on the ideas of the Thomist philosopher Josef Pieper and certain strands of existentialist thinking, an argument will be presented that intends to show how the spiritual can be accessed in all activities including elite sports such as Premier League football. This line of reasoning will then lead to a consideration of how existential phenomenological psychology can be usefully applied to begin to acknowledge and classify the different types of spirituality that may be encountered in the game. This will extend to examining the role of the sport psychologist in this task within a Premiership football club, and discussing the importance of support from other key staff in this environment.

The material presented in this chapter is based upon eight years of one-to-one sport psychology work with Premiership players from five clubs, amounting to over 2,000 hours of applied practice in total. An important section of the chapter will analyze how the existential approach to anxiety and courage could lead to a greater appreciation of the importance of spirituality in football and other sports.

A further aim of this work is to encourage others to consider the work of Pieper (1998), who has drawn on Thomist philosophy to differentiate clearly between the notions of human spirit and religious spirituality. Finally, brief mention will be made about the role of football fans, and the possibility that their involvement in the game can be understood socioculturally, psychologically and also from a spiritual perspective.

## SPIRIT IN SPORT PSYCHOLOGY

During the past decade there has been evidence of a growing interest in the relationship between psychology, spirituality and sport. Two books in particular have emerged as very important resources for those wishing to examine psychological perspectives on the spiritual dimensions of sport. Murphy and White's (1995) version of an earlier book contains sections on peak experiences and flow, and provides an annotated biography of 1,550 studies and articles addressing this topic. This is supported by Cooper's

(1998) work specifically addressing what sports performers often refer to as "the zone." In addition to these books we are finally beginning to see peer-reviewed articles in scientific journals investigating spirituality and team sports (Dillon & Tait, 2000) and prayer and sport (Czech et al., 2004).

However, to date there have been no articles or books focusing on spirituality and psychology in what is the biggest sport in the world in terms of both participants and financial resources. There are several possible reasons for this. Two of the most likely relate to the negative perception of sport psychology that has prevailed in professional football until quite recently. The explanation behind this has been well documented in several texts on applied sport psychology (Nesti, 2004) and includes skepticism about the effectiveness of mental skills training, coaches' perceptions about the role of sport psychologists and claims about the unique environment of professional football. On those rare occasions that sport psychologists have studied professional football it has often been in relation to talent development or mental toughness (Thelwell et al., 2005) or it has focused on junior players at the academy level.

Questions around spirituality, religious belief and the concept of spirit (as these factors impact psychologically on professional football players) have never been considered systematically, or investigated empirically. This is rather surprising since team spirit is often referred to by coaches and team managers in professional football to explain one of the key qualities of exceptional performers and outstanding teams. Sport psychologists have tended, with some recent notable exceptions (Ravizza, 2002), to ignore the concept of spirituality, or to argue that it does not exist in sport (Crust, 2006). Nesti (2004) has suggested that, most often, researchers have tried to reconceptualize spirit to mean self-confidence, and at other times it has been described in terms relating to intrinsic motivation.

In their review of spirituality in sport psychology, Watson and Nesti (2005) highlighted a number of recent studies that have examined the role of prayer in sport (Czech et al., 2004), spirituality and team sports (Dillon & Trait, 2000) and spirituality and excellence in sport performance (Sverduk, 2002). In many ways these studies are closely related to earlier work on peak experiences in sport (Ravizza, 1977) and flow (Czikszentmihalyi, 1975). The notion of peak experiences in particular shares much with the concept of spirituality. Emerging from the work of Maslow (1968) and the humanistic psychology movement, peak experiences refer to those deeply personal, subjective and apparently mystical states that can accompany exceptional performances. Such experiences are usually described in very positive terms and have been reported by athletes in relation to motivation towards their sport.

Sometimes the unpredictable nature of sporting contests can test the spiritual qualities of the person. As has been discussed previously by Pieper (1989) and Nesti (2007), courage, selflessness, spontaneity and hope may be more fully understood as spiritual terms rather than as psychological constructs or philosophical concepts. In the highly charged, emotionally volatile environment of professional sport, it is not uncommon for sports performers to suffer a poor run of form and defeats that may lead ultimately to losing their jobs, or at least facing financial penalties.

Although Premier League football is currently one of the wealthiest sports in the world, this does not in itself protect individuals from the pressures associated with failure and loss. To those outside of this world it is easy to imagine that greater resources would somehow ameliorate the stress and anxiety associated with the competitive process. In some ways the reverse may be true: the more one has, the greater the concern about losing it. This empirical fact has been commented upon by psychologists such as Fromm (1989/1942) and May (1977) as well as by philosophers (Pieper, 1998) and theologians (Ker, 1990). They have pointed out that the ever-increasing material wealth in the West has been associated with greater numbers of people suffering from psychological disturbances and spiritual crises.

Many of the Premiership players I have worked with during the past 15 years have mentioned frequently how aware they are that material and financial affluence could undermine their capacity to give all of themselves in training and matches across their careers. These players often highlight what appears to be a paradox: the more money they have, the more important it is for them to remain "pure" in their motives, and faithful to their calling as professional athletes. Whilst sports psychologists have referred to this in terms of intrinsic motivation, and being able to maintain a task focus rather than an ego orientation, the players I have engaged with in dialogue have convinced me that much more is actually at stake. They invariably talk about pride, doing one's duty, putting all of oneself on the line and holding nothing back. These terms arguably go beyond motivation, focus and goal-setting and are much closer to the spiritual qualities and attributes of the person (Nesti, 2007).

One very important concept that relates closely to the spiritual ideas of courage and hope is that of anxiety. This type of anxiety differs from the competitive anxiety that has been discussed so extensively in the sport psychology literature (Jones, 1995), in that it describes an emotion we encounter whenever there is a threat to the status quo. Nesti (2004, 2007) has described this *existential anxiety* as being fundamentally an anxiety about meaning, or identity. In relation to this, Maslow (1954) claimed that European existential psychology added greatly to humanistic theory through its emphasis on the importance of personal meaning, which Maslow translated as identity. The existential anxiety experienced by an individual is the result of uncertainty about personal identity when facing a key moment of transition. During those occasions when a team loses week after week, the air is filled with existential anxiety. Literally, this is anxiety about existence! It is no exaggeration to say that, subjectively at least, the feeling is one of helplessness and despair. The annihilation of Premiership status, playing careers and staff job security is a real and present danger. It is at times like these that many managers and their coaching staff in the Premiership demand evidence of collective and individual spirit. Note that it is spirited performances and the display of team spirit that managers ask for. Motivation, concentration, focus and confidence are often also mentioned during these critical periods. However, it is the spiritual terms of character, courage and resilience that are given predominance.

When the Premiership managers and players talk about courage, they are keen to stress that this is something quite different from bravery. Unlike much current academic writing in psychology and sports psychology, these professional sportsmen (who are largely uneducated in terms of high-level academic qualifications) insist upon making clear distinctions between words that are obviously related but discrete! Bravery is used to describe acts where an individual instinctively attempts to do the right thing, and often where there is an element of physical or mental danger. In contrast, courage is a more deeply personal act. They describe courage much more closely to the sense of Aquinas or Aristotle (Corlett, 1996b), which involves accepting a challenge and acting upon it in a situation where the individual has the option to hide from his responsibility. Players and staff have confided in me over years of working in Premiership football that, whilst bravery is commonplace in professional sport, it is the spiritual quality of courage that separates the true champion from the others.

This notion of courage is inextricably linked to the concept of existential anxiety. According to this view (May, 1975), the courageous person does not avoid the anxiety of going it alone by hiding in the group, or by evading a challenge or a decision. Such a player, in front of 35,000 passionate supporters, asks to receive the ball once again despite losing it easily on the previous three occasions, or shoots when the easier option is to pass the ball out wide having just missed the target with their two previous attempts.

Another closely related term to courage is that of spontaneity. This may seem an unusual claim because spontaneity is usually associated with acting on impulse, and is frequently described as something that accompanies effortless and natural behaviors. However, Fromm (1994), after over 50 years' work as a therapist, claimed that the capacity to be spontaneous was *the* single most important sign of mental health. This suggests that spontaneity is deeply connected to our self-identity and our capacity to think and act authentically. When a sports performer, or anyone else for that matter, displays spontaneous behavior, we are likely to see the very best (as well as, sometimes, the worst) from that person. It is so attractive a form of human behavior (when it is oriented towards constructive behavior) that it can only be understood as evidence of human freedom and our capacity to act.

At an analytical level, the attribution of spontaneity can be seen as evidence of a holistic account of human being. When we attribute spontaneity we attribute the act to the person; no one would find it satisfactory to account fully for spontaneity in terms of instinctual drives, reinforcement schedules or genetics. As has been pointed out by Pieper (1998) and Nesti (2007), spirit may be better described as *the* human quality where our freedom and free will resides. A spontaneous act cannot be forced, or explained away in terms of deterministic psychology or materialist philosophy. Psychologically and philosophically speaking, I am fully responsible for my spontaneous act. All of these factors partly explain why spontaneity is universally admired. It has been pointed out by Novak (1994) and others that sport and play are two of the clearest examples of human activities infused with spontaneous behavior.

In relation to Premiership football, where the stakes are often so high, inventive, imaginative and creative behavior is highly valued. It is during these moments of imagination that matches can be turned and game-breaking events occur. To be spontaneous with so much to gain or lose requires the spiritual quality of courage. In other words, the players must be courageous enough to "throw" themselves into the task without inhibition. This can only be done when the individual's mind and body act in unison, and are bound together by spirit.

It is for these reasons that the four Premiership managers with whom I have worked closely during the past eight seasons have repeatedly stressed that they want in their teams, above all else, players with spirit. They know that top players will already possess high levels of mental skills, physical capabilities and technical and tactical know-how. But my role has been to help to develop the team and individual spirit of players in their charge.

For the same reasons, these managers and their senior coaches are often so very dismissive of sports psychologists and the dominant academic view of sport psychology, which is materialistic, positivistic and conceives of human agency in deterministic terms. This remarkable learning experience for me as a sports psychologist is all the more surprising because not one of the 18 Premiership staff I have been fortunate to work alongside has studied any philosophy, psychology or theology at advanced levels. Their understanding has been gained from reflections on their lived experience over many years in professional football. As I have pointed out before (Nesti 2004), these data are in many ways similar to phenomenologically derived accounts of sport practices and, because of this, they can legitimately be described as empirical.

It could be argued that for far too long, psychology and sport psychology have been unable or unwilling to fully accept terms like 'spirit' and 'courage.' As has been discussed previously, this situation is due to the philosophical roots of most approaches in psychology. Giorgi (1970) has argued that the discipline has been based on the methods of natural science. Such methods are ill-suited to the study of individual experiences and subjective phenomena. Vitz (1994) has pointed out that due to the materialist and deterministic philosophical underpinnings of modern psychology, the discipline has been unable to satisfactorily examine religious belief and spiritual practices. Most within sports psychology have followed (often unwittingly) this limited approach to psychology. Nesti (2004, 39–41) has suggested that sports psychology should be more prepared to use phenomenological methods in its research. Phenomenology, which involves the empirical study of essences and personal meaning, is one way in which prayer, team spirit and religious faith could be investigated within sport. A small body of work has begun to explore these ideas within sport psychology research. Although not addressing spirituality directly, research by Fahlberg et al. (1992) and Dale (1996) have demonstrated the value of using a phenomenological approach in sport psychology. Phenomenology is primarily interested in providing description of events and experiences, rather than identifying cause-and-effect relationships. Such an approach would be opposed to the rather arrogant scientist perspective, which typically rejects the concept of spirituality and the term 'spirit,' by translating these terms to mean confidence, motivation or even mental toughness.

## ENCOUNTERS AND SPORT PSYCHOLOGY COUNSELING

It should be noted that following Pieper's (1998) attempt to use Thomist perspectives to examine human and religious notions of spirit and to identify their relatedness and points of difference, it is important to acknowledge that many Premiership players hold strong religious beliefs. In my experience, managers view this positively where it is clear that this part of a player's identity provides them with a strong sense of self which is not likely to shrivel when arduous tasks are faced, such as possible relegation from the league, serious injury or repeated deselection. As a sports psychologist who has been fortunate to work one-to-one with over 200 premiership players, I have been able to reflect on the importance of human spirit and religious belief in these individuals and their lives as highly paid professional athletes.

What follows is an account of a typical encounter with a player in this environment. Whilst this does not represent work done with any particular individual, it draws on discussions and issues that I have dealt with during the past eight seasons. Before presenting this, it is important to explain my approach to sport psychology practice. I have a background in both traditional mental-skills-based sports psychology and mainstream psychology. My approach to counseling players draws in part on theistic perspectives in existential phenomenological psychology. These approaches are open to the spiritual dimension, and conceive of human being in terms of mind, body and spirit (for a fuller account of this, see Nesti, 2004).

Following this approach, one-to-one meetings with players sometimes involve use of the encounter. This has been described, by counseling psychologists from within various existential traditions, as being an example of person-to-person meeting. For existential writers such as Marcel (1948) and Frankl (1984), this encapsulates a holistic mode of communication which at its most fundamental level requires the psychologist to be spiritually available to the person with whom they are working. This requires empathy, spontaneity, passion and authenticity on behalf of both parties. In this way these particular strands of existential philosophy and psychology emphasize that genuine communication cannot be achieved by skills or techniques alone. Instead, what is required is that the focus is on the person first and their role as a Premiership player second, and that it is the encounter itself which may be of more benefit to the athlete than any new goals, tasks or psychological skills that they attempt to work on.

Sometimes, players reach a stage in their professional careers where they are established in a team or squad, and find themselves financially secure. Encounters with players in these situations can prove extremely valuable opportunities for reflection on what the individual hopes to achieve in the next stage of his life. Within existential psychology these moments are referred to as boundary situations. Issues can arise around many different factors, some largely within the player's control and others less so. However, the common element is that the player is prepared to wrestle with the choices available to him at the time. The example that follows highlights ways in which some of this process can be understood from a spiritual perspective:

> *I had worked with this player for 19 months and had seen him become a confident and established member of the first team squad. He had agreed a contract worth £1.5m per year and had recently got married to his long-term girlfriend. It seemed as though much of what he had dreamt of as a young player was now becoming a reality.*
>
> *We agreed to meet in our usual room, which was down at the stadium away from the training ground. As I always did, I reminded Vince (not his real name) that our sessions were completely confidential and that the manager fully supported this process and understood how important it was that all discussions remained private between us. Very soon into our dialogue Vince explained that he was surprised at how quickly his excitement about the new contract and his marriage had begun to fall away. He talked about feeling somewhat guilty about how quickly he was beginning to take these two wonderful things for granted. He admitted that, although he was really happy with things in his life and career, he somehow felt that this was becoming a problem for him.*
>
> *We discussed his performances in matches and at training and our dialogue revealed that, despite the outward appearance of success, he felt increasingly anxious about what he could achieve next. So far as he could ascertain, no one on the coaching staff nor other players had sensed that something was wrong with him. However, despite achieving outstanding performance data in training and competitive matches, he knew that he was not progressing as he should. Part of the*

*way through the encounter, Vince asked if he was being greedy to want more, given the fantastic year he had just lived through.*

*After analyzing what this meant to him, he came to recognize that his anxiety was around whether he was beginning to settle into a static and fixed identity, and whether this might ultimately lead to a decline in his performances and impact negatively on his broader life. The dialogue at this stage centered on the more spiritual aspects of healthy psychological functioning. For example, Vince began to describe how he had always been prepared to give his all as a player and a person, and that this was because he believed that this was the way to truly experience joy in one's success, and was the best way to deal with inevitable failure and defeat.*

*Although at no time did he describe himself as a spiritual or religious individual, from a phenomenological perspective the terms he used, such as 'choosing to give my all,' 'putting myself on the line for the team,' and 'always trying to show the real me,' clearly related to notions of selflessness, authenticity and personal meaning. It goes without saying that this particular 1-hour 45-minute session was an emotionally draining and passionate experience.*

*The reason for both the duration and intensity of this encounter was because the sport psychologist and the player were discussing the most important aspects of personality. We were not engaged in a discussion around cognitive or behavioral techniques that can be used by an individual to alleviate symptoms (Corlett, 1996a). Neither was the session about discussing better time management, dealing with the media or handling manipulative agents. Quite simply, we were engaged in dialogue about the spiritual core of a person and the process of recognizing that this quality of human being must be constantly attended to, sustained and nurtured.*

*It is important to add that these types of encounter take place equally with players who are not committed to a particular religious belief and those who practice a faith. However, it is fair to say that where a player has a religious belief the process is somewhat different. Most usually, they are quicker to acknowledge that the most important element that contributes to their ability to perform in the exciting, volatile and ruthless world of Premiership football is that their self-worth is ultimately guaranteed by the unconditional love of God. No matter what they experience in their career and lives, God as the ultimate source of spirit will be with them as their careers progress, and in the end, inevitably decline.*

One of the most important aspects of the encounter is that it provides an opportunity for a fully confidential meeting to take place where the key focus is on matters deemed most important by the players themselves. Although, as a sports psychologist working in Premiership football, my main concern is with helping to enhance performance, no distinction can be made between narrow sport-focused issues and those relating to broader life. In my experience, players are acutely aware that their sport performance and their personal lives are inextricably linked. It is not uncommon to find that players spend more time talking about their need to be true to themselves and to take some control over events within football and across the rest of their lives.

Given the demands placed upon a Premiership player regarding fitness and dietary requirements, media expectations, performance attainment and huge financial rewards, one of the most important challenges relates to the need for meaning beyond the transient rewards and pressures experienced as a player. Although not discussing elite professional sports performers, Balague (1999) highlighted how important it was for athletes to have a clear identity and values that were based ultimately on something beyond their sporting achievements.

The approach I employ in my work acknowledges that for many athletes the most important source of meaning, values and identity is that of a spiritual belief. This could be in the form of a religious belief, or it could be connected to an acceptance that life and its meaning cannot be reduced to mere possessions, temporary successes and fame. In my dealings with Premiership players I have often witnessed both of these expressions of spirituality.

Within an encounter the aim is to help the footballer to grasp more fully his freedom to choose a particular path and to reject other opportunities. This freedom comes with responsibilities and duties to self and others, and has been differentiated by Clark (1973) from several strands of humanistic psychology where the focus is exclusively upon complete freedom to do as one wishes. Indeed, in its more extreme form, such a one-sided account of freedom and free will has led to analyses in terms of the 'postmodern condition' in which all values are relative and are centered on self. As I have said before (Nesti 2007), such a self-centered ethic is of little value in the world of sport, where individuals are often required to leave behind their own individual desires on behalf of the team. Again, it is this objection to postmodern thought (with its relativity of values) and humanistic psychology that is so clearly evident in the beliefs and practices of the Premiership football managers and coaches I have worked with.

During encounters with players there is an attempt to maintain what Buber (1958) has referred to as an I-Thou relationship. This requires the sport psychologist to approach the client as a person first and an athlete second. The aim is to engage in a kind of personal dialogue where the relationship between the parties is the key factor rather than where each focuses on their specific roles. In other words, in an I-Thou mode the differences between the psychologist and the player dissolve and a passionate, authentic and spontaneous encounter takes place in an environment of care and respect. This does not mean that difficult feelings will be avoided in the session or that an aimless conversation will take place. The I-Thou dialogue is broken when one party only sees the other as one who can do something for them. I-Thou moments, in contrast, are those where both player and psychologist maintain a directness and vitality of communication, and remain in an attitude of spiritual availability for one another. 'Disponibilite' (Marcel, 1948) or the notion of spiritual availability has been referred to as a presence "that belongs to those persons who listen not with their minds alone but with their hearts, minds and whole being" (Nesti, 2004: 82).

Although Buber's work has been described by many leading theologians, philosophers and psychologists as one of the most important books of the 20th century, its impact on sport psychology has been minimal. I have suggested (Nesti, 2004) that this situation is largely due to the dominance of materialist and determinist approaches to psychology in sport such as psychoanalysis (e.g., Andersen, 2000), behaviorism and cognitive approaches (Cox et al., 1993). Each of these in turn rejects the possibility of the spiritual, and in so doing is logically incapable of including psychospiritual terms such as courage, passion, meaning and love in their analysis.

This is very unfortunate, given that many Premiership players and senior staff expect their sport psychologist to have something to offer on these concepts! Clearly, they are not expecting sport psychologists to approach these topics in the same way as the club chaplain, whose main concern is with the soul. However, they are quite adamant that sports psychologists should be able to speak convincingly about spiritual qualities and have knowledge and professional competencies that will allow them to develop the spirit of individual Premiership players.

During an I-Thou relationship, the dialogue between the sports psychologist and the player becomes one where the dominant features are spontaneity and honesty in communication. It is in these situations that it becomes clear that a nonutilitarian philosophy underpins this work. It is no exaggeration to say that such dialogue confirms the full worth of the person beyond his instrumental role as psychologist or Premiership player. The focus is not on the person as a means, but as an end. Although it may seem strange to our ears, this type of dialogue can only really take place where the psychologist accepts that there is sacredness about human life, and that this alone is the ultimate foundation of our value beyond any material achievement or success. Such an anthropology is rooted in a spiritual perspective, since it rests on the belief that we are more than the sum of our physical attributes, psychological capacities and environmental histories. We are human beings endowed with free will (our essence) on a journey where our identity is always in a state of flux (our existence).

## THE FOOTBALL FAN

One area in the future that would benefit from being considered from a spiritual dimension is that of the football fan. The passion, commitment and intensity of football supporters is well known to all, and yet explanations of this behavior often seem to ignore that it has more in common with love than anything else. It is not really good enough to describe football fans as motivated towards their clubs, or to claim that they live vicariously through the great deeds of their teams. It seems more accurate to suggest that followers (such a more evocative word than 'supporters') of a team are spiritually committed to their club. The experience of being a fan involves moments of immense joy and great despair. It demands loyalty through difficult times and can bring about feelings of collective euphoria on occasion. All of these terms and many others associated with this experience appear closely linked to ideas of spirit, spirituality and even religious belief and practices.

The managers and coaching staff I have worked with in Premiership football are in no doubt about the important role that the fans can play in lifting the spirit of the team. As a sport psychologist, I have been asked to speak to the media at certain times during a season to point out how important the fans are to help the team to play with courage, passion and belief. These concepts, as has been explained in this chapter, can be understood from both a spiritual and a psychological perspective. It would be interesting to investigate whether football supporters saw their role more in line with the spiritual account, as has been discussed here, or whether they were more inclined to discuss their influence in more clearly psychological terminology and concepts.

The language used by the fan when describing great games and unexpected defeats could provide a deeper insight into this topic. Phenomenology would be an ideal method to collect this data and understand it prior to theories and preconceived notions. For example, the fan often refers to the importance of "getting behind the team," especially when the media are unfairly castigating players and coaches. Those who are familiar with the passions and traditions of the game know that the loyalty of fans for their club is often shared across the generations in families, and that great value is placed on "sticking together" in good times and bad. A more phenomenological approach would be unlikely to describe this experience in terms of psychological constructs and hypothetical causes. This approach could begin to throw some light on why football fans often see it as their right to criticize *their team,* whilst refusing to acknowledge the legitimacy of a professional media class to do likewise. This type of research could be described as an attempt to understand the spirit of the football fan. Quite possibly, fans might explain their involvement with the club in language often associated with religious belief and spiritual practice. Such a list could include words like suffering, despair, joy and even love. Hopefully in the future, sports psychologists will be prepared to adopt truly empirical approaches that will allow them to study the people's game in the language of the people!

## BIBLIOGRAPHY

Andersen, M.B. (Ed.) (2000) *Doing Sport Psychology,* Champaign, IL: Human Kinetics.

Balague, G. (1999) Understanding Identity, Value and Meaning When Working with Elite Athletes, *The Sport Psychologist*, 13: 89–98
Buber, M. (1958) *I and Thou*, trans. W. Kaufmann, New York: Charles Scribner's Sons.
Caruso, I.A. (1964) *Existential Psychology: From Analysis to Synthesis*, London: Darton, Longman & Todd.
Clark, M.T. (1973) *The Problem of Freedom*, New York: Meredith Corporation.
Cooper, A. (1998) *Playing in the Zone*, Boston: Shambhala.
Corlett, J. (1996a) Sophistry, Socrates and Sport Psychology, *The Sport Psychologist*, 10: 84–94.
Corlett, J. (1996b) Virtues Lost: Courage in Sport, *Journal of the Philosophy of Sport*, 23: 45–57.
Cox, R.H., Qui, Y., and Liu, Z. (1993) Overview of Sport Psychology, in R.N. Singer, M. Murphy and L.K. Tennat (Eds.), *Handbook of Research in Sport Psychology*, New York: Macmillan, 3–31.
Crust, L. (2006) Challenging the 'myth' of a spiritual dimension in sport, *Athletic Insight*, 8,2: 62–73.
Csikszentmihalyi, M. (1975) *Beyond Boredom and Anxiety*, San Francisco, CA: Jossey-Bass.
Czech, D.R., Wrisberg, C.A., Fisher, L.A., Thompson, C.L., and Hayes, G. (2004) The Experience of Christian Prayer in Sport—an Existential Phenomenological Investigation, *Journal of Psychology and Christianity*, 2: 1–19.
Dale, G. (1996) Existential-Phenomonology: Emphasizing the Experience of the Athlete in Sport Psychology Research, *The Sport Psychologist*, 10: 158–171.
Dillon, K.M., & Tait, J.L (2000) Spirituality and Being in the Zone in Team Sports: A Relationship?, *Journal of Sport Behaviour*, 23(2): 91–100.
Fahlberg, L.L., Fahlberg, L.A., and Gates, K.W. (1992) Exercise and Existence: Exercise Behaviour from and Existential-Phenomenological Perspective, *The Sport Psychologist*, 6: 172–191.
Frankl, V. (1984) *Man's Search for Meaning: An Introduction to Logotherapy*, New York: Simon & Schuster.
Fromm, E. (1942) *The Fear of Freedom*, London: Ark Paperbacks.
Fromm, E. (1994) *The Art of Listening*, London: Constable.
Giorgi, A. (1970) *Psychology as a Human Science*, New York: Harper & Row.
Jones, G. (1995) More Than Just a Game: Research Developments and Issues in Competitive Anxiety in Sport, *British Journal of Psychology*, 86: 449–478.
Ker, I. (1990) *Newman the Theologian: A Reader*, London: Collins.
Kingston, F. (1961) *French Existentialism: A Christian Critique*, London: Oxford University Press.
Lipscombe, N. (2004) The Relevance of the Peak Experience to Continued Skydiving Participation: A Qualitative Approach to Assessing Motivations, *Leisure Studies*, 18: 267–288.
Marcel, G. (1948) *The Philosophy of Existence*, London: Harvill.
Maslow, A.H. (1954) *Motivation and Personality*, New York: Harper & Row.
Maslow, A.H. (1968) *Toward a Psychology of Being*, New York: Van Nostrand Reinhold Company.
May, R. (1975) *The Courage to Create*, New York: Norton.
May, R. (1977) *The Meaning of Anxiety*, New York: Ronald Press.
Murphy, M. and White, R. A. (1995) *In the Zone: Transcendant Experience in Sports*, London, Penguin.
Nesti, M. (2004) *Existential Psychology and Sport*, London: Routledge.
Nesti, M. (2007) Persons and Players, in J. Parry, Robinson, S., Watson, N. J., and Nesti, M. (2007) *Sport and Spirituality: An Introduction*, London, UK: Routledge: 135–150.

Nesti, M. and Littlewood, M. (2009) Psychological preparation and development of players in Premiership football: Practical and theorectical perspectives, in T. Riley, A. M. Williams and B. Drust (eds). *International Research in Science and Soccer*, Londaon, UK: Routledge: 169–176.

Novak, M. (1994/1967) *The Joy of Sports: End Zones, Bases, Baskets, Balls and Consecration of the American Spirit*, New York: Basic Books.

Pieper, J. (1989) *Josef Pieper: An Anthology*, San Francisco: Ignatius Press.

Pieper, J. (1998) *Leisure: The Basis of Culture*, South Bend, IN: St. Augustine's Press.

Prebish, C.S. (1993) *Religion and Sport: The Meeting of the Sacred and the Profane*, Westport, CT, USA: Greenwood Press.

Ravizza, K. (1977) Peak Experiences in Sport, *Journal of Humanistic Psychology*, 17: 35–40.

Ravizza, K. (1984) Qualities of the Peak Experience in Sport, in J. Silva & R. Weinberg (Eds.), *Psychological Foundations of Sport*, Champaign, IL: Human Kinetics, 452–461.

Ravizza, K. (2002) Spirituality and Peak Experiences. Symposia conducted at the Annual Conference of the American Association of Applied Sports Psychology: Tuscon, Arizona, October 30–November 3, 2002.

Ravizza, K. (2002a) A Philosophical Construct: A Framework for Performance Enhancement, *International Journal of Sport Psychology*, 33: 4–18.

Sartre, J.-P. (1958) *Being and Nothingness: An Essay on Phenomenological Ontology*, trans. H. Barnes, London: Routledge. (Original work published 1943)

Sverduk, K. (2002) Spirituality and Performance: Pathways to Excellence. Symposia conducted at the Annual Conference of the American Association of Applied Sports Psychology: Tuscon, Arizona, October 30–November 3, 2002.

Thewell, R., Weston, N. and Greenlees, I. (2005) Defining and understanding mental toughness within Soccer, *Journal of Applied Sport Psychiology*, 17: 326–332.

Vitz, P. (1994/1977) *Psychology as Religion: The Cult of Self-Worship*, Grand Rapids, MI: Williams Eerdmans Publishing.

Watson, N. (2007) Muscular Christianity in the Modern Age: Winning for Christ or Playing for Glory?, in J. Parry, Robinson, S., Watsion, N. J. and Nesti, M. (2007) *Sport and Spirituality: An Introduction*, London,UK: Routledge: 80-94.

Watson, N.J. and Nesti, M. (2005) The role of spirituality in sport psychology consulting: An analysis and intergrative review of literature, *Journal of Applied Sport Psychology*, 17: 228–334.

# 7 Flow, Sport and the Spiritual Life

*Patrick Kelly, S.J.*

*You cannot serve God and mammon.*

(Luke 16:13, NAB)

*I came so that they might have life and have it more abundantly.*

(John 10:10, NAB)

*I have told you this so that my joy may be in you and your joy may be complete.*

(John 15:11, NAB)

For many people in America and elsewhere, sports have always been a natural topic of conversation. Over the last few decades, they have also become an area of inquiry for scholars from disciplines such as philosophy, history, sociology and psychology. More recently, scholars of spirituality have joined the conversation. Far from idle chatter, the water cooler conversations and academic discussions about sport have focused on such problems as the ethics of the exorbitant salaries of professional athletes, the commercialization of intercollegiate athletics, performance-enhancing drug-use scandals, and abusive coaching techniques employed by youth coaches or the all-too-frequent negative experiences of young people in Little League and school settings. The conversations also touch on the meaning of sport practices themselves and how the attainment of wealth and fame, which is possible for elite level athletes today, is related to human fulfillment.

With respect to the last issue, practitioners themselves are also engaged in the conversation. Legendary NBA coach Phil Jackson writes in dramatic fashion about the realities facing today's NBA players:

> The battle for players' minds begins at an early age. Most talented players start getting special treatment in junior high school, and by the time they reach the pros, they've had eight or more years of being coddled. They have NBA general managers, sporting goods manufacturers, and assorted hucksters dangling money in front of them and an entourage of agents, lawyers, friends, and family members vying for their favor. Then there's the media, which can be the most alluring temptress of all. With so many people telling them how great they are, it's difficult,

> and, in some cases, impossible, for coaches to get players to check their inflated egos at the gym door. (Jackson & Delehanty, 1995: 90)

According to Jackson and Delehanty, players' attachments to external goods such as wealth and fame have a corrosive influence on team dynamics and on players' ability to experience the genuine human and spiritual values associated with playing basketball. In his estimation, and that of some scholars today, the game has its own rewards. According to Jackson and Delehanty (1995: 79), it is these rewards that are important to most players:

> Whether they're willing to acknowledge it or not, what drives most basketball players is not the money or the adulation, but their love of the game. They live for moments when they can lose themselves completely in the action and experience the pure joy of competition. (Jackson & Delehanty, 1995: 79)

In Jackson's view, "one of the main jobs of a coach is to reawaken that spirit" (Jackson & Delehanty, 1995: 79).

From the earliest days, Christians have been in dialogue with the broader cultures in which they lived. St. Paul, for example, was a Greek-speaking Jew who was sensitive to Greek categories of thought and lived cultural realities. When writing to the citizens of Corinth, who were very familiar with the Isthmian games, Paul compared the Christian life to a race: "Do you not know that the runners in the stadium all run in the race, but only one wins the prize? Run so as to win" (1 Cor. 9:25, NAB). John Paul II commented on such passages in Paul's writings in a speech he gave in 1984 to 80,000 young athletes from all over the world: "St. Paul had been acquainted with the sporting world of his day. . . . And he did not hesitate to include sport among the human values which he used as points of reference for dialogue with the people of his time" (April 24, 1984: 3). John Paul II encouraged Christians in our time to continue the dialogue with sport. He emphasized that Christians today should pay attention especially to topics such as the meaning of games and sport and the quality of human experience in sport. Most importantly, he insisted that the dignity and integral development of the person needed to be kept front and center when considering sport practices and policies.

## FLOW THEORY AND SPORT

As was mentioned earlier, sometimes athletes choose to make their lives a narrow-minded pursuit of external goods such as wealth and fame. Or they might approach their sport itself merely as a venue for dominating others or inflating their own egos. In such cases it is difficult to see how the sports practices can be a context for personal development or self-transcendence or have much civic value. But it is important to recognize that there are human goods associated with games and sport. This point seems obvious, given the fact that human beings have engaged in such activities in all cultures throughout history (with distinctive characteristics and emphases in different times and places, to be sure). Because God's grace does not do away with what is human, but rather elevates it to another level, identifying the human goods associated with sport is indispensable for the development of a spirituality of sport.

One rich resource for understanding the human goods of sport is the flow theory of psychologist Mihaly Csikszentmihalyi, who wanted to understand the phenomenology of human development and well-being in general. He was critical of psychological theory for attending too exclusively to the negative aspects of human experience. In the process of his research he discovered a common experiential state which people described during their participation in activities such as games and sport, dancing and rock climbing, as well as in some work settings. He referred to this as *flow* because this was a word that the respondents themselves sometimes used when asked about their experience. Flow, as he uses that word, "denotes the wholistic sensation present when we act with total involvement. It is the kind of feeling after which one nostalgically says: 'That was fun,' or 'That was enjoyable'" (1975a: 43).

Enjoyment is central to the experience of flow; however, Csikszentmihalyi makes a distinction between enjoyment and pleasure. Most people, he writes, when thinking of the kinds of experiences that improve the quality of life first think of pleasurable experiences associated with "good food, good sex, all the comforts money can buy" (Csikszentmihalyi, 1990: 45). He points out that pleasure is an important part of the quality of life, but that on its own it does not lead to happiness (Csikszentmihalyi, 1990: 46).

According to Csikszentmihalyi, when people ponder further about what makes their lives rewarding, "they tend to move beyond pleasant memories and begin to remember other events, other experiences that overlap with pleasurable ones but fall into a category that deserves a separate name: *enjoyment*" (Csikszentmihalyi, 1990: 46). People describe themselves as experiencing enjoyment when they are engaged in challenging activities that require skills and their complete attention.

Such activities usually are or become *autotelic* activities. The word 'autotelic' derives from the Greek words *auto*, self, and *telos,* goal, and suggests that the goal is within the activity itself. A composer once pointed out to Csikszentmihalyi that he doesn't compose music for the money or the fame, but because he loves doing it: "This is what I tell my students. 'Don't expect money, don't expect fame or a pat on the back, don't expect a damn thing. Do it because you love it'" (Csikszentmihalyi, 1975a: 54–55).[1]

People's emphasis on the enjoyment they experience when engaged in autotelic activities led Csikszentmihalyi to a view similar to Jackson's with regard to the question of the relationship of wealth and fame to happiness.

For Csikszentmihalyi, external goods such as these are powerful symbols of happiness, but it is illusory to think that the possession of them will make one happy. Rather, happiness depends on the quality of experience in our lives.

In America, with the lingering effects of our Puritan heritage, we tend to be suspicious of enjoyment. Csikszentmihalyi's work invites us to reconsider the significance of the enjoyment we experience in activities like games and sport, as well as the relationship between such experiences and the spiritual life.

## ELEMENTS OF FLOW

One of the first indications that a person is experiencing flow is that he is intensely absorbed in the activity or experience. Csikszentmihalyi refers to this using the Buddhist term "one-pointedness of mind" or the "merging of action and awareness." The person's perspective is nondualistic; what he is doing and thinking about are one and the same thing. According to former San Francisco 49er quarterback John Brodie, a player needs to have such a one-pointedness of mind in sport:

> A player's effectiveness is directly related to his ability to be right there, doing that thing, in the moment. . . . He can't be worrying about the past or the future or the crowd or some extraneous event. He must be able to respond in the here and now. (Murphy &White, 1995: 22)

A high school basketball player describes a similar dynamic that occurs when he is playing basketball:

> The court—that's all that matters. . . . Sometimes on court I think of a problem, like fighting with my steady girl, and I think that's nothing compared to the game. You can think about a problem all day but as soon as you get in the game, the hell with it! . . . Kids my age, they think a lot . . . but when you are playing basketball, that's all there is on your mind—just basketball. . . . Everything seems to follow right along. (Csikszentmihalyi, 1975a: 47)[2]

Flow is most likely to occur when the activity has clear demands for action and provides immediate feedback about how well one is doing. If a person is playing tennis, she knows that she wants to return the ball over the net into the other side of the court, and knows immediately whether she has achieved her goal. According to Billie Jean King, such clear demands require her to focus only on the task at hand: "It's like I'm out there by myself. . . . I concentrate only on the ball in relationship to the face of my racket, which is a full-time job anyway, since no two balls ever come over the net the same way" (Murphy & White, 1995: 107–108).

Flow experiences typically require a great energy output from the person and a considerable amount of discipline as well. Such expenditures of energy and discipline are common in sports where athletes undergo lengthy periods of training. After prolonged training, there is typically an ease or an effortlessness to one's action and even a sense of being carried along by a current. At these times, "action follows upon action" seemingly without the need for conscious intervention on the athlete's part. As one female long-distance runner put it: "You are going faster, and yet it seems easier. . . . It is hard to describe in words unless you experience it. . . . Just that it is like you know . . . you're going as fast as you can go, and yet you're doing it quite easily" (Jackson & Csikszentmihalyi, 1999: 75).

During flow experiences, because of the enjoyment and the intense absorption in the activity, the person forgets about herself temporarily, or experiences an "ego-lessness." This doesn't mean that the self disappears, but simply that explicit reflection on the self stops for the time being. The activity requires all of the person's attention. Consequently, she doesn't have the psychic energy left over to be wondering "What do they think of me?" or "What will I get out of this?" And yet when the activity is over and the person reflects on herself anew, the self she is reflecting on has changed and grown. Csikszentmihalyi explains this dynamic:

> In flow a person is challenged to do her best, and must constantly improve her skills. At the time, she doesn't have the opportunity to reflect on what this means in terms of the self—if she did allow herself to become self-conscious, the experience could not have been very deep. But afterward, when the activity is over and self-consciousness has a chance to resume, the self that the person reflects upon is not the same self that existed before the flow experience: it is now enriched by new skills and fresh achievements. (1990: 65–66)

Flow experiences, while experienced in the consciousness of individuals, are not individualistic. On the contrary, what is deeply satisfying is letting go of ego concerns and experiencing oneself as a part of something larger than oneself. Even the most gifted players in team sports need to learn how to do this. Phil Jackson writes about how Michael Jordan put on virtuoso performances repeatedly in his early years with the Chicago Bulls, but the team could not win consistently. Other teams noticed that Jordan's teammates were not very involved in the offense and would simply focus on stopping him. It was only when Jordan was willing to step back so that his teammates could grow as players and everyone could be involved in the offense that the Bulls were able to win their NBA championships (Jackson & Delehanty, 1995).

During flow, time is experienced as "out of the ordinary" and unlike regular clock time. Several hours might go by in what seems like a few minutes. On the other hand, sometimes time seems to slow down and something that took a few seconds seems to have lasted much longer.

Csikszentmihalyi points out that if a person has a reasonably stable or secure sense of self it will be easier for him to enter into flow experiences. And such a sense of self will more likely develop if a young person has had the experience of being accepted, respected and loved (Csikszentmihalyi, 1990: 89–90).

> It stands to reason . . . that a child who has been abused, or who has been often threatened with the withdrawal of parental love—and unfortunately we are becoming increasingly aware of what a disturbing proportion of children in our culture are so mistreated—will be so worried about keeping his sense of self from coming apart as to have little energy left to pursue intrinsic rewards. (Csikszentmihalyi, 1990: 89–90)

Other scholars have written about similar themes. In her article "Meanings of the Body," Lynne Belaief writes about the importance of an experience of "ontological security" which "includes not only a firm sense of one's own existence but of the *rightness* of that existence" (Belaief, 1977: 59). For Belaief, when ontologically secure, we can enter into experiences for their own sake—we can play. And when we are playing, she points out, we are not following external orders, "but our own freedom" (Belaief, 1977: 59).

Our games today, which have their human appeal in large part because they are activities engaged in for their own sake, have become overencumbered with external goods, such as money and fame. It is winning, of course, that leads to the acquisition of these goods. And so, our energy and resources are often exclusively put into figuring out how to make use of the latest technologies and techniques in order to win more often. We tend to become obsessed with outcomes, with the bottom line. In such a context, it is a struggle to keep in touch with the aspects of sports participation that give them their human significance: the joy of playing, absorption in the activity, effortlessness, the experience of selflessness and unity with others and an altered sense of time. But athletes *do* experience these things from time to time, even at the highest levels of sports competition. And it is such experiences that make sports participation so rewarding. These are also the aspects of sport participation that are associated with personal development and self-transcendence.[3]

## FLOW, SPORT AND CHRISTIAN SPIRITUALITY

Several themes in Christian spirituality can be correlated with the insights of Csikszentmihalyi and practitioners like Phil Jackson with regard to sport. One of the first that comes to mind is the recognition that we get off track in a spiritual sense when we become too attached to money and status. Throughout the gospels, Jesus warns of the dangers of greed, and he repeatedly reminds his followers not to be so concerned with their own status.

Ignatius of Loyola writes in his *Spiritual Exercises* that it is characteristic of the enemy of our human nature to tempt people in the following way:

> People find themselves tempted to covet whatever seems to make them rich, and next because they possess some thing or things they find themselves pursuing and basking in the honor and esteem of this world. Then getting such deference raises up the false sense of personal identity in which a blinding pride has its roots. (Fleming, 1996: 113).[4]

Ignatius is identifying a dynamic that he says can "ensnare" people; it is associated with disorder and dysfunction, both in human societies in general and in sport. But, as we have seen, when people are experiencing flow while playing sports, their participation is associated with personal development and self-transcendence, positively affecting persons and communities. What might the significance of such experiences be from the perspective of Christian spirituality? What follows are a few suggestions along these lines.

From a Christian spiritual perspective, one of the more important aspects of participation in sport is to be found simply in the enjoyment that is experienced when doing something for its own sake. For Thomas Aquinas, it is these two elements that make play very much like contemplation. As he puts it:

> There are two features of play which make it appropriate to compare the contemplation of wisdom to playing. First, we enjoy playing, and there is the greatest enjoyment of all to be had in the contemplation of wisdom. As Wisdom says in Ecclesiasticus (24:27, NAB) 'My spirit is sweeter than honey.'
>
> Secondly, playing has no purpose beyond itself; what we do in play is done for its own sake. And the same applies to the pleasure of wisdom. If we are enjoying thinking about the things we long for or the things we are proposing to do, this kind of enjoyment looks beyond itself to something else which we are eager to attain, and if we fail to attain it or if there is a delay in attaining it, our pleasure is mingled with a proportionate distress. As it says in Proverbs (14:13, NAB), 'Laughter will be mixed with grief.' But the contemplation of wisdom contains within itself the cause of its own enjoyment, and so it is not exposed to the kind of anxiety that goes with waiting for something which we lack. This is why it says in Wisdom (8:16, NAB), 'Her company is without bitterness' (the company of wisdom, that is) 'and there is no boredom in living with her.' It is for this reason that divine Wisdom compares her enjoyment to playing in Proverbs 8:30, 'I enjoyed myself every single day, playing before him.' (Tugwell [ed. & trans.], 1988: 527–528).

Thomas also describes the dynamics of contemplation itself in terms of play and as analogous to the flow experience. He comments on the text from

Ecclesiasticus which reads, "Run ahead into your house and gather yourself there and play there and pursue your thoughts" (32:15–16, NAB). During contemplation, he writes, "it is . . . necessary that we ourselves should be fully present there, concentrating in such a way that our aim is not diverted to other matters" (Tugwell [ed. & trans.], 1988: 527).

> Accordingly the text goes on, 'And gather yourself there,' that is, draw together your whole intention. And when our interior house is entirely emptied like this and we are fully present there in our intention, the text tells us what we should do: 'And play there.' (Tugwell [ed. & trans.], 1988, 527).

The close relationship between play and contemplation suggests that the person who is learning how to play may also, at the same time, be learning something about the dynamics of the contemplative life. In this sense, one's participation in games and sports can have a much more profound and lasting influence on one's life than any amount of money or fame could ever have.

Csikszentmihalyi has pointed out that a person is more easily able to enter into activities he enjoys for their own sake when he has a sense that he is of value, that he is loved and accepted. And this is why growing up in a loving and supportive environment is so important. Belaief writes about the importance of having a sense of "ontological security," which enables a person to play in freedom.

The importance of knowing that one is loved and this leading to fullness of life is also a central theme in Christian spirituality. For the apostle Paul, love was far more important than anything else in the Christian life. And according to the author of the 1st letter of John, "God is love" (1 John 4:16, NAB). Jesus tells his followers, "As the Father loves me, so I also love you. Remain in my love" (John 15:9, NAB), and he exhorts them to love one another. He tells them these things, he says, "so that my joy might be in you, and your joy might be complete" (John 15:11, NAB). Some contemporary theologians point out that a person who has experienced God's love and remains in this love has a sense of "ontological security" and hence is able to play. As the Jesuit Hugo Rahner puts it: "The person who has faith and truly loves God is also the one who can truly play, for only he who is secure in God can be truly light of heart" (1967: 57–58).[5]

The experience that athletes sometimes have of belonging to something larger than themselves—as can happen when playing on a team—also resonates with the emphasis on community in Christian spirituality. This emphasis has its roots in the Hebrew experience of being called as a *people*, and is given repeated expression in Paul's writings with images such as the body of Christ, used to describe the church. For Paul, each member of the body of Christ is accountable to the other. "If one parts suffers, all the parts suffer with it," he writes. "If one part is honored, all share its joy"

(1 Cor. 12:26, NAB). Jesus gathers disciples around himself and a community is formed in the Spirit in the wake of his resurrection, which is to be characterized by love and service. His disciples would be judged by the way they treat, not just one another, but those without food or clothing, the sick and imprisoned, and by how warmly they welcome the stranger (Matt 25:31–46, NAB). This emphasis on community and outreach to the poor and the afflicted has always been present in the monastic traditions associated with St. Benedict and in other religious communities, and in institutions such as hospitals run by the churches. But it is present as well (in varying degrees) in the day-to-day life of any diocesan parish or school in our time.

## FLOW, SPORT AND THE REST OF THE SPIRITUAL LIFE

Csikszentmihalyi recognizes that sometimes athletes who experience flow while they are playing their sport live lives of dissolution or meaninglessness when not engaged in their sport. The same is true of artists and others. For this reason, he was interested in mining the resources of the flow experience for insights about how all of the aspects of a person's life could be made more meaningful. In this next section, I will be making some connections between the dynamics of the flow experience and the dynamics of the Christian life in a general sense, drawing on the insights of Ignatius of Loyola.

Some of the major themes in Ignatius' spirituality are analogous to themes expressed in the literature on the flow experience. It is an understatement to say that Ignatius was very single-minded. After his leg was shattered by a cannonball at Pamplona and he had his transformative experience while convalescing, he lived the rest of his life with the intention of having everything he did devoted purely to the service, honor and praise of God. "The eye of our intention," he wrote, "ought to be single" (Ganss, 1991: 161). One of his most important contributions to spirituality is his *Spiritual Exercises* and the guidelines for discernment which accompany them, which provide a way for people to come to an understanding of how to live their lives and make choices in a way that "descend(s) from above, from the love of God" (Ganss, 1991: 164) and hence give greater glory to God.

The purpose of the Spiritual Exercises is to help a person experience greater interior freedom, so that they can make choices that are a generous response to the love of God. And so, the retreat provides many opportunities for the person to consider where they might have "inordinate attachments." We have already seen how attachments to money, fame or what others think of us can interfere with our ability to play games well. Attachments can also be disruptive in our life in general. It might be that a person feels he needs all of the material possessions he has right now or has envisioned owning in the future and this keeps him from moving in a particular direction. Or he might be so attached to other people having a good opinion of him that this keeps him from taking seriously his desire to work among the poorest of the poor in India, or to start up a computer company (because of fear of failure, for example). The common feature of our attachments is that they keep us from being free enough to follow the inspiration and leading of the Spirit of the risen Christ which leads to life for ourselves and others.

For Ignatius, we grow in the Christian life by paying attention to, and learning from, all aspects of our lived experience. He felt that it was particularly important, however, to pay attention to one sort of affective experience that he called *spiritual consolation*. By spiritual consolation he means the same thing that the term 'consolation' ordinarily means, that is, affective experiences such as sweetness, gladness, peacefulness. What makes consolation spiritual is that these experiences have a noticeable affect on a person's (or a community's) relationship to God. Spiritual consolation is associated with, for example, an increase of faith, hope and love and brings "tranquility and peace" in the "Creator and Lord" (Ganss, 1991: 202).

Because grace perfects nature, it is not surprising that the experience of consolation is analogous to the flow experience in many ways. For Ignatius, consolation is associated with "genuine happiness and spiritual joy" (Ganss, 1991: 205), for example. Consolation is also associated with effortlessness; the experience is gentle and easy, like water falling into a sponge or like coming into one's own house through an open door. It feels like obstacles are being removed so the person can move forward in doing good. But this effortlessness usually comes after much disciplined attention and practice. Finally, consolation is related to the growth and development of the person, helping one move from good to better in the Christian life (Ganss , 1991: 201–207). [6] For Ignatius, one's major decisions should be made related to and building on experiences of consolation. [7]

On the other hand, the person who was trying to go from good to better would also experience something Ignatius called *spiritual desolation*, which he characterized as the contrary of consolation. The experience is noisy and disturbing, like water falling on a rock; one is agitated and disturbed, bitter and discouraged; it is difficult to be energized about going forward; and one feels separated from God (Ganss [ed]., 1991:202). Ignatius expects that every Christian would experience *both* consolation and desolation. And he gives advice about how to deal with desolation, which includes: be patient and remember that consolation will return; be faithful to one's prayer, perhaps practice some penance and make a closer examination of oneself and one's life of faith; remind oneself that one can do much with the grace and strength God provides at all times (Ganss, 1991: 202–205).

The important point with respect to our discussion is that Ignatius counsels that a person should never change a decision which she made during consolation *while* she is in desolation. Consolation and desolation are affective experiences, but they are also typically associated with different kinds of thought processes. When in desolation, it is very easy to begin to doubt one's own giftedness, capacity for ministry, to want to withdraw from the challenges of life, and so on. According to Ignatius, thoughts such as these, which are so common during experiences of desolation, are not to be trusted because they are not coming from "the good spirit" (Ganss, 1991: 202).

Of course, the experiences associated with consolation as they are described by Ignatius have a broader reach than the flow experiences as they have been described up until now in the research. The genuine happiness and spiritual joy associated with consolation can be experienced in the forgiveness of sins, for example. The peace associated with consolation can be experienced in the midst of sorrow or suffering because of an awareness of union with Christ. But this fact does not make the experiences of flow we have while at play and in other activities unimportant for the spiritual life. Such experiences are enjoyable and rewarding in themselves and are also "signals of transcendence." They point out to us what we are made for and help us to understand how, as Thomas said, "grace perfects nature" (Aquinas [trans. 1947]: 308).[8]

## NOTES

1. I recognize that the idea of doing something for its own sake can make some theologians nervous, on the grounds that all of our activities need to be directed to God as our ultimate end. For Csikszentmihalyi, however, doing something for its own sake means primarily that one is not engaged in the activity for extrinsic rewards, such as money or status, etc. And in this sense, his views are consistent with some of the core emphases in Christian spirituality. What Csikszentmihalyi's research does is help us to understand the dynamics that lead to life to the full when people are not "ensnared" by money and status. That is, it unpacks for us the positive side of the picture. An understanding of such dynamics is important for a tradition whose founder is quoted as saying, "I came so that they might have life and have it more abundantly" (John 10:10 NAB).
2. Flow experiences can become problematic when they are a part of the reason that a person does not pay attention to other areas of his life to which he should be paying attention. Such a case can be seen in the experience of former star NFL wide receiver Lance Rentzel, who exposed himself to young girls on two different occasions in 1966 and 1970, which led to his career unraveling. In his autobiography *When All the Laughter Died in Sorrow* (1972), Rentzel wrote about the way his experiences playing football had shaped him as a young person and how these experiences were related to the development of his problems off the field: "One trouble was that I had become an expert at repressing any emotions that threatened me. I could hide things about myself that I didn't want to see and thus could avoid untoward feelings. This is a good quality to have on the football field. It has enabled me to concentrate completely on catching the ball, repressing the fear of getting hit or dropping it. Under normal conditions this overdeveloped ability to repress allowed me to go through a full game without emotional interference or distraction. Well, that was fine when I was playing football, but it's no

way to spend your whole life. Football was—and is—very important to me; but life isn't football, and football is only one part of the life of even the most devoted player" (Rentzel, 1972: 240).

3. Tennis legend Billie Jean King reminds us of the importance of attending to these kinds of experiences: "When it happens I want to stop the match and grab the microphone and shout '*That's* what it's all about.' Because it is. It's not the big prize I'm going to win at the end of the match, or anything else. It's just having done something that's totally pure and having experienced the perfect emotion, and I'm always sad that I can't communicate that feeling right at the moment it's happening. I can only hope people realize what's going on" (Murphy & White, 1995, *In the Zone*, 126).
4. This quotation is taken from Fleming's contemporary reading of the literal text of Ignatius' *Exercises*.
5. I have amended the English translation of this text to make the language more inclusive with respect to gender.
6. Ignatius has in mind persons who are "purging away their sins" and progressing from "good to better" in the service of God when he writes about the experience of spiritual consolation. For him, persons who are not interested in the things of God and are living a fundamentally self-centered life, "going from one mortal sin to another" (Ganss, 1991: 201), would experience God's Spirit in a different way than is described in this section. So too would people who are "going from good to better" in general but who have an area of their life where they are actually regressing. In the case of the first kind of person and with respect to the area of regression in the second, the Spirit of God would use the person's own reflection on moral problems to sting his conscience with remorse in the hope of getting him to change the fundamental direction of his life.
7. Ignatius describes spiritual consolation as an experience where the "soul is aflame with the love of its Creator and Lord. As a result it can love no created thing on the face of the earth in itself but only in the Creator of them all" (Ganss, 1991: 202). The point about loving no created thing in itself might seem at odds with the notion of an autotelic experience, where a person participates in the activity for its own sake. As was mentioned earlier (see footnote #1), for Csikszentmihalyi doing something for its own sake means primarily that the person is not engaged in the activity for extrinsic rewards, such as money and fame. In his first article (Csikszentmihalyi, 1975a: 44) and book (Csikszentmihalyi, 1975b: 37) he pointed out that the phenomenology of the flow experience is analogous to the phenomenology of meditation and religious experiences.
8. Ignatius would write later in his rules that consolation itself needs to be discerned. The angel of darkness, he wrote, can take on the "appearance of an angel of light" (Ganss, 1991: 206). And so, good people can get off track, typically by consolation associated with pious or holy thoughts. The way one knows whether one is being deceived or not is by paying attention to the "beginning, middle and end" of any train of thoughts. If these are all good and wholly good, then one can be confident that the thought originated with the good spirit. On the other hand, if the train of thoughts ends up leading to something bad, distracting or less good than what the person had originally proposed to do, or to disquiet, lack of peace, turmoil, etc., this is an indication that, in Ignatius' terms, the "evil spirit" is at work. While such experiences may be difficult to go through, one can learn from them and guard oneself in the future against such "characteristic snares" (Ganss, 1991: 206).

## BIBLIOGRAPHY

Aquinas, T. (1947) *Summa Theologica,* 3 vols., trans. by Fathers of the English Dominican Province, New York: Benziger Bros.

Aquinas, T. (1975) *Summa Contra Gentiles,* 4 vols., trans. Anton Pegis, Notre Dame: University of Notre Dame Press.

Aquinas, T. (1984) *Questions on the Soul,* trans. James H. Robb, Milwaukee: Marquette University Press.

Bailey, S. (1995) Permission to Play: Education for Recreation and Distinction at Winchester College, 1382–1680, *The International Journal of the History of Sport,* 12(1): 1–17.

Belaief, L. (1974–1977) Meanings of the Body, *The Journal of the Philosophy of Sport,* IV: 50–67, R.G. Osterhoudt (Ed.), published under the auspices of Philosophic Society for the Study of Sport.

Bushnell, H. (2000) *Christian Nurture,* New York: Wipf and Stock Publishers.

Callois, R. (2001) *Man, Play and Games,* Chicago: University of Illinois Press.

Caraman, P. (1990) *Ignatius of Loyola,* London: Collins.

Cox, H. (1969) *The Feast of Fools: A Theological Essay on Festivity and Fantasy.* Cambridge, MA: Harvard University Press.

Csikszentmihalyi, M. (1975a) Play and Intrinsic Rewards, *The Journal of Humanistic Psychology,* 15(3).

Csikszentmihalyi, M. (1975b) *Beyond Boredom and Anxiety: The Experience of Play in Work and Games,* San Francisco: Jossey-Bass.

Csikszentmihalyi, M. (1990) *FLOW: The Psychology of Optimal Experience,* New York: Harper & Row.

Csikszentmihalyi, M. (1993) *The Evolving Self,* New York: HarperCollins.

Csikszentmihalyi, M., and Csikszentmihalyi, I. (Eds.) (1988) *Optimal Experience: Psychological Studies of Flow in Consciousness,* Cambridge: Cambridge University Press.

Cusa, N. (1986) *The Game of Spheres,* New York: Abaris Books.

Daniels, B. (1995) *The Puritans at Play: Leisure and Recreation in Colonial New England,* New York: St. Martin's Press.

Fleming, D. (1996) *Draw Me into Your Friendship, the Spiritual Exercises: A Literal Translation and Contemporary Reading,* St. Louis, MO: Institute of Jesuit Sources.

Frank, R.W. (1935) "Protestantism and Play," in *Social Progress,* 26.

Ganss, G. (Ed.) (1991) *Ignatius of Loyola: The Spiritual Exercises and Selected Works,* New York: Paulist Press.

Garrison, R. (1993) Paul's Use of the Athlete Metaphor, *Studies in Religion,* 22(2): 209–217.

Gladden, W. (1866) Amusements: Their Uses and Abuses, North Adams, MA, USA: James T. Robinson & Co., Printers.

Guardini, R. (1997) *The Spirit of the Liturgy,* New York: The Crossroad Publishing Co.

Hearn, F. (1976–1977) Toward a Critical Theory of Play, *Telos,* 30.

Hogan, W. (1967) Sin and Sports, in R. Slovenko and J.A. Knight (Eds.), *Motivations in Play, Games and Sports,* Springfield, IL: Thomas.

Huizinga, J. (1968) *Homo Ludens: A Study of the Play Element in Culture,* Boston: Beacon Press.

Hyland, D. (1977) "And That Is the Best Part of Us": Human Being and Play, *Journal of the Philosophy of Sport,* 4: 36–49.

Hutton, R. (1994) *The Rise and Fall of Merry England: The Ritual Year 1400–1700,* Oxford: Oxford University Press.

Hutton, R. (1997) *The Stations of the Sun: A History of the Ritual Year in Britain*, Oxford: Oxford University Press.

Jackson, P., and Delehanty, H. (1995) *Sacred Hoops: Spiritual Lessons of a Hardwood Warrior,* New York: Hyperion.

Jackson, S., and Csikszentmihalyi, M. (1999) *Flow in Sports: The Keys to Optimal Experiences and Performance,* Champaign, IL: Human Kinetics.

John Paul II, Pope. (2000, October 29) Jubilee of Sports People, homily in Rome's Olympic Stadium, Rome: The Holy See. Available from http://www.vatican.va/holy_father/john_paul_ii/homilies/documents/hf_jp-ii_hom_200010'

John Paul II, Pope. (2000, October 28) During the Time of the Jubilee: The Face and Soul of Sport, homily in Rome: The Holy See. Available from http://www.vatican.va/holy_father/john_paul_ii/speeches/documents/hf_jp-ii_spe_2000102

John Paul II, Pope. (1984, December 10) Sports Offers Opportunity for Spiritual Elevation, *L'Osservatore Romano.*

John Paul II, Pope. (1984, April 24) International Jubilee of Sport: Homily at Olympic Stadium, *L'Osservatore Romano.*

John Paul II, Pope. (1984, April 4) The Most Authentic Dimension of Sport, *L'Osservatore Romano.*

John Paul II, Pope. (1982, October 4) Holy Father's Address to International Olympic Committee Meeting in Rome," *L'Osservatore Romano.*

John Paul II, Pope. (1980, November 3) To Participants in the Twelfth Youth Games, *L'Osservatore Romano.*

John Paul II, Pope. (1980, July 14) Human and Sporting Qualities Make Men Brothers, *L'Osservatore Romano.*

John Paul II, Pope. (1979 September 17) Sport, a School of Human Virtue," *L'Osservatore Romano.*

John Paul II, Pope. (1979, June 18) The Discipline of Sports for Complete Human Formation, *L'Osservatore Romano.*

John Paul II, Pope. (1979, May 28) Pope to Milan Football Team, *L'Osservatore Romano.*

Kallendorf, C. (Ed.) (2002) *Humanist Educational Treatises*, The I Tatti Renaissance Library, Cambridge, MA: Harvard University Press.

Kelly, S.J., P. (1992) Sport in Human Development, *Human Development*, 13(3).

Lee, R. (1964) *Religion and Leisure in America: A Study in Four Dimensions,* New York: Abingdon Press.

Lonsdale, D. (2003) *Eyes to See, Ears to Hear: An Introduction to Ignatian Spirituality,* Maryknoll, NY: Orbis Books.

McLean, Teresa. (1983) *The English at Play in the Middle Ages,* Slough, UK: The Hollen St. Press.

Meier, K. (1995) Embodiment, Sport and Meaning, *Philosophic Inquiry in Sport* (2nd ed.), Champaign, IL: Human Kinetics.

Meier, K. (1995) An Affair of Flutes: An Appreciation of Play, *Philosophic Inquiry in Sport* (2nd ed.), Champaign, IL: Human Kinetics.

Mehl, J. (1990) *Les Jeux au rouyame de France du XIIIe au debut du XVIe siècle,* Paris: Librarie Artheme Fayard.

Merdrignac, B. (2002) *Le sport au Moyen Age*, Rennes, France: Presses Universitaires de Rennes.

Miller, D.L. (1971) Theology and Play Studies: An Overview, *Journal of the American Academy of Religion*, 39: 349–354.

Miller, D.L. (1970) *Gods and Games: Toward a Theology of Play*, Cleveland, OH: The World Publishing Company.

Modras, R. (2004) *Ignatian Humanism: A Dynamic Spirituality for the 21st Century*, Chicago: Loyola Press.

Moltmann, J. (1972) *Theology of Play*, New York: Harper & Row.
Murphy, M., and White, R. (1995) *In the Zone: Transcendent Experience in Sports*, New York: Penguin Books.
Neale, R. (1969) *In Praise of Play: Toward a Psychology of Religion*, New York: Harper & Row.
Orme, N. (2001) *Medieval Children*, New Haven, CT: Yale University Press.
Pfitzner, V. (1967) *Paul and the Agon Motif*, Leiden: E.J. Brill.
Pieper, J. (1965) *In Tune with the World: A Theory of Festivity*, trans. R. Winston and C. Winston, New York: Harcourt, Brace and World.
Pieper, J. (1963) *Leisure: The Basis of Culture*, New York: Random House.
Plato. (1970) *The Laws*, New York: Penguin.
Rahner, H. (1967) *Man at Play*, New York: Herder and Herder.
Reeves, C. (1998) *Pleasures and Pastimes in Medieval England*. Oxford: Oxford University Press.
Rentzel, L. (1972) *When All the Laughter Turned to Sorrow*, New York: Saturday Review Press.
Roochnik, D.L. (1975) Play and Sport, *Journal of the Philosophy of Sport*, 2: 36–44.
Ruhl, J.K. (1984) Religion and Amusements in Sixteenth- and Seventeenth-Century England: "Time Might Be Better Bestowed, and besides Wee See Sin Acted," *British Journal of Sports History*, 1(2): 125–165.
Sawyer, F. (1847) *A Plea for Amusements*, New York: D. Appleton and Company.
Schall, J.V. (2001) *On the Unseriousness of Human Affairs: Teaching, Writing, Playing, Believing, Lecturing, Philosophizing, Singing, Dancing*, Wilmington, DE: ISI Books.
Schall, J.V. (1976) *Far Too Easily Pleased: A Theology of Play, Contemplation, and Festivity*, Beverly Hills, CA: Benziger.
Struna, N. (1977) Puritans and Sports: The Irretrievable Tide of Change, *Journal of Sport History* 4 (Spring): 1–21.
Strutt, J. (1876) *The Sports and Pastimes of the People of England*, London: Chatto and Windus.
Toner, J. (1981) *A Commentary on St Ignatius' Rules for the Discernment of Spirits*, St. Louis: Institute of Jesuit Sources.
Toner, J. (1991) *Discerning God's Will: Ignatius of Loyola's Teaching on Christian Decision Making*, St. Louis, Institute of Jesuit Sources.
Toner, J. (1995a) *Spirit of Light or Darkness? A Casebook for Studying Discernment of Spirits*, St. Louis: Institute of Jesuit Sources.
Toner, J. (1995b) *What Is Your Will, O God? A Casebook for Studying Discernment of God's Will*, St. Louis: Institute of Jesuit Sources.
Tugwell, S. (Ed.) (1988) *Albert and Thomas: Selected Writings*, New York: Paulist Press.
Turner, V. (1982) *From Ritual to Theater: The Human Seriousness of Play*, New York: Performing Arts Journal Publications.
Turner, V. (1987) *Anthropology of Performance*, New York: PAJ Publications.
Verdon, J . (1996) *Le Plaisir au Moyen Age*, Paris: Perrin.
Verdon, J. (2001) *Rire au Moyen Age*, Paris: Perrin.
Verdon, J. (2003/1980) *Les Loisirs au Moyen Age*, Paris: St2/Tallandier.
Winnicott, D.W. (1971) *Playing and Reality*, New York: Routledge.

# Part III

# Transcendence in Movement, Play and Sport

# Part III Introduction

*Jim Parry*

## INTRODUCTION

One of the concepts central to an understanding of spirituality is 'transcendence,' which carries at least two meanings: firstly, going beyond certain limits, surpassing or exceeding; and secondly, superior or supreme. Both meanings are clearly apparent in talk of God. The transcendent deity is seen both as a being who goes beyond our world, nature, the universe, time, and so on; and as one who is seen as omnipotent—as superior to us mortals, as supreme.

But there are many other contexts involving our spiritual life that employ the term, too. Empathy requires the transcendence of the self (Robinson, p. 46); community and solidarity require the transcendence of blood ties; seeing oneself as a citizen of the world requires the transcendence of race and nation; a commitment to the global environment (or simply an awareness of the natural environment) takes us beyond the here and now (Robinson, p. 27). And a search for meaning in life may transcend all of the preceding.

Simon Robinson (2007 pp. 56–57) provides further explication:

- Transcendence involves a 'going-beyond' or a 'reaching-out,' but this doesn't mean a separation, or an escape—but rather an engagement, or an articulation.
- Transcendence is of the limitations of the self and of the present—it opens possibilities for change and development.
- Transcendence is potentially transformative, in the finding of new meaning, purpose, practice and partnership.

In this part, four chapters explore notions of transcendence in movement, play and sporting activities. In Chapter 8, Scott Kretchmar examines the spiritual potential of games. He begins by noting that Western thinking is replete with dichotomies and any number of other neat and tidy (if overly simplistic) ways of understanding our world, and that religion is not exempt from this tendency. One of its favorite dualisms—the sacred versus the secular—can certainly enlighten us, but Kretchmar suggests that it also has potential for mischief, since such dichotomies have provided a skewed vision of games and play.

Kretchmar argues that the full value of these activities cannot be appreciated by forcing them toward either the sacred or the secular—that games and play are spiritually ambiguous. This is partly because the genealogies of both are intertwined. Games emerged in our history from work and rest, increasing intelligence and efficiency, boredom and malaise, chance or good fortune, logic . . . and play.

To put this in religious terms, they can both be part and parcel of "Kingdom living" here and now, albeit unevenly. Games and play can be understood as "gifts of God," and can help us to appreciate the fact that the Kingdom is truly at hand.

The argument for play and games as spiritually ambiguous entities takes us to an analysis of the relationship between the two, and also to the potentially surprising conclusion that play has been typically overrated in theological treatments, while games have too often been unjustifiably ignored. Games, it turns out, may be one of the greatest gifts of God.

Susan Saint Sing's Chapter 9 is a journey through time and across many disciplines examining what the great minds have expressed in regards to energy, God and play. The chapter is set up as a series of questions based on key, pivotal phrases such as Carl Jung's insight and description of a collective unconscious. According to Jung, archetypes create myths, religions and philosophical ideas that influence and set their stamp on whole nations and epochs, including ideas of play and sport.

This chapter examines a broad range of writers, physicists, theologians, philosophers, artists, all speaking in similar, collective terms about play—considered under the headings of: God playing with his creation, forming things to play, describing this energy as dancing, and God playing with us. Through many such examples, this energy we have to play is seen to be connected to the spiritual, to the nature of God.

According to Susan Saint Sing, sport philosophers can make a spiritual contribution to their field today by tapping into the collective unconscious of scholars, poets, physicists, mathematicians, sport philosophers, writers, athletes, Olympians, theologians, scripture, popes and sculptors—through a vast collection of descriptions or symbols which reveal that play echoes to us, resonates within us from the origins of the universe. This 'energy continuum' helps modern sport philosophers to understand where we have been, where we are, and where we are going, in that the impetus to play is intended to help us transcend our base nature and advance humankind as part of the energy of the expanding universe.

In Chapter 10, Irena Martínková and Jim Parry begin by introducing some of the main ideas of Zen Buddhist thinking in relation to movement, such as non-dual experiencing, the illusion of the ego and its dissolution, emptiness, aimlessness and fearlessness. They go on to describe what meditation in Zen means and, since this does not only have to be practiced while sitting motionlessly in *zazen* or slowly walking in *kinhin*, they also discuss it in relation to the everyday life of the practitioner. Then, they introduce the movement forms of Zen, that is, the martial paths, with their relation to their Zen features explained, especially the important concept of 'no-mind' (*mushin*).

We are now in a position to see what Zen has to offer to enrich sport experience, and this is possible because sports work on the same experiential base as Zen. Practicing sports in the Zen spirit can suggest a change in the present predominant orientation on results and performance, and the general instrumentalization of sports practice. Instead, we direct our attention to a full experiencing of the activity, which facilitates a joyfulness, a fluency, an effortlessness and incidentally also an efficient and improved performance.

In Chapter 11, Ivo Jirásek examines the idea of the pilgrimage as a mode of travel, from the perspective of kinanthropology, which may be defined as the discipline that applies philosophical analysis and methodology to the understanding of human movement activities. He seeks to show that pilgrimage is not only a topic in the study of religion or history, and even that religious passion is not necessary for such a journey.

Whereas there are many words on a continuum from tourism to pilgrimage for such movement activities as hiking, wandering, walking, journeying and so on, Jirásek wants to examine them from the perspective of the sacred and the profane. Whilst some of these activities are closer to the profane (with the cognitive or enjoyable and pleasant aspects of traveling dominating), others seem more closely related to the sacred (in which case, spiritual interests are more important for the itinerant). However, of course, some aspects are common to all of these activities: bodily endeavor and effort, meeting a challenge in foreign or unusual places, and the challenge and adventure that come with difficulty.

After considering Cohen's five 'modes' of tourism (recreational, diversionary, experiential, experimental and existential), Jirásek proposes five 'experiential modes' (the aim, the 'attuning,' the mode of experience, the approach to a question, and the focus of attention), arguing that it is the 'mode of experiencing,' rather than the motive for travel, or the nature of the place visited, that marks out a trip as one with spiritual import. He sees an opportunity for teachers in sport, leisure or tourism studies to emphasize the possibility of deeper levels of traveling, rather than just taking pictures or shopping for souvenirs. For example, simply walking with a sensitivity to nature is just the kind of activity through which we might explore physical and movement spirituality. Jirásek advocates being a "*pilgrim with a light heart*," with the primary aim not only of visiting and seeing places, but of finding inspiration, feeling and deep experiencing.

## BIBLIOGRAPHY

Robinson, S. (2007) The Spiritual Journey, in J. Parry; S. Robinson; N. J. Watson; and M. Nesti (2007) *Sport and Spirituality: An Introduction*, London, UK: Routledge: 38–58.

# 8 Why Dichotomies Make It Difficult to See Games as Gifts of God

*Scott Kretchmar*

## INTRODUCTION

Those who were raised in the Judeo-Christian tradition[1] believe that God will provide . . . if not now, then later; if not exactly in the ways we expect, then in accord with God's own purposes. But in whatever manner this drama of human need and divine Providence works out, believers still face the future with a "blessed assurance." They encounter the uncertainties of life with a faith-based confidence that springs from the twin promises that God's grace is sufficient (2 Cor. 12:9) and that nothing can separate them from the love of God (Rom. 8:35).

All this is good and reassuring. But figuring out what counts as an authentic gift of God and what does not has never come easy. Believers look for answers in holy scripture. They pray for clarity. They try to fortify faith-based conclusions with reason. Still they often end up shaking their heads and are forced to conclude that God works in "mysterious ways." To complicate matters further, the faithful discover that the forces of evil have a similar *modus operandi*. For these reasons it is difficult to tell a gift of God from things that come from other potential donors.

I plan to wade into these murky waters by arguing that divine provisions are more expansive than we often think. This broader understanding of the "gifts of God," however, is a complicated one. It is complicated by the fact that many such provisions, as I will be describing them, are ambiguous.

God's gifts paradoxically are needed and not needed, assets and liabilities, welcome and unwelcome, blessed and dangerous . . . at the same time! Admittedly, this sounds more than slightly illogical, but I hope to make some sense of it in the pages that follow. The primary impediment to this messy understanding of God's provision can be found in our tendency to divide the world up into neat compartments. So, it is with the simple categories provided by dichotomies and dualisms that we must begin our journey.

## THE TENDENCY TO SEE THE WORLD IN PAIRS

We face choices when trying to characterize the world in which we live. A favorite option has been to divide things neatly into twos, often as polar opposites or mutually exclusive alternatives. My own mother was no exception to the rule. When I was a child, one of her favorite moral injunctions went something like this. "Good people don't do that sort of thing." So, I learned early on that people came in two basic varieties . . . good and bad, and that (at least on occasion) I was in danger of falling into the latter category.

This particular bifurcation that focused on good and bad people, however, had company. Over the years, I was also introduced to right and wrong, part and whole, rural-urban, severe-mild, strong-weak, stimulus-response, reward-punishment, laugh-cry, found-lost, explicit-implicit, irrational-rational, and so on. My own experience, I learned, was not unusual.

Kelso and Engstrom (2006), for example, give evidence for what they see as a more or less universal human tendency to divide reality into opposable pairs. They provide over 2,300 examples of dichotomies that are common in human thought and can be found in lexicons around the globe. Most all of us, it would seem, have chosen to characterize the world in terms of dichotomies.

Why such a proclivity for divisions and dualisms, it could be asked? The most direct answer is this: it is simply the way things are. Just like male and female, north and south, straight and crooked, things tend to come in pairs. On this line of thought, our mental tendencies to divide reality into opposites and our corresponding verbal conventions merely reflect reality. "We call 'em as we see 'em," sport referees like to say, unaware of the profound metaphysical and epistemological implications of their words. And we apparently "see 'em," at least in most cases, as either-or, white or black, true or false—that is, as dichotomous.

To be sure, there is an element of truth to such claims. Some reality does come in twos. Or to say the same thing more pragmatically, dividing the world dichotomously can be useful. This is surely the case when teaching youngsters which snakes are dangerous and which are not, or which mushrooms can be eaten and which are poisonous. And, as my mother knew, dichotomies are useful in teaching unambiguous lessons about ethical behavior and good people. Shades of gray, when it comes to such things as snakes, mushrooms, and ethics, may do more harm than good . . . at least for youngsters who need to be kept out of harm's way and have to learn right from wrong.

Dichotomies, however, have their limitations. One of them can be found on the flip side of the metaphysical coin previously mentioned. While some things come in pairs, many do not. And even though certain parts of reality *can* be described dualistically, it may be harmful or misleading to actually *do so* on a regular basis. The common dichotomy of play and work can serve as a case in point. These aspects of life might be more helpfully discussed as a complementary pair (play~work) that exhibit greater and lesser degrees of intrinsic satisfaction. Work, it could be argued, tends to have lesser amounts of *intrinsica* while play has more. But that does not exclude the intrinsic from work or the extrinsic from play. Any given experience at work or at play may, therefore, be ambiguous, with a kind of residual tension existing between the two poles. In short, a simple dichotomous understanding of work and play might be replaced by an infinite number of possible mixtures of worklike and playlike experiences. Later we will see how games have roots in both work and play.

Such worries about the utility of dichotomous characterizations are not new. A number of writers have raised questions about the unwarranted simplicity (and potential simplemindedness) that goes with dualistic portrayals of reality. Pragmatists like Dewey (1922/1988) and James (in McDermott, 1967/1977) were notoriously suspicious of dualisms. Analysts of Eastern approaches to life like Suzuki (1949/1961) and Herrigel (1953/1964) felt that abstract bifurcations did relatively little work and often stood in the way of enlightenment. Modern philosophers and social scientists, including Gould (2003), McGinn (1999), Kelso and Engstrom (2006), and Prokhovnik (1999/2002) and even C.P. Snow (1959/1986) of "Two Cultures" fame who called "2" a "very dangerous number" (p. 9) have weighed in against dichotomies. Some physicists have joined literary and philosophical types by suggesting that the ultimate stuff of the universe is neither a particle nor wave but somehow ambiguously both . . . at the same time!

In light of all this, it would appear that dichotomies, as ways of understanding reality, are coming under attack all the way "up" to the most profound cognitive or spiritual reality that can be intuited, believed, or experienced and all the way "down" to the smallest physical thing—so tiny that it cannot even be seen or measured. Even so, in most any conversation, treatise, debate, dialogue, work of fiction or nonfiction or injunction from one's own mother, dichotomies are likely to play a prominent role . . . whether helpfully, not so helpfully, or somewhere in between. Even when they deserve to be retired or killed and buried, dualisms die hard.

## DICHOTOMIES AND DUALISMS IN RELIGION

This dualistic durability is seen in religion and spirituality just as it is in the rest of life. Dualisms continue to attract, and it is simply difficult to get our intellectual arms around opposites as compatible. Descartes's mind and body serve as a case in point. As this French philosopher knew, is difficult to grasp the notion that ideas are tethered to the meat in our heads. After all, meat and ideas are so different . . . so radically different as to defy reconciliation (McGinn, 1999; Midgley, 1994). Yet, we well understand that our ideas do not come from nowhere. Modern neuroscience has demonstrated that brain states and experiences are connected. Neither one takes place without the other. But still, electrical charges and ideas are so different as to be incommensurable.

On the spiritual side of our lives, some reconciliations are just as challenging. It is difficult to reconcile Augustine's city of man with his city of God. One is the locus of sin and approbation, the other of holiness and salvation. It is hard to live in both places at once. A person has to make a choice, and this choice cannot be "both at the same time."

The Bible too can be read in a way that reinforces the apparently exclusionary options available to the person of faith. "No servant can serve two masters. For either he will hate the one and love the other, or he will be devoted to the one and despise the other. You cannot serve God and mammon" (Luke 16:13). Recommendations for behavior are clear and equally extreme. The faithful person will have to "sell all that [he or she has] and follow me" (Luke 18:22). The rich young ruler might have preferred a third option, but none was given.

The notion of spiritual conversion is also laden with dichotomous thinking. When asked if one has been born again, it is not normally acceptable to say, "sort of," or "about two-thirds." Either one is born again . . . or not. Salvation seems to be just as difficult to reconcile with ambiguous descriptions. After all, can a person be partly saved? Or saved in degrees? When Judgment Day comes, it would seem that the verdict will be of the "all or nothing" variety. Either we get in or we don't. How could a believer, after all, be "in" and "not in" *at the same time*?

It is interesting, however, that the Christian religion rests squarely on the compatibility of one of the most striking incompatibilities of all time. The historical Christ figure was said to be both God and man . . . at the same time, not one after the other, not as a composite of two separate parts. In other words, the standard dichotomies of divine or human, sacred or profane, omnipotent or weak, omniscient or fallible, bulletproof or vulnerable do not work very well when describing Christ. If there were ever a messy, illogical, difficult-to-figure-out individual, this God~man would have to be among the leading contenders for the honor. This oil~water person of Jesus even provoked Tertullian (circa 200/1956) to comment, "Credible est, quia ineptum est." (It is credible because it is ridiculous.)

If orthodox Christianity was among the leaders in embracing certain absurdities, Zen Buddhism has not been far behind. It too is grounded in the elimination of handy dualisms—the distinctions, for example, between wanting and having, striving and being, winning and losing, even self and other. Enlightenment for the Buddhist involves an experiential overcoming of these "obvious distinctions." This is why Herrigel (1953/1964) reported obscurely in *Zen and the Art of Archery* that, after a considerable amount of spiritual progress had been made, the arrow began to shoot itself. Somehow, this German-philosopher-turned-Buddhist-monk was both the shooter and target . . . at the same time. For Herrigel, the dichotomy between self and world had been overcome, if only incompletely and temporarily, and only after years of meditative practice. Once again, dualisms die hard . . . both conceptually and practically.

Yet in Chinese philosophy, Zen Buddhism, and other eastern holistic traditions, a tension exists between yin and yang. In Christianity, a similar tension characterizes the relationship between the sacred and the profane. This complementary way of looking at the world does not eliminate polarities, differences or tensions. It merely suggests that dichotomies and other exclusionary conceptualizations have limited utility. Moreover, these limitations can have profound and unfortunate effects on how we think, what we value, and how we order our lives. This is no more clear than in the world of play, games and sport.

## JUDEO-CHRISTIAN BIAS FOR PLAY OVER GAMES

The church, theologians, and laypersons, at least in the Judeo-Christian heritage, have long had difficulty figuring out what to do with play and games. Should they be embraced as ends in themselves, exploited for theological purposes, actively avoided or simply ignored? Are they part of God's provision, a handy vehicle for promoting institutional goals, a source of temptation, a product of human depravity or of so little ultimate consequence that not much needs to be made of them one way or another? To put matters clearly and bluntly, does God put God's stamp of approval on such activities or not?

These questions, however, exemplify the brand of thinking that gets us into trouble. They are dangerous because they aim at clean and tidy, usually dichotomous, nonambiguous responses. They suggest that the world can be divided neatly into things that receive God's blessing and things that do not. They also suggest that things come into existence by means of two independent sources. They are the product either of divine or human agency. Indeed, the Christian treatment of play and games shows these very tendencies.

In fact, in both religious and secular literature, play has been treated more extensively and kindly than games. This makes some sense. Of the two, play is the broader phenomenon. Both animals and humans play, whereas formal gaming activity, replete with conventional rules and purposes, seems to be restricted to humans alone or at most, humans along with a few advanced species of animals (Burghardt, 2004; Tomasello, 2008). Play, in short, is ubiquitous across species, history and culture.

On the other hand, games in general, and competitive games in particular, are not as universal in scope. The tendency to play is natural, hardwired into the system, as it were. No similar tendency presents itself when considering participation in games. Playful responses can be found anywhere that sentient beings find "delightful distractions" (Bekoff & Byers,

1998). Games seem to require something more—something on the order of rules, means, ends, scoring systems and specified consequences for breaking rules. For all of these reasons, play, in contrast to games, has been regarded as the more fundamental and expansive phenomenon. It is understandable, in other words, that it has received the greater amount of scholarly attention.[2]

But play has also received more normative support. Commentators from both religious and secular perspectives have been inclined to sing the praises of play more than games. Aristotle set the tone when he argued that a life dedicated to ends is superior to one that focuses on means (Ethics, Book X). Joseph Pieper (1952) said much the same thing about the proper relationship between ends and means from a Christian perspective. Huizinga (1950) may have provided the most flattering account of play when he argued that culture itself (literature, religion, law, language and the like) develops in and through play. Civilization, in other words, is play dependent.

These accolades seem to be merited when considering the nature of play. Play, by most accounts or definitions, is the kingdom of ends. Play is good in itself. In more technical terms it is called autotelic. In play, the doing is its own reward. In this sense it is also relational. It stands "outside" our normal trafficking in the world, outside our normal survival activities which would have us "getting and spending." Thus, play is something of a respite, a change of pace, a temporary break from how we spend much of our time (Suits, 1977). This respite is salubrious for any number of reasons. Thus, the good life, according to Aristotle, Pieper, Huizinga, Suits and many who have followed their lead, is one that includes a good measure of play. We ought to work in order to play, on their view, not the other way around. The kingdom of ends trumps the kingdom of means.

Games, by way of contrast, are often treated in less friendly terms. Because they are associated with the vagaries of culture, their worth typically rises and falls with the particular circumstances under which they were invented and utilized. The Roman games received poor reviews, and for very good reasons. The gaming tables found in Las Vegas, the manipulative games that people play with one another (Berne, 1964) and various contests in which roosters, dogs or other animals fight one another to the death—all of these provide additional examples of games that raise serious moral questions. Even more benign games like baseball and football can fall prey to competitive excesses, crass commercialism, win-at-all-costs attitudes and other cultural ills.

Consequently, it might be argued that play deserves most of the praise it has received. The best part of us, according to Plato, is our playful nature (Plato, The Laws, 803c). Human beings are often "at their best" in some sense when lost in play (Schiller, 1794/1965). Life generally goes well when it is played. The same sweeping claims cannot be made about games.

For games, a contingent endorsement seems more appropriate. When they are organized and conducted in appropriate ways, they have considerable value. It may even be the case that play itself is what redeems games (Clifford & Feezell, 1997). That is, when games are conducted in the spirit of play, their value increases.

The upshot of these judgments about games and play is that we may be at risk of underestimating the significance of games. Could it be that dualistic thinking has contributed to a premature or unwarranted undervaluation of games? Are dualisms preventing us from seeing games as genuine "gifts of God"? Have we spent too much time on "theologies of play" when a "theology of games" might be just as sensible? I believe that dualistic tendencies have, in fact, had these kinds of impacts and would point to the following three dichotomies as examples of simplistic bifurcations that have promote such rash or exaggerated judgments.

## INNOCENCE AND CONTAMINATION

Play is associated with innocence. Puppy dogs play. Children play. Neotenous adults dance and cavort. Play happens spontaneously, without calculation, without hidden agendas, often without planning. The player, in many cases, cannot resist the call of serendipity and thus cannot be blamed for kicking up his or her heels. Play is a natural response to success, satiety, completeness. Who could blame a person for doing a jig or singing a thankful song of praise at the end of a hard week of work?

Let them come to me "as children," Jesus suggests. That is, those who are looking for a new life should approach this change full of innocent wonderment, trust and a readiness to commit fully. We approach play in like manner. We give ourselves to play; we submit to the call of play. We are required to exercise trust in play when we forget duties, lose track of time, try things we have never tried before. We play as if we were fools . . . at least temporarily. Indeed, both play activities and the play spirit would seem to belong to the domain of innocence, childhood and the becoming kind of foolishness that accompanies them.

Games, on the other hand, are activities that are constructed. They are the product of their rules. In this sense they are artificial, fabricated, invented. Games are made by human hands. James Naismith, for example, was given an assignment to find a suitable wintertime activity for the late 19th-century youth of the Springfield YMCA. He settled on a location, added a bit of equipment, and developed a few rules. The result was the game of basketball. This was an inherently self-centered activity. Basketball, in other words, was invented to serve a human need. Games, in this sense, are homocentric because they are made by us and for us.

In addition to the fact that games seem more self-centered than play, the easy manipulation of games and game rules opens up additional possibilities for those who have ulterior motives. Gaming might be used, for example, to suppress the masses or provide a palliative for the restless. It might be employed to promote one's national identity or prestige. Games might be used by capitalists for personal profit, by erstwhile lovers to impress a would-be mate or by weekend warriors to lose weight. Because games are built by us and for us, they can be genuinely played, on the one hand, or they can be used for any number of licit or illicit purposes, on the other. Games, in short, seem open to contamination in ways that play is not.

## THEISM AND HUMANISM, NATURE AND CULTURE

Play is the kind of thing that could have been present in the Garden of Eden prior to the fall. When God rested on the seventh day and declared that his creation was good, he may well have had play in mind . . . along with the many other things that made this special garden the Eden that it was. Adam and Eve, in fact, may have had a life that was one of unadulterated play. That is, they were created to take delight fully and eternally in the fruits of the garden and in one another. The world created by the hand of God, in other words, was playfully "sufficient" in all senses. No striving, no need, no deficits, no work, no embarrassments, no guilt—none of this could be found anywhere, at least not until our ancestors decided to remove God from God's seat of authority and take apples and other matters into their own hands.

This is when games and the rest of culture came about. While the conventions of society—government, religion, law, language, ethical mores, music, art—have their redeeming qualities,[3] they all carry the taint of human construction. They all show elements of hubris. Games and the rest of culture are, on this view, essentially products of the fall. The imperfections that accompany all humanism, all self-made artifacts, all attempts to place ourselves in the center of things characterize games, as well. Thus, rule-breaking, doping, hooliganism, excess partisanship, nationalism and other ills of the contemporary world of games come as no surprise. Games are imperfect conventions. They are the product of brash humanism, not respectful theism.

## COOPERATION VS. COMPETITION, SHARING VS. KEEPING, GIVING VS. TAKING

Play may be the orientation to life that promotes community and sharing better than any other. We dance together; we enjoy the feast together; we fantasize, make believe, wade on the beach, dig in the sandbox together. It is more fun that way, and in most settings, there is enough play spirit to go around. The more the merrier. Playing is typically about sharing.

Sharing is less likely in many game environments, particularly those that are competitive in nature. In fact, competitive games are, at least in one sense, zero-sum affairs. Some individual or some team wins, and all others lose. Someone goes home happy. Someone else goes home defeated and without the prize.

Competitive games seem to require taking . . . or at least the attempt to take something that others want as well. In territorial games, we want to take more ground. In skill-oriented games, we want to take more bases or take more good shots. In all games, we want to possess more points or whatever surrogate is used to measure superior performance. And of course, all competitors want to take home the trophy . . . a reward, as noted earlier, that cannot be shared.

## PRELIMINARY DICHOTOMOUS CONCLUSIONS

Based on these kinds of arguments and comparisons, the better part of reason would suggest that play be embraced and games be used, if at all, with caution. God may endorse play *ipso facto*, but God needs to know more before giving a divine blessing to any game. Play is part of the creation that God identified as "good." Games came later and show elements of the hubris and imperfections that invariably result when humans take charge. Play is communal and often cooperative. Games are typically competitive and exclusionary.

While these conclusions may have a degree of validity to them, they probably fall short of the more nuanced view of play and games that would better guide our attitudes toward and involvement with them. This requires, however, that we grow more comfortable with blurred edges and admixtures of apparently incompatible ingredients. It requires that we see our world as sacred and profane at the same time. It asks us to take the reality of the "first fruits" seriously, while acknowledging that these spiritual blessings are homogenized with all that is temporal, incomplete and imperfect. It asks us to see that the "kingdom is at hand," here and now, but only in a kind-of, get-a-glimpse-of, through-a-glass-darkly way. To appreciate the homogenization of the sacred and secular, we need to look more closely at games to see the entangled roots from which they grew.

## THE AMBIGUOUS GENEALOGY OF GAMES

Games are conventions and, as such, take their place among other elements of what might loosely be called human culture. Games, like all conventions—whether they be linguistic, artistic, or political—are governed by constitutive rules that stipulate relationships and meanings. As Searle put it, constitutive rules indicate that "X counts as Y in context Z." In sport, propelling a ball through a rectangular target without using one's hands counts as a goal in the context of soccer. Linguistically, "d-o-g" stands for a tail-wagging furry creature in the context of the English language.

Conventions, in the evolutionary scheme of things, came late—probably within the past 100,000 years or so (Tomasello, 2008). Burial ceremonies, the appearance of trinkets or jewelry, the production of Upper Paleolithic cave paintings, and hypothesized capacities for prelinguistic communication—all of these conventional or quasi-conventional activities showed up near the end of our 2.4-million-year journey from the emergence of the species homo to the present day.

Games, as relative newcomers, have roots that can be traced back across the millennia. Much of this is speculative, but the broad outlines of what has happened can be reconstructed with a certain degree of confidence. These outlines show without question that games grew from many different roots. Among them are work and rest, play, increasing intelligence and success, emotions, luck and logic.[4]

Work and rest came first. They had to be there at the beginning because they are required for survival. The inexorable laws of homeostasis—calories out and calories in, breaking down and building up, expenditure and restoration—provided early animals with a foundation for surviving and reproducing and thus for passing on their genes.

Primitive animals were undoubtedly hardwired to engage in requisite work and restoration behaviors. They faced challenges and needed to solve problems—to secure food, find a safe habitat, reproduce, avoid predation or premature death from other sources. This was their work. From the beginning, animals were problem solvers. From the beginning, animals were predisposed to meet challenges successfully. So they worked, and they rested.

Games bear a strong relationship to work. In fact, if one foundation for games were to be singled out, it might well be work. This is the case because games, in a sense, are artificial forms of work. They present us with challenges. They require us to find solutions to those challenges. They remind us that there are consequences if we are not successful. In short, they allow us to exercise our problem-solving capabilities but with a twist.

Part of this twist comes with the evolutionary emergence of play. Play, we might speculate, came after work because it is grounded in a more complex relationship with the world—one that includes affect and evaluation (Kretchmar, 2007). In other words, animals needed to be smarter. They needed to have a more sophisticated central nervous system if they were to "interrupt the appetitive process" and play. The capacity to be distracted from the work-rest cycle requires the ability to discriminate between positive and negative affect. It requires the primitive capacity to make judgments about the relative goodness of an experience.

When animals were able to make such discriminations, their existence moved from one of work and rest to one that also had to accommodate play. They gained the ability to be distracted. They began to encounter what we now call intrinsic satisfaction, something (as noted previously) that Aristotle regarded as the *sine qua non* of the good life. These animals became less predictable than their hardwired predecessors because invitations to play could strike at any time, even when prudence would suggest that such invitations not be accepted.

Games are grounded in play because problem solving is replete with intrinsic potential. One of the most gratifying things that problem-solving creatures can do is precisely to solve problems! When difficulties match capabilities, when demands are balanced with resources, when success hangs in the balance, when improvements can be noticed, when competence and excellence are experienced . . . the activity that includes these things can be exceedingly engaging (Csikszentmihalyi, 1990). Or to put it more simply, the attempt to solve good problems well can be great fun. Play, in short, provided an intrinsic twist to workaday problem solving.

For millions of years, it is likely that animals lived a stable and agreeable tripartite existence, one that included good measures of work, rest and play—a mixture of expenditures at the hands of necessity (work), expenditures and restorations through diversions (play) and simple recuperation (rest). As long as the needs for work, play and rest remained balanced, this arrangement had a degree of evolutionary stability to it.

According to some anthropologists, however, this balance was disrupted some 50,000 years ago when our ancestors crossed an evolutionary Rubicon of sorts (Alexander, 1990). Relationships among work, play and rest shifted, paradoxically enough, as a result of the increasing intelligence and success of our hominid predecessors. To put it simply, they worked too efficiently. They had better tools. They began to cooperate with one another. Their ability to communicate improved (Alexander, 1990). As a result, work was finished before the day was over. Even when normal play activities were relied on more heavily, time remained. Hours with nothing left to do weighed heavily on our predecessors.

For the first time in our long evolutionary history, boredom and malaise announced their presence (Kretchmar, 2007). The emotional lives of our ancestors were turned upside down. And the culprit was less work, less stimulation from the potentially engaging problems provided by work, less satisfaction from tackling good problems with equally good skills.

With the onset of such a powerfully negative emotion, the stage was set for games. To ward off the potentially debilitating effects of boredom and malaise, a surrogate for work was needed. If only our ancestors were smart enough to invent and engage in games.

Unfortunately, at least at this point in evolutionary history, they were not. This is where chance or luck comes in. The first "games" were undoubtedly accidental occurrences. That is, many of the requisites for good games came into existence by chance. Two of these requisites are well-fitted means and ends. The means permitted to solve the problem have to be matched carefully to the end. If the means are too loose relative to the end, the game becomes too easy. Conversely, if the means are too restricted, the game becomes too hard. By chance, however, a good balance might be struck.

A thunderstorm might delay a hunt just long enough to make the sojourn unusually and delightfully challenging. A lack of rain might deplete the tribal stores so that a future hunt is unusually and delightfully meaningful. Two wrestlers might be so well matched that the outcome of their activity is unusually and provocatively uncertain. Drama, uncertainty, challenge, bold initiatives, perseverance and excitement are the stuff of good games. Occasionally, by chance, we can speculate, these things were injected into the lives of our ancestors. They noticed that life was good under these enhanced conditions. All that was left for them to do was to connect the game dots—the satisfactions provided by "just-right" work, the intrigue of play, the recent decline in work, increasing experiences of boredom, and those wonderfully challenging activities that, by chance, sometimes came their way. All that was needed was to create the effects of the thunderstorm, the drought, and the well-matched wrestlers *by rule*—that is, by taking the production of "just-right" problems into their own hands.

Eventually somebody or some group of precocious hominids was able to do exactly this. They made the momentous move into conventions by stipulating relationships between things. These stipulations took the form of rules. With rules came the first freestanding games in the history of the human race.

At least three kinds of logic were needed for the development of games. The first is conventional logic. We already saw that this takes the form of "X counts as Y in context Z." A second kind of logic allowed our ancestors to embrace problems. It could be called gratuitous logic. It addresses the paradox of "harder is better." It allows gamewrights and game players to see that problems, oddly enough, are good things. A third kind of intellection that is needed for games can be called the logic of formalism. This is the thinking that connects means to ends and is the foundation of game ethics. If one does not play by the rules, in other words, one is no longer (really) playing that game. Without the logic of formalism, participants could seek success in any way that they wanted to. Game playing would become chaotic and results would be meaningless.

For millions of years conventional, gratuitous and formal logic were beyond the grasp of our ancestors. Because of this, games were also well beyond their reach—even though they were involved in the problem solving of work and the delights of play. They were restricted to the natural world of duties and pleasure, instincts and distractions, predictable behavior and unpredictable deviations from the requirements of prudence. However, they were not able, as it were, to break into the second world of conventions and culture, of games, language, government, art and religion.

The lineage of games is complex and ambiguous. As I have speculated, games would probably not have come about were it not for work. Games are, in a sense, ideal surrogates for work. They fit our human nature as problem-solving individuals very well. Games would probably not have come about without the influences of play and boredom. Play was the intrinsic engine that drove quest for games. *Intrinsica* is good. More of it is better. Boredom was the powerful, negative affect that placed the evolutionary spotlight ever more squarely on games. If life were to be intrinsically satisfying in a world of decreasing satisfaction from work, *Homo sapiens* would have to turn elsewhere.

Chance events undoubtedly helped our ancestors see where this "elsewhere" might be. "Accidental games" preceded actual games. All that was needed at this point in human history was the intelligence to negotiate the requirements of conventional logic. With such intellectual capabilities in place, and with the fortification provided by the logic of gratuity and formalism, games gained a foothold in our world along with other elements of culture.

In short, games are not isomorphic phenomena that stand in stark and clear contrast to play. If my account is at all on target, games emerged from work and rest, play, increasing intelligence and efficiency, boredom and malaise, chance or good fortune and at least three kinds of logic. Given an appreciation for that messy genealogy, we can return to the central question at hand. Does it still make sense to identify games as gifts of God? My tentative answer is "sort of."

## GAMES AS POTENTIAL GIFTS OF GOD

The "sort of" answer begins to make more sense when we examine other items that are associated with God's intervention and providence. Biblical references to manna from heaven, the wine at the wedding feast, the fish and bread for the feeding of the 5,000, the restoration of the beggar's ability to walk and other provisions might be considered similarly ambiguous. Nourishment, after all, can be used for any number of purposes—both good and bad. Food, as we well know in this era of childhood and adult obesity, can be consumed in moderation or excess. Drinking wine can be part of a celebratory feast that honors the divine, or it can lead to any number of destructive behaviors. The beggar could use his newly found ambulatory capability to walk humbly in the presence of the Lord or to head in other directions.

For these reasons it is difficult to identify any particular human capability or anything that people want and need as unequivocally "of God" or "of the world." It depends on how it is appreciated and used. Thus, it may be more accurate to say that the attribution of both worth and parentage to any item lies in the relationship between the person and that particular thing rather than in the thing itself. While things that we want and need have good qualities to them, they are not unequivocally good, at least not from a perspective that honors ambiguity.

This view of the world undercuts dualist theologies and again raises important questions about the adequacy of understanding reality in terms of dichotomies. One brand of dualism suggests that the world that God created was, *ipso facto*, good. Given this assumption, any human interactions with the world that lead to trouble reflect more on us than on God and the goodness of God's creation. In traditional terms, the fall of man from grace blocked our original access to the inherent goodness of the world. On this view, God and God's created world are good while we humans are thoroughly bankrupt and in need of help.

But we can also think of ourselves as ambiguous individuals, at once made in the image of God but also capable of very ungodly attitudes and activities. We are at once Kingdom-capable and Kingdom-challenged. The challenge comes from the difficulty in living God's promise, in cultivating our better nature, in living in faith and humility (Niebuhr, 1951: 25.) And so ambiguous people living toward an ambiguous world get a good taste of Kingdom living. But we get a whole lot else in addition.

This brings us back to games. It might be said that in games too we can get a taste of Kingdom living, but we can experience a whole host of other things too. This is due both to us and to the games we play.

Games are both lovely and dangerous . . . at the same time. They are lovely because they are not mere pastimes. They affect us much more deeply and personally than that. Games speak to who we are. We are problem solvers extraordinaire. We look out onto the world and immediately see things to make and do. We watch somebody perform a task and we imagine how it could be done better. When we are told that something is impossible to do, we often resist and try to prove that person wrong. At work and at play, in all seriousness and in the spirit of gratuity, we are problem seekers through and through. A just-right problem, particularly when it is encountered in the domain of play, can be a wonderful gift indeed.

At the same time, games are dangerous. The drive to succeed can overwhelm us. Interests in beating an opponent can become excessive. Success can lead to inappropriate self-congratulation. Training programs directed toward improvement and excellence can become addictive and, as a result, we can become game-dependent. But, for those of us who love games, the risks are worth it.

In order to support this risk-taking point of view, we could argue that the old cliché has it right. People do not live by bread alone. Our understanding of God's provision needs to take that fact into account. God provides for the whole of us—our physical, social, aesthetic, psychological and spiritual needs and desires.

And so, when hunter-gatherer efficiencies many years ago threatened our predecessors with boredom, and when tedium and too little to do cast a pall over God's creation, our *Homo sapiens* ancestors needed some "manna." It did not come all at once, but it showed up piecemeal in the form of artificial problems with increasing levels of sophistication and value. These activities eventually became our lovely~dangerous games.

God's world is not dichotomous. It is messy but full of hope. Games are risky, ambiguous phenomena with an uncertain genealogy. But they can also be experienced as wonderful gifts of God. In games there are moments, as Novak once put it, when we can see into the "fiery heart of the Creator" (Novak, 1976: 151). In games we can experience purpose, determination, grace, friendship, forgiveness, and excellence. In the sensuous physicality of games we can encounter the many aesthetic joys awaiting us in God's creation. In the spell cast by games we can encounter the world as bright and interesting. It all depends on the relationship. So, spiritually oriented problem seekers, in faith and humility, look for moments of Kingdom living in the games they play. They know, however, that other kinds of experiences will show up as well.

## NOTES

1. In this article I emphasize the Judeo-Christian tradition. Nevertheless, the article is designed to be compatible with other faith traditions as well.
2. Of course, sport (often regarded as a species of games) has received a great amount of attention, particularly in recent times. Nevertheless, play is the topic that has more frequently attracted traditional scholars. This is particularly true in the discipline of philosophy.
3. Luther was famous for calling culture in general, and the state in particular, a dike against sin. While culture, for Luther, was the imperfect product of fallible human beings, it was still useful.
4. Obviously other roots exist as well. Bipedalism, protein-rich diets, and the increasing size of the cranium are only three of them.

## BIBLIOGRAPHY

Alexander, R. (1990) How Did Humans Evolve Reflections on the Uniquely Unique Species, *Museum of Zoology Special Publication No. 1*, 1–38, Ann Arbor: University of Michigan.

Aristotle. (350 BCE) *Nicomachean Ethics*. Trans. by D. Ross. Retrieved April 15, 2009, from http://classics.mit.edu/Aristotle/nicomachaen.html

Bekoff, M., and Byers, J. (Eds.) (1998). *Animal Play: Evolutionary, Comparative, and Ecological Perspectives*, Cambridge/New York: Cambridge University Press.

Berne, E. (1964) *Games People Play: The Psychology of Human Relationships*, New York: Grove Press.

Burghardt, G. (2004) *The Genesis of Animal Play: Testing the Limits*, Cambridge, MA: MIT Press.

Clifford, C., and Feezell, R. (1997) *Coaching for Character: Reclaiming the Principles of Sportsmanship*, Champaign, IL: Human Kinetics.

Csikszentmihalyi, M. (1990) *Flow: The Psychology of Optimal Experience*, New York: HarperCollins.

Dewey, John. (1922/1988). *Human Nature and Conduct, 1922. The Middle Works, 1899–1924, Vol. 14*, Boydston (Ed.), Carbondale: Southern Illinois University Press.

Gould, S.J. (2003) *The Hedgehog, the Fox, and the Magister's Pox*, New York: Harmony Books.

Herrigel, E. (1953/1964) *Zen in the Art of Archery*, New York: Pantheon Books.

Huizinga, J. (1950) *Homo Ludens: A Study of the Play Element in Culture*, Boston: Beacon.

Kelso, J.A.S., and Engstrom, D. (2006) *The Complementary Nature*, Cambridge, MA: Massachusetts Institute of Technology.

Kretchmar, R.S. (2007) The Normative Heights and Depths of Play, *Journal of the Philosophy of Sport, XXXIV*, 1, 1–12.

McDermott, J. (Ed.) (1967/1977) *The Writings of William James: A Comprehensive Edition*, Chicago: University of Chicago Press.

McGinn, C. (1999) *The Mysterious Flame: Conscious Minds in a Material World*, New York: Basic Books.

Midgley, M. (1994) *The Ethical Primate: Humans, Freedom and Morality*, London and New York: Routledge.

Niebuhr, H.R. (1951) *Christ and Culture*, New York: Harper & Row.

Novak, M. (1976) *The Joy of Sports: End Zones, Bases, Baskets, Balls, and the Consecration of the American Spirit*, New York: Basic Books.

Pieper, J. (1952) *Leisure: The Basis of Culture*, New York: Pantheon Books.

Plato. (360 BCE) The Laws. Trans. by B. Jowett. Retrieved April, 15, 2009, from http://classics.mit.edu/Plato/laws.html

Prokhovnik, R. (1999/2002) *Rational Woman: A Feminist Critique of Dichotomy*, 2nd ed., Manchester and New York: Manchester University Press.

Schiller, F. (1794/1965) *On the Aesthetic Education of Man*, translated with an introduction by R. Snell, New York: Frederick Unger.

Snow, C.P. (1959/1986) *The Two Cultures: And a Second Look*, Cambridge/New York: Cambridge University Press.

Suits, B. (1977) Words on Play, *Journal of the Philosophy of Sport, IV*, 117–131.

Suzuki, D.T. (1949/1961) *Essays in Zen Buddhism: First series*, New York: Grove Press.

Tertullian (1956) *Tertullian's Treatise on the Incarnation (De Carne Christi)*, Ernest Evans (Trans. and Ed.), London: SPCK.

Tomasello, M. (2008) *Origins of Human Communication*, Cambridge, MA/London: The MIT Press.

# 9 The Energy of Play

*Susan Saint Sing*

There has been much speculation in physics on the origins of the universe, string theory, and the understanding of the ethereal fabric of which we are made. This fabric that pertains to the essence of matter and energy in the universe includes the human imprint from the Creator at the moment of creation. Can we link this energy in a continuum from the moment of the origin of the universe to the modern athlete and beyond? For if this energy continuum can be seen as plausible, then it fills a gap and aids the modern sport philosopher in understanding how the impetus to play within the element of sport helps us transcend our base nature, and advance humankind as part of the energy of the expanding universe.

This chapter is a journey through the ages of time and across many disciplines and discourse communities examining what the great minds have expressed in regards to energy, God and play. The chapter is set up as a series of questions to promote thought and plausibility based on key, pivotal phrases such as Carl Jung's insight and description of a collective unconscious. Jung describes a collective unconscious which carries primordial archetypes—foci of energy—that issue forth as images and symbols, which influence all people through the ages along the continuum. This collective unconscious is akin to a collective knowledge, passed from generation to generation since the inception of humankind's origins. Reflections of this collective unconscious reveal themselves to us through the images and symbols by which we name things, identify things and describe things—a common thread. This chapter will consider this broad-based thread of expression in terms of play, energy and the origins of the universe. Some archetypes of the unconscious include the trickster, the mother and the hero. According to Jung, archetypes create myths, religions and philosophical ideas that influence and set their stamp on whole nations and epochs (Jung, 1956a). Would they not influence and set their stamp on play and sport?

Considering the preceding—if, through the ages, a broad discourse of people: writers, scientists, theologians, philosophers, artists, all speak in similar terms of experience—they are probably reflecting more than just their opinion; they are probably expressing, or being *moved to express*, a similar unifying human understanding. According to psychiatrist Alexander

A. Weech, Jung's theory of collective unconscious can be looked upon as this type of dynamic. In this collective understanding, then, can we recognize descriptions of play that give us clues to the origins of the energy of play that link us and place us in a continuum with the moment of the creation of the universe—and therefore with the Creator? Let us take a journey along the continuum and across several disciplines

To begin, let us consider that scientists, mathematicians, poets, theologians and artists all reflect, name and describe *energy* as part of the moment of creation, as part of the essence and the intention of the Creator. It would not be uncommon to find science considering energy. Energy is certainly expressed in the arts and humanities—let us examine how energy and God are used together across all these disciplines.

What do some Nobel Laureates in physics say about energy, creation and God? Albert Einstein: "Energy evolved in very regular ways." It had purpose. Einstein never accepted that the universe was governed by chance: "God does not play dice." And continuing, what about the first moment of creation—the first moment of when energy was sent forth? Leon Lederman, a Nobel Laureate in physics, calls this moment of preexistence a time of the "God Particle . . . We don't know anything about the universe until it reaches the mature age of a billionth of a trillionth of a second" (Lederman & Teresi, 1993, *The God Particle: If the Universe Is the Answer What Is the Question?*). Stephen Hawking infers that God is something of a mathematical necessity for the universe to exist under the laws which it does (Hawking & Mlodinow, 2005, *A Briefer History of Time*). That Hawking infers a "necessity" for God is not entirely new. Earlier, along the continuum, in 1250 C.E., Aquinas describes aspects of God—goodness, necessity, intelligence—in collective terms as "understood by all," aspects which "everyone understands to *be* God" (Thomas Aquinas, *The Summa Theologica*). Perhaps Hawking is expanding on Aquinas's insights through the collective unconscious.

At the moment of creation in order for the near instantaneous creation of the known universe to exist, there was a burst of energy that formed the matter and antimatter that many physicists now believe consists of "strings." String theory is very complicated but it consists of a way of expressing the smallest particles of energy that exists in *all* parts and circumstances of the universe, thus perhaps providing a unifying theory between quantum physics and Newtonian physics. Physicist Briane Greene states, "According to string theory we would find that each [particle] is not point-like, but instead, consists of a loop . . . each particle contains an oscillating, vibrating, *dancing* filament" (Briane Greene. 1999, *The Elegant Universe*).

With strings we have energy likely to be present in all matter and antimatter, present in good energy and dark energy that is "described" and "recognized" by scientists in the language of play as—*dancing*. Interesting! Going back to Jung, if we describe what we "see," what we recognize and name based on previous learning models and experience, stemming from the collective past, then the physicist Greene, who was moved to describe the energy of strings as *dancing*, might be identifying this movement as so because it strikes a chord, memory, some visual link to a past occurrence where energy danced, where energy was intended and was part of the fabric and the very essence of the Creator.

What do the poets say? T.S. Eliot: "Except for the point, the still point, there would be no dance, and there is only the dance. I can only say *there* we have been: but I cannot say where" (Eliot, *The Four Quartets*). What is Eliot seeing in his mind when he writes that there is a still point without which there would be no dance—what is this "still point" out of which and around which all things dance? Is it God? Or the Trinity, or perhaps he is referring to Aristotle's Prime Mover?

What do the theologians say of the dance and the still point? St. Bonaventure states that the love of the Trinity is like a dance; its love is so great it becomes creation (Bonaventure's *Collected Works*). Aquinas says, "Therefore it is necessary to arrive at a first mover, put in motion by no other; and this everyone understands to *be* God" (Thomas Aquinas, *The Summa Theologica*). The still point is the beginning, the moment just before Creation, after which everything is in motion. Do we have any idea of what this moment of creation was like? Are there any clues that there was a moment in time through which the beginning of time passed? Can we link what the poets and theologians are talking about with science? Yes. Astrophysicist Neil de Grasse Tyson and Goldsmith (2004), in their book on the universe entitled *Origins*, states that cosmic background radiation (CBR) carries the imprint of a portal through which all of us once passed.

Dare we call this portal the moment of creation? What do the artists show us about this? Is it represented in Michelangelo's "touch" between God and Adam on the ceiling of the Sistine Chapel? Is this what he is creating from his collective unconscious? If the Creator loosed this energy in the universe setting forces in motion, is one of the energies on this imprint the urge to play? Is play part of the fabric of God?

What does scripture tell us? Adam and Eve were made in God's image (Gen 1:26, 27). Adam and Eve were made according to God's likeness. Does this likeness include play? Scripture tells us, "When he set the heavens in their place I was there, when he girdled the ocean . . . Then I was at his side each day, his darling and delight, *playing* in his presence continually, *playing* on the earth, when he had finished it . . ." (Proverbs 8:27–31).

We have looked at physicists, theologians, artists, scripture and psychotherapists—what do philosophers say about this energy of play? What is play? Kretchmar and Huizinga say play is a "state of fundamental prerational spontaneity which is freely chosen and entered into for the simple sake of *wanting* to do so. It is of a nature outside of the reality of the present, yet is equally as real to the player or players as the present is to an observer . . ." This description contains many of the elements and experience of the spiritual, doesn't it?

Play can take many forms, as many forms as any individual or group of individuals fancies entering into. Since physicist Briane Greene used the descriptive of energy dancing when describing strings, let us examine the example of play as dancing and see what the collective body of knowledge might be telling us. "The connections between playing and dancing are so close that they hardly need illustrating. It is not that dance has something of play in it or about it, rather it is an integral part of play: the relationship is one of direct participation, almost of essential identity . . . dancing is a particular and particularly perfect form of playing" (Johan Huizinga, 1955: 165, *Homo Ludens*). Dance, being an integral part of play, a perfect form of play, is also a prime example of play and should therefore be reflected throughout the collective unconscious.

If the impetus to play is from the Creator, it would have to have been there since the beginning. So when does the impetus, the intention, the energy to play come in? Has it always been with human kind? What do the anthropologists say? Anthropologists state that all civilizations have recorded play of some sort. So this continuum of play is part of our historical collective fiber. For the spiritual being what comes before civilization as we know it? The Garden—the mystical Garden of Eden, a time when we were one with God. Does/did play exist there?

Well, one could argue that if we are in God, and God is in us, and we are in one another, and since we are never outside of the omnipresent God, then the Garden is always present to us, which prompts us, collectively, to move toward play. Moreover, there is historical evidence for this as playfulness is throughout scripture in the Judeo-Christian tradition. What else does scripture say? Let us consider God arguing creation with Job: Can you lead about the crocodile with a hook? Can you play with him [crocodile] as with a bird?" (Job 41:1,5, *New American Bible*). ". . . Strength is lodged in his neck and untiring energy dances ahead of him [the crocodile]" (Job 41:22, *New English Bible*). And again, "Here ships ply their course; here Leviathan your creature which you formed plays (Psalm 104:26). ". . . your creature Leviathan which you formed to play . . ." (Psalm 104:26, *Holman Christian Standard Bible*). In Exodus 15:20, Miriam danced, and David danced before the Lord with all his might (2 Sam. 6:14).

Three examples of play have thus far been shown to be centered in the spiritual:

1. God playing with creation
2. God forming things to play
3. God describing this energy of play as dancing.

Continuing, what do the writers say? Barbara Ehrenreich, in her book *Dancing in the Streets*, states, "There was without question, a tradition of collective ecstasy among the Hebrews." And that the archaic roots of ecstasy involve play: we can infer that these scenes from prehistoric rock art are *depicting dancing figures*, which have been discovered at sites in Africa, India, Australia, Italy, Turkey, Israel, Iran and Egypt, among other places. "Whatever else they did, our distant ancestors seemed to find plenty of time for the kinds of activities the anthropologist Victor Turner described as liminal, or peripheral to the main business of life" (Ehrenreich, 2006, *Dancing in the Streets*).

Ehrenreich gives multiple examples that the ancients played. What about the Middle Ages? There are various examples of toys and games, sports stemming from the Middle Ages up through to modern time. Play as far back as the ancient Olympics and the Middle Ages has been associated with religion and at times even spirituality. Victor Turner considered St. Francis of Assisi, 13th-century mystic, one of the most profound examples of the liminal man. Francis played a mystical violin throughout the countryside. All cultures played. There are myriad examples and styles of play through the ages. Humans play. Even animals play. Play is part of the fabric of God's creative energy.

Play could be considered an invitation, passing back and forth between the energy of God and the energy here in this world's creation; then, when the urge to play comes upon us, we, like children, respond to it in glee—and then it is gone for a time. The response, the communion, is returned and exchanged with and to the Creator until the next time. We have within our power the will to engage or refuse that Presence; and in the refusal we lapse into the shadow of our darker nature (Saint Sing, 2004, *Spirituality of Sport: Balancing Body and Soul*).

What is it that unites body, mind and soul into the mind/body/soul? What is the body electric that poet and philosopher Walt Whitman talks about? What is it that we know when something greater is there, out there on the field, or in the gym? What we are responding to is the experience of *grace*. A human effort has been graced by God. We, in our creaturehood, having come from the Creator, and still being enlivened by the energy and spirit of the Creator inherently respond to this communion—it resonates with a template within us. The template is the memory or recognition of godliness. Play is a return to that, a memory pushing through layers of consciousness and breaking surface like a wave on a beach where we, like children, press our toes in the sand for a moment and then it is gone, to resurface later. Play is an archetype of goodness and joy, a cluster of energy mirroring the last memories of the perfect human state and union with God—the Garden of Eden.

With this additional possibility, what do the poets say? Dante writes, "Thus, even as he wheeled to his own music, I saw that substance sing, that spirit-flame above whom double lights were twinned; and he and his companions moved *within their dance* . . ." (disappearance of the Roman Emperor Justinian and his fellow spirits in the wake of hymning and dancing, *The Divine Comedy*, Dante Alighieri, "Paradiso," Canto VII 4:7)

Going on, what do biologists, physiologists, sport philosophers and journalists say? How do we make this inner information useful to us? If we have a collective unconscious, might we have a collective kinetic blueprint or template also? Can we decipher the physical to explain the ethereal? Recent interests in studying muscle myelin and talent seek to examine physical muscle tissue and makeup and use the findings to explain something as ethereal as "talent." Is it possible to dig into tissues and say, "Ah, there it is, *that* is talent." Yet scientists are doing exactly that and coming up with the explanation that we are "hardwired" to exhibit certain talents when we play.

Our search for the energy play is similar. We "see" the energy of God that gives rise to all matter and the intention of that energy is to interact, create, vibrate, oscillate, even to dance. Are science and philosophy joining hands? Does this playfulness pass and develop in a collective kinetic unconscious akin to Carl Jung? If so, historically, it would be logical that play evolves as civilizations and intelligence and curiosity evolve—as the need for diversion and entertainment evolves. Darwin teaches us of survival of the fittest, that we evolve to suit our needs because we must adapt to survive—we get bigger brains and better hands—yet there is also a need, apparently, to be spiritual and to *play* and when something is beyond the physical, beyond the natural laws, can we take it to the metaphysical or supernatural realm and see play as evolving? If it does evolve, wouldn't kinesiologists want to put an imprint of spirituality on it? If we aren't doing these things, are we hindering or muting its development?

Wilson (2002) writes in *Darwin's Cathedral*: "It might seem disadvantageous in terms of foraging for sustenance and safety, for someone to favor religious over rationalistic explanations that would point to where the food and danger are." Religion seemed to use up physical and mental resources without an obvious benefit for survival. He continued, "Today the effort has gained momentum, as scientists search for an evolutionary explanation for why belief in God exists—not whether God exists, which is a matter for philosophers and theologians, but why the belief does. This is taking place not between science and religion but within science itself, specifically among scientists studying the evolution of religion. These scholars tend to agree on one point: that religious belief is an outgrowth of brain architecture that evolved during early human history." In short, we are hardwired to believe in God and if believing in God is part of our brain architecture wouldn't play be also?

Maybe sport philosophers can answer this, bridge the gap between biology and philosophy with the fact that we are hardwired to believe in God in the same manner that we are hardwired to play—play is part of the mind/body/spirit makeup that is part of the Creator. Our energy for play, games, sport is the "stuff" of God, the "stuff" of life—of the very matter from which we are created.

Play is vital to life. What do the great writers and philosophers say about play and life? Bertrand Russell writes, "We no longer play because we grow old, we grow old because we no longer play." Eugene Fink writes,

"Originally play was the strongest unifying force. . . . "Play is a fundamental phenomenon of existence. . . . Play has the coloring of joy" (Fink, *The Ontology of Play*). Might the spiritual aspects of play and the lack of these same aspects wither the body in aging, contribute to depression, contribute to a state of physical illness and decline? Aren't sport philosophers studying the benefits and intricacies of the mind/body/spirit called to research these vital connections? Yet, we as educators in sport shy away from the spiritual when it seems that the spiritual is inherent to play.

What can we learn if there is a spiritual energy intending for us to play? What communion are we entering into when we play? The preceding examples have shown that there is a spiritual connection to play. The spiritual makes us more playful—but, as educators, can we take this idea further along the continuum to explore if when we play we are becoming more spiritual?

What does a pope say about play contributing to our spiritual welfare? "With this celebration the world of sport is joining in a great chorus, as it were, to express through prayer, song, play and movement a hymn of praise and thanksgiving to the Lord" (Jubilee of Sports People, John Paul II, 29 October 2000). He includes play as part of the spiritual whole of the expression of praise to God.

What do the philosophers believe? Merleau-Ponty (1962) discusses "mythical consciousness" and the phenomenology of movement, and Michael Novak distills the power of athletic experience in the revelatory moments of perfect form, and likens them to being part of or coming from another plane. "Tens of thousands of passes are thrown every year . . . occasionally however, a player or a team executes a play so perfectly—it is as though they cease for a moment to be pedestrian and leap into a realm of the Gods. A great play is like a revelation, the curtains of ordinary life part and perfection flashes for an instant before the eye" (Novak, 1976, *The Joy of Sports*).

What is this plane that Novak alludes to? What is beyond the empirical? The collective kinetic blueprint of play—can we recognize it from evidence? Is there a bridge from empirical to mythical? Enter "Breakthrough Kinesis." What is it? There are moments when performance barriers are broken, such as Bannister and breaking the 4-minute mile, Glendon and the 1920 Olympic win that set up the longest winning streak in Olympic history—both coming about as if a door has opened and all of a sudden the logjam on the other side rushes through. The collective unconscious has pushed through the performance barrier and advanced humankind. When a breakthrough kinesis takes place, when an athlete accomplishes the heroic act, others are somehow emboldened and enabled—a rebirth of hope and heightened ability. The hero soon has company—contributing to the unfolding creation beyond the empirical. The human kinetic moment joins the mystical (Saint Sing, *Quest*).

Again, dare we call a breakthrough event *grace*? It is as if grace has entered the equation and the collective kinetic blueprint has been thrust forward, moved by a nonempirical means—beyond the natural explanation to the supernatural—metaphysical, the mystical. Are we hardwired for this kind of grace as we are hardwired for belief and talent, and breakthrough moments of performance because these are part of our molecular physical being with which *all* matter *dances*? It seems plausible that we are. Why are we hardwired for these? Because all of these are part of the energy of Creation, the fabric of the Creator, the essence of who we have been and will be—they are the very matter of our makeup.

What do the ancients say? There is a rune stone from 1100 C.E. which has the inscription "God within me, God without, how can I ever be in doubt, I am the sower and the sown, God's self-unfolding and God's own." To be the sower *and* the sown, to be the unfolding of God, is a concept which helps us see our relationship as both creature and part of the Creator. Since we are created in the likeness of God, does God play? Does God play with us? What do the poets and writers say? "With no warning, a wave of energy swept my body. I was tossed again and again, gently and playfully in an exhilarating but helpless fashion, like a juggler tosses a ball . . . This ecstatic experience went on and on and I found myself shouting, 'God is playing with me!' " (Pearce, 2002, *The Biology of Transcendence*). Furthermore, Rilke states, "So long as you only catch what you yourself toss up 'tis only skill of a minor range. Only when you suddenly catch the ball thrown by your eternal Companion of play, against your center in a perfect gesture in one of the arcs traced against the great bridge of God, does knowing how to seize it really count—not for yourself *but for the world*" (Rilke, as presented by Fink in *The Ontology of Play*).

In conclusion, we have considered: play comes from God at the moment of creation and is imparted to us and made part of us spiritually and physically—we are "hardwired" to play—and play unites us to God. We have considered many examples of the energy of play emanating from the Creator:

1. God playing with his creation
2. God forming things to play
3. God describing this energy as dancing
4. God playing with us

We have looked at many examples through the ages and across disciplines of this energy we have to play being a connection to the spiritual, the nature of God and therefore of ourselves. So, how can we as sport philosophers make a spiritual contribution to our field today? Through the collective unconscious of scholars, poets, physicists, mathematicians, sport philosophers, writers, athletes, Olympians, theologians, scripture, popes and sculptors a vast collection of descriptions or symbols reveals that play echoes to us, resonates within us from the origins of the universe.

If we are "hardwired to play" and play is part of the energy of God, shouldn't we be including the spiritual component in our writings, our coaching, our classrooms? Shouldn't we honor the vast collection of descriptions and symbols which reveal that play echoes to us, resonates within us from the origins of the universe, stemming from the Creator at the moment of Creation to us, *for us*? For if this energy continuum can be seen as plausible, then it is worth considering, for it fills a gap and aids the modern sport philosopher and future sport philosophers in understanding—where we have been, where we are, and where we are going—in that the impetus to play is intended to help us transcend our base nature and *advance* humankind as part of the energy of the expanding universe. Play matters, so play as if it matters . . .

## BIBLIOGRAPHY


Alignieri, D. (cited in Musa, M. Ed.) (1995) *The Portable Dante*, New York, USA: Pengiun.

Aquinas, T. (1981) *Summa Theological*, Notre Dame, IN, USA: Christian Classics, Ave Maria Press.

Bonaventure, Saint (1978) *The Classics of Western Spirituality*, Mahwah, NJ, USA: Paulist Press.

Campbell, J. (Ed.) (1982). *The Portable Jung*, New York: Penguin Books.

Capra, F. (1985) *The Tao of Physics: An Exploration of the Parallels between Modern Physics and Eastern Mysticism* (2nd ed.), Boston: Random House.

Capra, F., Steindl-Rast, D., & Matus, T. (1991) *Belonging to the Universe: Explorations on the Frontiers of Science and Spirituality*, San Francisco: Harper.

Ehrenreich, Barbara. (2006) *Dancing in the Streets*, New York: Henry Holt and Company.

Eliot, T.S. (1991) *Collected Poems*, 1909–1962, New York, USA: Harcourt Brace.

Fink, E. (1968) *The Ontology of Play*, New Haven, CT, USA: M&M Publishing.

Foer, F. (2003) *How Soccer Explains the World: An Unlikely Theory of Globalization*, New York: Harper Collins.

Freeman, E. (Ed.) (1912). *Man a Machine and the Natural History of the Soul—Julian Offray de la Mettrie*, Chicago: Open Court Publishing.

Greene, Brian. (1999) *The Elegant Universe: Superstrings, Hidden Dimensions, and the Quest for the Ultimate Theory*, New York: Random House.

Harris, J. (1994). *Athletes and the American Hero Dilemma*, Champaign, IL: Human Kinetics.

Hawking, S., & Mlodinow, L. (2005) *A Briefer History of Time*, New York: Bantam.

Huizinga, Johan. (1955). *Homo Ludens: A Study of the Play the Element in Culture*, Beacon.

John Paul II (2007) *Jubilee of Sports People*, Catholic Online, retrieved from http://www.catholic.org/international/international_story.php?id=32333

Jung, C.J. (1956a) *The Archetype and the Collective Unconscious: The Collected Works of C.J. Jung* (Bollington Series), Princeton, NJ: Princeton University Press.

Jung, C.J. (1956b) *The Undiscovered Self. The Collected works of C.J. Jung* (Bollington Series). Princeton, NJ: Princeton University Press.

Kretchmar, R.S. (1994). *Practical Philosophy of Sport and Physical Activity*, Champaign, IL: Human Kinetics.

Lederman, L., & Teresi, D. (1993) *The God Particle: If the Universe Is the Answer, What Is the Question?* New York, Boston: Houghton Mifflin.

Merleau-Ponty, M. (1962) *Phenomenology of Perception* (Colin Smith, Trans.), London: Routledge and Kegan Paul. (Original work published 1945)
Novak, M. (1976). *The Joy of Sports.* New York: Basic Books.
Pearce, Joseph C. (2002). *The Biology of Transcendence: A Blueprint of the Human Spirit*, VT: Park Street Press.
Saint Sing, S. (2004) *Spirituality of Sport: Balancing Body and Soul,* Cincinnati: St. Anthony Messenger Press.
Singh, S.S. (2003) Breakthrough Kinesis, *Quest*, 55(4): 306–314.
Tyson, N. de Grasse, & Goldsmith, D. (2004) *Origins: Fourteen Billion Years of Cosmic Evolution*, New York and London: Norton.
Wilson, D.S. (2002) *Darwin's Cathedral: Evolution, Religion, and the Nature of Society,* Chicago: Chicago University Press.

## Other Sources

Thomas Aquinas, *Summa Theologica,* collected works.
T.S. Elliot, *The Four Quartets,* collected works.
Albert Einstein, collected works.
*New York Times*, "Darwin's Cathedral," by Wilson.
*New English Bible*—Proverbs 8:27–31, Samuel, Mathew, and Genesis 1:26, 27.
*New American Bible*—Job 40:29, 41:22.
*Holman Christian Standard Bible*—Psalm 104:26, Exodus 15:20.
Bertrand Russell, collected works.

# 10 Zen, Movement and Sports

## Focusing on the Quality of Experiencing[1]

*Irena Martínková and Jim Parry*

At first glance, it may seem inappropriate to attempt to connect Zen and sports. To a layperson in the West,[2] Zen Buddhism is often considered a mystical religion that has nothing to do with the development of the human body and movement. On the other hand, to a Zen practitioner, it would seem unsuitable to associate Zen with sport and its promotion of development through competition, since this is antithetical to Zen's view of reality. How then can Zen and sport be reconciled? If we wish to relate these two approaches to human development, we need to set aside the abovementioned prejudices and discover what the two have in common. The common basis of Zen and sport which we shall propose, and with which we shall work in this text, is the focus on practice and the quality of experiencing.

Firstly, it is necessary to provide a brief introduction to Zen Buddhism, as it may not be familiar to the Western reader. It is impossible to fit Zen into Western categories. In the Western context, Zen is often referred to as a religion or as an Eastern philosophy. But if we understand religion as a set of beliefs and a relation to God, Zen cannot be referred to as a religion. Sometimes Zen is called a religion of no religion—it is not a religion in the sense that it does not have any set of beliefs, but rather allows us to get rid of beliefs altogether (Watts, 2000: 25, 121). However, neither is Zen a philosophy, describing what there is. In fact, in Zen, conceptual thinking is rejected because of the limitations of concepts. Concepts are considered as mere approximations of reality, which necessarily influence and modify our perception of reality. If Zen uses concepts, it is for purposes other than philosophy. For in philosophy concepts are meant to describe reality, to say how things are. Zen does not use concepts to describe reality but instead uses them to help practitioners to experience reality directly, without the mediation of concepts. What is important here is not the kind of *wisdom* that is kept in concepts and that is to be transferred to new generations, but rather the quality of *experiencing* of the practitioner. With regard to this, it may be suitable to refer to Zen as a way of liberation or a way of life or a 'path' (cp. Watts, 1957: 3).

## EXPERIENCING AND ZEN

As the main objective of this text is to explore the topic of experiencing in Zen and sport, let us firstly consider the process of our experiencing as Zen works with it. To do so, let us begin by exploring our everyday experiencing. Primarily we get to reality through different concepts that we do not even recognize as concepts, because we usually think that what we experience *is* reality. We do not usually think much about the *way* we experience, but rather are interested in *what* we experience, without feeling any requirement for reflection on the process of experiencing. However, we do not experience reality directly—rather, our experiencing derives from what we have learnt and from what we experience with our senses, which are also influenced by prior learning, and directed by our expectations, aims, wishes, etc. Thus our experiencing is not direct, but conditioned by various concepts. Concepts modify the sense experiences of reality and give us a different picture of what there is. Suzuki describes this with a following example:

> When we see a mountain, we do not see it in its suchness, but we attach to it all kinds of ideas, sometimes purely intellectual, but frequently charged with emotionality. When these envelop the mountain, it is transformed into something monstrous. This is due to our own indoctrination out of our 'scholarly' learning and our vested interests, whether individual, political, social, economic, or religious. The picture thus formed is a hideous one, crooked and twisted in every possible way. Instead of living in a world presented to the Primary Nature in its nakedness, we live in an artificial, 'cultured' one. The pity is that we are not conscious of the fact. (Suzuki, 1988: 175)

This kind of experiencing conditions our life, the way we are, the way we relate to others, the way we make our decisions, etc. It shapes our existence.

However, our experiencing does not have to be determined in this way. Zen can help us in this. One motif in Zen practice is to highlight the problems of experiencing in relation to concepts, leading to the dissolution of the concepts through which we experience. Gradually, through Zen practice, one starts to experience reality directly, becomes more and more fully immersed in immediate reality and through it remakes his or her life. Thus Zen offers a way out of our conventional conditioned experiencing, and leads to a direct experiencing of what there is, without 'capturing' it and fixing it with concepts.

Fixing objects is what concepts do, whereas in direct experiencing, reality is empty of form and is in perpetual flux (Nhat Hanh, 1988; Suzuki, 1988: 108). So, 'what there is' excludes fixed objects that we have captured from the flux of reality. To capture something would mean to alter this transient and continuously changing reality into an artificial and static form. Knowing this, the practitioner of Zen unlearns the habit of capturing and fixing things, while understanding that everything (including one's own self) is empty of form. However, it is necessary to note that emptiness and transience are also concepts in the face of a direct experiencing. Zen uses the concepts of emptiness and transience as suitable concepts for *approaching* direct experiencing. Thus, these concepts are to be abandoned, too.

Direct experiencing goes hand in hand with non-dual experiencing. Duality arises through conceptual thinking. Dualistic thinking means differentiating the 'unity of reality' and atomizing it. When this happens it often takes the form of preferring one differentiandum over another—sometimes, for example, as establishing two extremes (beauty and ugliness, good and evil), which encourages a tendency to prefer one extreme over the other as the appropriate one to pursue. When we abandon concepts, there are no opposites, no contradictions, nothing to pursue. This revelation changes one's life dramatically. (See more in Suzuki, 1988: 94; Watts, 2000: 38.)

The aim of Zen (that is, enlightenment or awakening in English, or *satori* in Japanese) relates to this state of direct and non-dual experiencing. Of course, any description of *satori* will again employ concepts that are meant to help us to understand what *satori* is. What *satori* is can be fully understood only in the experiencing of it. *Satori* is a radically different kind of experiencing in contrast to our common everyday experiencing, which relies on concepts; it opens an unexpected angle of perception:

> Whatever this is, the world for those who have gained a satori is no more the old world as it used to be; even with all its flowing streams and burning fires, it is never the same one again. Logically stated, all its opposites and contradictions are united and harmonized into a consistent organic whole. This is a mystery and a miracle, but according to the Zen masters such is being performed every day. Satori can thus be had only through our once personally experiencing it. (Suzuki, 2000: 230)

Nevertheless, to say that we gain *satori* is not an appropriate way of speaking about it. *Satori* is not to be 'gained'—rather, it is a way of experiencing that we already 'have,' and have always 'had,' but which is usually clouded by our concepts. The presupposition of Zen is that we are already enlightened, although we may be unaware of it, because our concepts obscure the possibility of experiencing the enlightened state (Dürckheim, 2001: 12; Watts, 1957: 154). Zen masters are examples of 'beings' who experience in this way. This radically different way of experiencing in enlightenment leads some to refer to Zen as a mystic religion, but, from the point of view of Zen, the state of enlightenment is our natural state.

## ZEN PRACTICE—ZEN MEDITATION

Zen practice is based on the abovementioned attitude. For attaining direct experiencing, various techniques are used. However, learning to experience directly is not like learning a new skill. Rather, it means to get rid of the concepts through which we normally experience. When no concept is left, the experiencing is direct. One of the techniques of breaking the hold of conceptual thinking is meditation. Although in different schools of Buddhism there are different ways of meditating, generally we can say that meditation is mediation to the immediate. The main characteristic of meditation in Zen Buddhism is that it does not have an object to relate to. It is not meditation about something, but rather it is meditation without any object. Therefore Zen meditation is not a kind of concentration in the usual sense of the word, but rather a quiet awareness of whatever happens (Watts, 1957: 155).

The meditation that is specific for Zen is called *zazen* (sitting meditation) or *kinhin* (walking meditation). In *zazen* one is advised to assume an upright sitting posture, but it should not be stiff. The hands rest on one's lap. The legs are either crossed with the feet soles upward on the thighs—that is, in a full lotus position (*kekkafuza*), and if this is not possible some easier position can be assumed, such as a half lotus position (*hankafuza*)—or the practitioner can be in a kneeling position (*seiza*) using a bench or a cushion (*zafu*). *Kinhin* is a walking meditation—the Japanese word *kinhin* means to 'go straight.' It is a very slow and smooth kind of walking as if one were standing in one place. From the waist up, the posture should be the same as that in *zazen*. In both *zazen* and *kinhin* the eyes are open and look about one meter to the front. They do not search for any object in particular, but rather bring awareness to the whole surrounding situation. The position itself is stable, but it is not a stiff but rather a dynamic stability (Hirai, 1997: 43).

*Zazen* is usually practiced in a room with few distractions. Thus one is taken from the common busy-ness of his or her everyday life with nothing to which to attach one's awareness. When sitting in *zazen* one's thoughts often become dominant. When thoughts emerge during a meditation, they should not be controlled. One should just leave them without pursuing them. The stable body position supports the quietness of the mind (Sekida, 2005). Maintaining the proper posture is generally sufficient to help to deepen breathing and to permit emotions and disturbances to subside.

When sitting or walking quietly, one can stop being busy with developing or following ideas, and can become aware of what is going on in the here and now. The mind gradually gets used to not creating thoughts and starts *doing nothing*. In this way, the mind becomes no-mind (*mushin*; Kamata, 1992: 22; Suzuki, 1988: 94). The no-mind is not limited, however, only to the mental state. It means experiencing with our entire being. *Not-doing* is not sleeping or dozing, but rather full awareness. In case the awareness is missing, the master overseeing the meditation comes with his stick (*keisaku*) and helps the practitioner regain awareness with a hit.

If this kind of meditation is hard to achieve for those who are used to constantly developing chains of thought, then meditation might be preceded by concentration. Concentration helps to stop the chain of thoughts and the various disturbances that arise through our attachments to our concepts. Concentration is realized through focusing one's attention on something, for example, on counting one's breaths (Hirai, 1997: 37ff). Then, when the object of concentration is taken away, the mind is not so busy with generating and following ideas as before, but is much more free to be quietly aware, without the distraction of concentration. As a result of meditation the mind gets used to not clinging to concepts, and one thus stays relaxed, flexible, joyful and open to new situations, allowing one to see what is there with one's naked senses (Watts, 2000: 121).

In this way the meditating person welcomes and encourages the enlightened state to arise. Because true Zen practice is a practice without any wish to gain enlightenment, it makes no sense to do something to bring the enlightenment about. Rather, through not-doing, the desired state can *happen* by itself, when favorable conditions for its arising have been established. That is also why Taisen Deshimaru (1993: 24) can say that *zazen* itself is *satori.* Watts explains this as follows:

> Whereas it might be supposed that the practice of Zen is a means to the end of awakening, this is not so. For the practice of Zen is not the true practice so long as it has an end in view, and when it has no end in view it is awakening—the aimless, self-sufficient life of the 'eternal now.' (Watts 1957: 154)

So, enlightenment arises during quietude—whilst thinking nothing and doing nothing. However, *zazen* and *kinhin* do not mean that in Zen one ends up sitting or slowly walking for the rest of one's life. Formal meditation just supports the awakening of direct experiencing. Practice does not mean a period of opposition to some real life, but rather the period of meditation is to be expanded into the whole life of the practitioner (Suzuki, 1988: 5). Through quietly sitting or walking, one gets used to this state and it comes to permeate all areas of life; and for this reason, we can speak of Zen as a way of life.

Kamata (1992: 23) says that Zen can create an infinity of forms. It can also be seen in moving forms, that is, in various forms of Japanese martial paths (*budō*). Let us have a look at the union of Zen and martial paths more closely.

## ZEN AND MARTIAL PATHS

The term *budō* is a term denoting certain Japanese martial paths,[3] which arose at the end of 19th and the beginning of 20th centuries and which deemphasized the lethal aspects of martial arts of samurai times in favor of educational purposes. Martial paths are influenced by Japanese culture and mainly by Shinto, Confucian, Daoist and Buddhist ideas. In the context of this chapter we will be talking about those Japanese martial paths (*budō*) that are closely connected to Zen Buddhism, as discussed, for example, in the works of Taisen Deshimaru, Eugen Herrigel, Shigeo Kamata and Daisetz T. Suzuki. However, the influence of Zen in relation to the many different schools of *budō* was variable. The schools most influenced by Zen were usually the *dōjō*[4] affiliated with Zen temples, while the teachings of the masters in the *dōjō* associated with local authorities were influenced to a lesser degree.

Zen was first accepted into the martial arts by the samurai of the Kamakura era (12th–14th centuries) because they sought a means to cope with death, since they always stood at its door, given the lethal character of their battles (Kamata, 1992: 23; Suzuki, 1988: 182). In order to accept one's own death, an understanding of the flowing and transient nature of reality, which supports the realization of the unfettered state of mind, was helpful:

> First, when a samurai faced his opponent, with his sword drawn, fear inevitably arose. What was the source of this fear? The opponent? The sword that was thrust toward him? The Buddhist response is that fear is created by one's own mind. The samurai had to conquer the fear within oneself before he could conquer the opponent. (Kiyota, 1990: 26)

Zen proved worthwhile for the practice of certain schools of samurai, and it considerably changed the practices of those samurai who accepted it. While samurai usually tried to master the techniques of their school, mastering a technique and winning a fight were not necessarily ends in themselves. This attitude is discussed, for example, by D.T. Suzuki in his book *Zen and Japanese Culture*, in which he presents a manuscript about the school 'The Sword of No-Abiding Mind' founded by Hariya Sekiun in the 17th century (Suzuki, 1988: 170 ff). For this school, the mastering of martial technique was a secondary thing; it was the same as mastering any other activity in everyday life. The most important thing was developing an understanding of the fundamental principle of life, which was sometimes described as 'Heavenly Reason' or 'Primary Nature,' which meant 'living in line with how things are'; that is, directly experiencing 'what there is.' Without this, even the most skilful swordsman was a slave to delusive thoughts, which would then influence his actions (disturbing thoughts, fear of death, striving for victories, etc.). The desired state was that of no conceptualization, no thinking—the state of enlightenment. In this state, everything would take care of itself:

> Sekiun now employed himself in learning how to perfect the art of swordsmanship along the line of Heavenly Reason or Primary Nature in the state of as-it-is-ness. He was convinced that such a principle was applicable to the art. One day he had a great awakening. He discovered

> that there was no need in swordplay to resort to the so-called technicality. When a man is enthroned in the seat of Heavenly Reason, he feels as if he were absolutely free and independent, and from this position he can cope most readily with all sorts of professional trickery. (Suzuki, 1988: 171)

Being enthroned in the state of no-mind (*mushin*), Sekiun became unbeatable by other swordsmen in his time.

With the end of the traditional four-tiered arrangement of Japanese society and thus with the end of the class of warriors in the late 19th century, martial techniques could no longer withstand the competition from new martial equipment and strategies. However, the martial techniques did not disappear and some of them evolved into *budō*. The aim of *budō* lies no longer in the winning of deadly fights but in the education of the human being. And in those *budō* that are closely related to Zen, the direction of this education is obviously derived from the Zen Buddhist point of view. In this context the Chinese/Japanese character *dō* can be understood as a path toward enlightenment.

The no-mind that is nurtured in Zen is of great importance for fighting. When one fights, one needs to be ready and open to what is happening at that very moment. When the mind is attracted to an object and stops on it, instead of flowing freely along with the whole situation, an 'opening' or 'stopping' is caused. Similarly, any clinging to the past or preparing for the future leads to an 'opening,' which results in an inadequate reaction. 'Stopping' thus causes disturbances in direct experiencing, with the emergence of different kinds of disturbing feelings, desires, moods, worries and thoughts (Kamata, 1992: 89; Suzuki, 1988: 95 ff). Any 'stopping' causes delay, which can be used by the opponent for an efficient counterattack. For example, a thought that leads to a prepared strategy can be misleading and countereffective, if the situation develops differently than expected. Worries may prevent one from fighting with one's full engagement, or desires may make one too impatient to act in an appropriate way. Without direct experiencing one becomes vulnerable and an easy target for an opponent. On the other hand, when the present moment is not disturbed by an expectation or a conceptual thought, reactions become adequate and timely. When the response to an attack is not prepared in advance nor blurred by thinking, and the mind is open to what is just happening, the reactions are spontaneous and, as innumerable Zen stories tell, enormously efficient.

This way of thinking influenced the actual practice of those *budō* that adapted the Zen way of thinking. Though in *budō* training, *zazen* may be used before the practice of techniques, the principles of Zen are used throughout the entire practice session. In *budō*, it is usually the endless polishing of one's techniques that invites the state of no-mind to settle in. *Budō* always put an emphasis on mastering the basics; the practice then consists, for example, of repeating the same movement for long periods of time towards the perfection of the whole movement (Donohue, 2005). For example, in archery it might be shooting into a target of 80 centimeters in diameter from a distance of 3 meters for a period of 3 years (Dürckheim, 2002: 30). This is no challenge and thus any pursuit of aims (e.g., hitting the target) is excluded and, in this way, the actual process of practice can come to the fore. During this long period of time, the body is regaining its balance, while one's thoughts settle down. On the whole the mind stops being active in producing thoughts and attaching itself to them, or to different objects that it recognizes, and frees itself to doing nothing, while mirroring the unblurred present moment (the here and now).

In *budō*, there is a specific approach to the control of movement. At first, attention is paid to the control of breathing and to the relaxing of unnecessary tensions. Through this control, however, a spontaneity of action arises. Spontaneity arises when the mind is flowing (no-mind) and not restricted (or 'stopped') by subjective thoughts, concepts and emotions. The movements are no longer initiated or controlled by the conscious self, but are direct reactions to what is happening here and now. Thus control is not the aim but is the means towards spontaneous action, which is often described as fluent, effortless, joyful, timely and efficient.

Nowadays, *budō* are not nearly as dangerous as the martial arts from which they developed, because of the safety precautions and protective gear commonly used. The majority of injuries now are usually caused by inadvertent or accidental contact with the opponent. Even though *budō* are no longer meant to be lethal practices, the idea of having one's life at stake has remained, but in a different sense—it is not simply 'life' in the sense of survival but rather the fully lived life, in the sense of the direct experiencing of reality. In Zen as well as in the martial paths, the state of no-mind is important since it is the nonillusory and natural way to be. With mature masters, the whole process of fighting is then not only perfect but also effortless, enormously efficient and last but not least beautiful to watch. The movement is flowing—responsive without stopping to whatever appears. In this way, the *process* of movement within the practice of *budō* is highlighted, while the *aims* gradually disappear.

## EXPERIENCING IN SPORT

In the previous section, we tried to show that Zen can be meaningfully applied to *budō*, and we discussed a specific kind of experiencing that is promoted in relation to Zen and *budō*. However, Zen practice is not restricted to formal practice, but is supposed to pertain to the whole life of a practitioner. Anything that one does (that does not require conceptual thought) can be done in the Zen way (Watts, 2000: 57 ff). Now we shall describe experiencing in sport and then we shall show how the Zen approach to sport could enrich an athlete.

At the beginning of this chapter it was said that we usually approach and experience 'reality' first and foremost through various concepts that we do not recognize as concepts because we think that what we directly experience is reality itself. This applies not only to intellectual activities but to any activities. Concepts direct our lives, and sport practice is no exception, so we should not be surprised that athletes' experiencing is informed and shaped by certain concepts that are based on more general concepts from outside of sport; among the most obvious being the importance of success, victory, self-affirmation, constant improvement and so on. These concepts support instrumental thinking in athletes, which influences their experiencing as well as the process of their performance. And whilst under the influence of these concepts, athletes are led away from experiencing the here and now, from experiencing the actual process of movement.

When athletes are led by these concepts, which produce attachments to expected ends (such as the importance of victory or the outcome) and/or which are related to past experiences (e.g., past defeat), it results in the generation of distracting expectations, ideas and emotions. An overemphasis on outcomes in sport (just as in daily life) puts enormous tensions on the performance of an athlete, and it disables him or her from performing in the best possible way. In turn, this influences the overall experiencing of the athlete, because expectations and distractions modify both the process of one's performance and also one's experiencing of it. Unable to be in the here and now, the athlete is likely to underperform, but also is likely to take an approach that underestimates the importance of the process.

Instrumental thinking in sport affects the quality of the movement itself. In this way, one's movement becomes just a means to some end (expected outcomes, concepts that motivate towards participation, etc). On the other hand, a concern with process emphasizes the quality of the movement itself, independently of ends and outcomes. Recall the earlier example of the archer who attends to the process of shooting, rather than its outcome.

Consider, for example, the question of balance: in sport, the general approach is that the overall balance of the athlete should be in focus just so far as it is required to support the necessary performance. That is to say: when movement is just a means towards an achievement, the actual quality of the human movement depends on the various levels of competition. This might be a complicated mixture of elements such as the following: the ranking of the league or tournament; the abilities of the competitors involved; the particular 'external' circumstances of the contest (weather, quality of conditions or equipment, etc.); the particular 'internal' circumstances of the contest (near the beginning or near the end; when one is winning or losing; when one has a particular opportunity, when a particular victory is of special or overwhelming importance) and so on. Therefore, usually, no more care is given to the quality of movement than is necessary for outperforming others in particular circumstances and, in fact, to give more care might even be seen as wasteful or inefficient. This is because instrumental thinking tends to be comparative, in the sense that the performance required for victory on a particular occasion is always comparative to another person's performance at that time. In this way, the end 'justifies' the means—the performance of the athlete has only to be 'good enough' to achieve its end—it does not necessarily have to be excellent (we can perform quite poorly, but still win).

To summarize, the conceptual thinking which gives rise to the instrumentality of sport is problematic because it overemphasizes results and underemphasizes process. When the end is more highly valued than the means, process becomes just a means to a goal. When the end overrides the means, the athlete fails to pay adequate attention to the means of his or her performance—to the quality of his or her movements. In this way athletes make themselves, as well as other beings, into an instrument for their aims; and thus may fail to treat themselves in an acceptable way, perhaps even harming themselves or others. This kind of approach also influences the quality of the athlete's experiencing, since experiencing which is driven by concepts and instrumentality differs from direct, nonconceptual experiencing, and may disallow the fluent, effortless, joyful, timely and efficient performance that flows from it.

## ZEN IN SPORT

We would like to show here that the Zen approach can enrich the sport experience by addressing the problem of conceptual thinking and the resultant instrumentality. At first glance it seems that the meanings of Zen and sport differ profoundly—sport is about performance and achievement, while Zen is about enlightenment. However, we think that it is possible to relate Zen to sport, because both are about the development of the human being and because both require an experiential basis. Without Zen practice one cannot learn what Zen is about. The same is valid for sport. One cannot learn what, for example, a long jump is about from merely reading about it or watching others performing it. Also, in Zen just as in sport, attention to the quality of one's movement is important, which is especially apparent in *budō* practice.

The Zen approach can highlight the importance of the process of movement in sport, drawing fresh attention to the quality of movement, emphasizing the necessity of balancing one's whole movement, and gradually leading to full immersion in the here and now. In this way, the Zen approach within sport can help to reduce an overemphasis on the outcomes of the performance, whose consequences include many problematic side effects, such as cheating, rule bending, harming others, injuries, treating members of the opposite team as enemies, taking performance enhancing drugs, and so on.

This emphasis on process is often difficult to draw to the attention of athletes, since the results of performance—both in terms of the internal and external goals of sport—are of immense importance to them. But if athletes are led to perform in the Zen way, with the focus on performing the movement in a relaxed and aimless way, every move gradually becomes more flowing, effortless and efficient without imbalances and perturbations from concepts. When thinking is extinguished, then nothing constrains and controls the movement. Unlearning the ingrained habit of living according to one's concepts changes one's experiencing. In the unconceptualized here and now, the athlete's movement is not limited by his or her subjective concepts any more, and becomes fluent, effortless and spontaneous in reacting to whatever arises in the situation. There is no individual human being who controls the activity, but the activity happens by itself:

> When the ultimate perfection is attained, the body and limbs perform by themselves what is assigned to them to do with no interference from the mind. The scarecrow, in imitation of a human figure, is erected in the middle of the rice paddies, holding a bow and arrow as if ready to shoot, and seeing this birds and animal are frightened away. This human figure is not endowed with a mind, but it scares away the deer. The perfect man who has attained the highest stage of training may be likened to this—all is left to the [unconscious and reflexive] activities of the body and limbs, whilst the mind itself stops, at no points, and with no objects.' (Suzuki, 1988: 100)

This can be compared to some of the activities of our everyday life. We do not have to control our legs to run—they know how to do it. But, unlike in everyday life, one learns that in the Zen way one is not influenced even to the extent of telling them the right direction, as all movement is balanced and flows in line with 'the pulsation of Reality' (Suzuki, 1988: 9).

In the end, we can ask a more fundamental question: Why promote the abovementioned experiencing in sport? Even though Zen could be applied to sport practice, why do so? It is because the Zen approach can bring to athletes a joyfulness, a fluency, an effortlessness and incidentally also an efficient and improved performance. Practicing sports in the Zen spirit can support the improved performance that we would normally desire through our practice of sport, without focusing on those ends—without attending to them. A perfect performance is then born out of perfect practice, and it is, as is described in Daoism, a 'marvelous' activity (Watts, 1957: 134). However, the performance is not intended to be 'perfect' nor to be compared to other performances. Just as in martial paths, an excellent performance is just an external proof of something that is more important; that is, the transformation of the practitioner (Dürckheim, 2002: 31; Herrigel, 1953: 8).

## NOTES

1. This chapter was written with support from a research grant from the Ministry of Education, Youth and Sports MSM 0021620864, Czech Republic.
2. We will use the words 'West/Western' when referring to the Euro-American cultural context, while the terms 'East/Eastern' will be reserved for the East Asian countries that have Zen Buddhism in their tradition.
3. It is necessary to distinguish martial paths (*budō*) from martial arts. Martial paths developed at the end of 19th and the beginning of 20th centuries from martial arts.
4. *Dōjō* is a place for the practice of *budō* and at the same time the term also means the site of enlightenment (Kiyota, 1990: 19).

## BIBLIOGRAPHY


Deshimaru, T. (1993) *L'anneau de la voie*, Paris: Albin Michel.

Donohue, J.J. (2005) Modern Educational Theories and Traditional Japanese Martial Arts Training Methods, *Journal of Asian Martial Arts*, 14: 2, 8–29.

Dürckheim, K. (2001) *Wunderbare Katze und andere Zen-Texte*, Bern, München, Wien: Scherz Verlag.

Dürckheim, K. (2002) *Hara. Zemský střed člověka*, Praha: Dobra.

Herrigel, E. (1953) *Zen in the Art of Archery*, London: Routledge and Kegan Paul.

Hirai, T. (1997) *Zazen*, Prague: CAD Press.

Kamata, S. (1992) *Zen and Aikido*, Tokyo, Aiki News.

Kiyota, M. (1990) Buddhist Thought in *Kendō* and *Bushidō*: The Tenshin Shōden School of Swordsmanship, in M. Kiyota and H. Kinoshita (Eds.), *Japanese Martial Arts and American Sports. Cross-Cultural Perspectives on Means to Personal Growth*, Tokyo: Nihon University, 17–28.

Nhat Hanh, T. (1988) *The Heart of Understanding*, Berkeley, CA: Parallax Press.

Sekida, K. (2005) *Zen Training: Methods and Philosophy*, Boston and London: Shambhala.

Suzuki, D.T. (1988) *Zen and Japanese Culture*, Boston; Rutland, VT; Tokyo: Tuttle Publishing.

Suzuki, D.T. (2000) *Essays in Zen Buddhism: First Series*, New Delhi: Munshiram Manoharlal Publishers.

Watts, A.W. (1957) *The Way of Zen*, New York: Pantheon Books.

Watts, A.W. (2000) *What Is Zen?* Novato, CA: New World Library.

# 11 Pilgrimage as a Form of Physical and Movement Spirituality

*Ivo Jirásek*

There are many words on a continuum from tourism to pilgrimage for such activities as hiking, wandering, walking, journeying and so on. Some of them are closer to 'profane' activities from the point of view of human experiencing (with the cognitive or enjoyable and pleasant aspects of traveling dominating), while some of them are more closely related to the 'sacred' path (and in this case, a spiritual interest is more important for the itinerant). However, some aspects are common to all of them: bodily endeavor and effort, the adventure that comes with difficulties and the challenge met in foreign places.

In this chapter I want to show that pilgrimage is not only a topic of religion or history, and that religious passion is not even necessary for such a journey. An opportunity for us in sport studies (kinanthropology), leisure studies (recreology) or tourism lies in stressing the possible deeper levels of traveling rather than just taking pictures of places visited or shopping for souvenirs. For example, a sensitivity toward nature is just the kind of spirituality without religious attitude which is often connected with human movement. Walking as such could be a good way to explore physical and movement spirituality.

Relations between tourism and pilgrimage have been seriously considered not only in a specific issue of *Annals of Tourism Research* (e.g., Rinschede 1992 19:1) but also in many other texts. However, the distinguishing attribute of the journey seems to be understood by the majority of researchers as the traveler's aim or motivation. If the religious motive prevails, the journey can be defined as a pilgrimage, whereas if a profane motive is primary, it is rather tourism.

The fact that there is behavioral continuity between both extremes was underlined by Cohen (1979), who elaborated a model of five different modes of tourism, distinguished by their relation to the individual's 'spiritual' (as well as cultural and social) center. The notion of 'center' has Eliade's (2006) meaning: not some hypothetical geographic center, but rather the center which for the individual symbolizes ultimate meanings.

*The Recreational Mode* is characteristic of travelers who look firstly for enjoyment and well-being in their journeys. They leave their own 'center' but don't look for another. They look for relief and relaxation, not spirituality. They travel to get relief and to find curiosities; they do not require re-creation (in another 'center'), but rather the regeneration of their powers for their everyday lives, and the renewal of adherence to the meaningfulness of their own center.

*The Diversionary Mode* is the characteristic mode of a postmodern person: he or she wants to avoid alienation in everyday existence, but not to find meaning. The postmodern person, characterized by existential vacuum and the absence of life meaning (Frankl 1994, 1997), looks for enjoyment in meaningless pleasure.

*The Experiential Mode* is a typical mode of a tourist looking for knowledge, in particular looking for inspiration in the meaning of others' lives. This does not mean a renewal of his or her own spirituality, or a search for authenticity in his or her own life, but rather a confirmation that others' experience can be really authentic. It is not a way of confirming his or her own mode of spirituality, but rather it is a contact with "otherness." Such a tourist doesn't feel as if he or she is a pilgrim, but watches with interest the authenticity of the other's experience.

*The Experimental Mode* characterizes the traveler who has lost his spiritual center (e.g., that of his own society) and looks for an alternative. Such a tourist wants to try to experiment with the authenticity of other societies' spirituality not only to watch passively but to experience it. Looking for himself or herself, however, has the effect of extending the findings of any response to this question, and so such searching and everlasting traveling can become a way of life, an effort to find new and ever newer possibilities without choosing just one of them.

*The Existential Mode* is a mode of tourism equal to pilgrimage. It is a search for authentic experience by the confirmation of a spiritual center of one's own culture and society, which might also be perceived somewhere else than in the place of one's residence. However, this could also take the form of a 'conversion'—the selection of another center, with the intention of leaving one's center permanently, accepting the values and experience of the other culture (as documented by Sharpley & Sundaram, 2005).

These models are not clearly defined, but they do create a certain line of continuum, along which it is possible to move. In various sections of his/her journey a traveler can then adopt a different mode, from pilgrimage to recreational tourism, depending on the given concrete experiences in this or that section of the journey.

Cohen's model is widely discussed and accepted. However, I would like to propose a different way of understanding this situation, which suggests a tourist-pilgrim continuum not with regard to the aim and motivation but to the way of behavior of a particular traveler at a certain place. The principal difference lies in the whether I arrive at a certain place only to see it or record it, and get just a shallow and first-sight impression; or whether I come prepared, ready, open, with a willingness to try to experience every possibility that is available at this place.

My proposal is based on a possibility of certain specification or 'classification' of tourist modes, or 'kinds' of tourism, in regard to the aims and motives of participants, which are, however, quite different from Cohen's model. For example, we use the terms "conference tourism" and "sex tourism" (which is a major problem—not only ethical, but also political) (Brennan, 2004; Pettman, 1997) and which cannot, however, be simplified as violence of men to women (Jeffreys, 2003; Sanchez Taylor, 2006). In the literature we often meet the terms "ecotourism" (Stronza, 2001; West & Carrier, 2004), "ethnic tourism" (Greathouse Amador, 1997) and "heritage tourism" (Yiping Li, 2003).

In a certain way, too, "space tourism" (Sawaya, 2004) or "traveling to frontiers" (Laing & Crouch, 2005) or expeditions and courses of Outward Bound (Daniel, 2007; Heintzman, 2003) are undoubtedly connected to spirituality or obtaining some deep experience. Moreover, some of the tourists' journeys can be perceived as a pilgrimage, but it is difficult to disambiguate these categories (Allcock, 1988; Sharpley & Sundaram, 2005), since "pilgrimage" does not have a clear description either. Besides classical "religious pilgrimage," that is, visits to religious centers, we can distinguish, for example, "cultural pilgrimages," which are journeys to cultural and arts monuments of the history, and also "political pilgrimages"—visits to places connected with war events or politicians activities (Cohen, 1979: 191). We can even unify both modes and consider "pilgrimage tourism" (Collins-Kreiner & Kliot, 2000), or relativize the boundary by the terms "secular pilgrimage" or "sacred tourism" (Singh, 2005) or "pilgrimage as tourism" (Rountree, 2002). However, I consider that comparing a trip to an entertainment center to a religious pilgrimage is far too simple a view, which does not respect the specifics of the sacred and the profane.

The definition of the line between pilgrimage and tourism loses its exactness and becomes even more unclear when we consider new aspects of the religious life in modern times. Religious phenomena are not easily classified within the framework of organized religious systems, but rather they are diffused and interconnected. Besides the traditional religions, the popularity of gnosticism as well as paganism, shamanism, witchcraft and various other cultic and spiritual practices seems to be on the increase. Trips to Neolithic monuments are organized, and inspiration is delivered by ethnic cults with rituals using, for example, African drums or Australian musical instruments, walking over fire, and so on.

The search for spirituality in a society thirsty for values thus leads many individuals towards searching for a kind of universal wisdom that can be explored in a plurality of forms which are available in various parts of the world. The inexactness of specifying pilgrims' versus tourists' behavior is documented by Rountree (2002) on journeys around goddess relics in Europe. On what basis do researchers differentiate individual modes? Who classifies "correctly" a certain journey as a tourist trip or a pilgrimage? Surely it is on the basis of the aims and motives which are notified to researchers by the travelers themselves (Collins-Kreiner & Kliot, 2000; Rountree, 2002; Sharpley & Sundaram, 2005).

It is even possible to search for certain demographic or socioeconomic factors:

> Those who defined themselves as "pilgrims" tended to describe themselves as belonging to a low socio-economic group, while those who described themselves as "tourists" tended to depict themselves as belonging to a high socio-economic group. (Collins-Kreiner & Kliot, 2000: 59)

Whether a respondent makes a decision in this or that way depends exclusively on his/her feelings and experience. The basis for my proposal is to underline this experience even more. I am not aiming at an exact classification, but rather at defining meaning fields in which we can meet behavior which is typical either of tourists or of pilgrims. I don't want to differentiate tourism from pilgrimage, but rather the tourist's behavior from the pilgrim's behavior.

Firstly, let's look at what they have in common. Naturally, the primary common attribute is traveling—leaving home and going back, the utilization of transport modes and services which are connected with traveling. At a time of easy accessibility to any place on the world, that is, in terms of globalization, the element of risks, danger and overcoming of barriers by one's own powers is reduced. I think that this is the moment which will later be worth special attention. Nevertheless, certain difficulties and strains remain undoubtedly connected with both modes. Souvenirs and memories from journeys (photographs, statues, meretricious objects and other memorabilia) are not characteristic only of tourists either—badges, pictures and pilgrims' marks have been brought home by pilgrims since old times. Naturally, we could find many more common characteristics, but this is fully sufficient for our needs now.

Secondly, let's look at ways in which they differ:

## 1. Aim of the Journey

If researchers agree more or less with the fact that the aim, intention or motive is the matter that distinguishes a tourist from a pilgrim, I agree with them. However, comparing to descriptive differentiation of religious and secular motivation (i.e., a religious aim of the journey, e.g., a place connected with a prophet of a certain religion, with wonders, with cults etc., versus a profane area which is not used by a cult of a concrete religious system), I would like to stress the point of the element of behavior. I think that a typical attribute of the tourist is his/her aim *to see* certain monuments (religious or profane), while the pilgrim's behavior shows rather forms of *experiencing*. A decisive aspect to differentiate the tourist and the pilgrim is not a geographic place, as even seemingly profane places not connected with the cult (not only natural curiosities) can offer certain possibility of musing , thinking, deep experience and certain exaltation—and these are attributes of spirituality.

## 2. Attuning

While a tourist arrives at (more often than walks to) a concrete place to *record* the seen picture, that is, the photograph, or at least to put it into his/her memory in a form of remembrances, or to bring a certain souvenir as a document of the place visited (the document not only for him/herself, but also for others who are necessary to share the journey with), a pilgrim concentrates on *a present experience*. The souvenirs brought are to remind him only of what happened, but they are not the substantial thing. The most important is attuning to a certain space. The openness to *genius loci*. If the tourist arrives to grasp a first-sight visual impression, the pilgrim attunes him/herself concentratedly in a visited place. He/she tries to grasp it not through visualization, but through complex experience.

## 3. Mode of Experience

The tourist looks for enjoyment and happiness. These experience states can be found in completely equipped centers, in ease and relaxation, but also in dynamic motion, in movement from one place to another or in getting knowledge. The pilgrim's experience, however, is rather based on passion, where pleasure and happiness are rather a consequence, resulting from perceiving the visited place in its fullness and complexity. The pilgrim's experience is defined in more substantial terms than simply a visualized proof—rather by perceiving with all senses the message that is represented by the place itself.

## 4. Approach to a Question

The tourist is looking for answers. He/she wants to see the magnetism that attracts crowds of people to the most popular and most ideal places. He/she wants to assure him/herself that the travel agencies' recommendations are valid—so that the question "Is it really so beautiful there?" has a clear answer that will be provided to him by his/her senses. However, the pilgrim relies on the questioning itself—he/she is immersed in the question, which is more important than any answer. He/she has not got a predefined question, because the journey to the place and the stay there are themselves a kind of questioning—in a way exploring step-by-step the specifics of the place and its spirit. Our personal engagement, our feeling of the energy of the place, our concentration on its exceptionality—these are not only visual but experiential.

## 5. Focus

The tourist's attention is volatile, jumping from one attraction to another, watching details in a shallow way without a necessity to synthesize them. On the contrary, the pilgrim's attention is concentrated on the wholeness of being (not only sensual relief), for the more interconnections that are discovered within a given place, the more the pilgrim can create a unique unity of personality, place and time. A personal unity without analytic segmentation of physical states from ideal devotion or social relations, but the experience of oneself as a personal unity which is fully integrated into the context of the place, that is, Heidegger's full being-in-the-world, enabling authentic existence.

If we summarize these five constitutive elements, these five experiential modes, which are too abstract in themselves, we can get a basic dichotomy of the tourist's approach versus the pilgrim's one to a selected place, not on the basis of a previous intention (motive) to perceive the journey as religious or profane, but on the basis of different criteria from those that had attracted researchers' attention up to now.

The identifying aspect, which is more important than an initial intention, more substantial than even a concrete visited place, is the mode of experience. Visualization and efforts at volatile picture recording of shallow attributes for the future are the tourist's approach, while the pilgrim's mode is a full attuning to a question which is said by the place to the person who is willing to open him/herself to it, and perceive in a concentrated way the energy of the place. It is not our acceptance of or involvement in a concrete religious system that is important, but the will to perceive the energy of the place with our whole being.

If we accept this view, if we stress the point about experiencing visited places as central for tourists' and pilgrims' journeys, then other aspects will be only external, shallow and unimportant. It is not a label of a name that we assign to a certain journey which is substantial here, but the experience that can be brought to us. A traveler might feel like a pilgrim just because he/she is going to visit a holy place of his/her religion and faith, but he/she can end up approaching the journey only in a tourist way.

However, he/she will visit the place; he/she will see and maybe record it but not *experience* it. The journey will not fulfill its symbolic spiritual purpose, because the necessary attuning and openness towards the given place will not be realized. On the contrary, the tourist who comes to the place that offers a spiritual dimension (and it doesn't have to be a purely religious center, but, for example, a natural curiosity that contributes to a deep authentic experience of a nature value, or a cultural building which is famous for its cultural value) without any previous intention can get an enriching spiritual impulse, regardless of whether he/she expects it at first place, and regardless of whether this place has religious significance for him/her, or even of whether he/she confesses a certain religion or not. Because the experience itself, its devotion, connection of personality with space, attuning and full being in the "here and now" decides the spiritual value of the stay.

The parallel can be found with rituals and ceremonies. Mostly, pilgrims participate in cultic ceremonies characteristic of a concrete place (prayer, sacrifices, supplication and other symbolic activities). If, however, they participate only in an external form, without involvement of the whole personality, they can certainly consider themselves as participants, but they cannot get the full value which the ceremony offers for those who are fully "immersed" in them, who become part of it, who experience it with full self-devotion. This interiorization of the place and time, not a shallow external participation, characterizes the distinction differentiating a full-value participation in the ceremony from its external (and maybe socially ostentatious) visually proved participation, but which is without deep internal authentic experience.

What such a distinction enables is the transfer of the same point of view also to the journey itself, not only to its aim, that is, the way of experience not only of a certain selected religious center or natural area with a deep spiritual impulse, but also to the motion itself, to the course of traveling. Because the thing that contributes to the concentration, to devotion, openness towards the visited place, to a full experience and not only its external visualization is time and motion. Time is necessary for the required preparation and attuning. Naturally, it is not possible to visit a certain place profitably without a previous attuning of ideas and a search for some understandings of it.

Naturally, though it is not possible to visit several places at a certain distance from one another during, say, one hour and suppose that those places can tell us all the content which is symbolically anchored in them. Without the willingness to invest sufficient time we cannot experience the journey in the pilgrim's mode of full experience. And motion, in particular physical movement that can contribute to attuning even more, is a factor that puts into the shade the time values of the travel industry. Adequate time can multiply the value of the visited place.

I don't want to state that the pilgrim's experience can be obtained exclusively by walking, while visiting a far destination by plane will make a deep experience impossible. This is certainly not the case, but, nevertheless, the constraints which appear when insufficient time and physical movement are assigned can interfere with an adequate understanding of the place in an authentic and in a significant way. Therefore the final part of the paper must mention the possibilities of the basic mode of the pilgrim's travel—walking.

Spirituality without a religious frame, that is, spirituality potentially existing in spheres that are usually considered profane, is absolutely evident in nature. A significant tree, well, rock—and also the sea, a storm or other gusts of energy forces have been understood as of spiritual origin, or spiritual significance from ancient times. They have been seen as holy places—as a place visited by the gods. Even a nonreligious person can feel the force of such a natural place or event, and it is a commonplace. Such an experience is conditioned by attuning to the place, with a sensitivity of perceiving. However, not only sensitivity towards nature can be a document of spirituality independent of religion. We are interested especially in the area of movement culture, in the area of physical movement.

Walking as such could be a good way to explore physical and movement spirituality. A pilgrimage requires sufficient physical strength and durability, self-denial and overcoming pain and loss, combining frequent danger with long-lasting trips. Each effort which leads to some marked-out goal is also a kind of pilgrimage. Each trip where we have to concentrate and sacrifice ourselves in some fashion (perhaps our fatigue, pain and discomfort), when we concentrate on a point which awaits us, when we look forward to something and prepare for it, when we focus perhaps with some effort at that locale and are able to get in tune with it—this is also a kind of pilgrimage. It is only with that kind of preparation that we can see and perceive, only with that kind of wandering can we truly understand and deeply experience something.

Or even, as Rupert Sheldrake (1994: 169) claims, I can actually strengthen that kind of place with energy, while tourists only suck energy away through their preoccupied presence. I would also agree with his faith that "a great deal of good would come about if tourists became pilgrims once again." In this fashion a tourist would become the secular form of a pilgrim (tourism would become a kind of true wandering) as opposed to merely moving from one place to another, in a kind of impatient and anxious roaming. Instead, the tourist would allow the visited locale to have an effect on him or her, with an attempt at authentic experiencing.

> In the present day of total mobility and the automobile nature of society, walking and pilgrimaging related to it, have been rediscovered not only as a short-term form of relaxation, but also as a forgotten way of natural communication which makes a deeper connection with nature possible as well as with oneself. (Zemánek, 2005: 9)

Is that spirituality? Perhaps it is. It is a spiritual level which does not require a religious dimension. Not every pilgrimage, or every trip in the labyrinth of the world, has to lead us to the otherworldly paradise of our heart, which consists of God's presence. We can remain unaffected by this method of experience as "*we are not given the gift of faith.*" This does not mean, however, that we cannot sufficiently realize the unique nature and strength of the place to which we wander, experience its holiness and enriching calm. It is definitely not a coincidence that seeking spirituality and its connection with physical movement has become a theme which has met with increased interest. The value-lacking and unanchored postmodern world is looking for new ways to obtain firm support. Perhaps some of us can actually find it in sport and physical activity and its potential spiritual dimension, as the existential vacuum in which we live is unsatisfying. Life in even the most atheist country can thus acquire a new dimension through the means of new ideological impulses, with possibilities for concentration and genuineness, the power of spirituality in sport performance.

The open society in which we live is a labyrinth of numerous possibilities which we have at our disposal. Nothing is forbidden; everything is allowed.

But if everything is allowed, what is most important and what is less essential? Which of the possibilities should we go for? We have lost a central point for decision making (as no general accepted values exist) and this gives us much more demanding requirements, placing us in unanchored situations. We are thrown into the labyrinth of all possibilities, where we have to choose from only some of them, but at the same time we lack any generally accepted criteria for choice. In this kind of situation, with the constant consuming and collecting of flat experiences (which can simply be bought), even the extremely ordinary equipment of a small rucksack and setting out on a trip can help—as a "*pilgrim with a light heart*," without attempts at trying to transform the world, without the need to make more money once again. With only one's own courage and faith, with the desire to see as much as possible of the labyrinth of the world and get to know it as deeply as possible. With an attempt at not only visiting and seeing, but also first and foremost finding inspiration, feeling and deep experiencing.

## BIBLIOGRAPHY


Allcock, J.B. (1988) Tourism as a Sacred Journey, *Society and Leisure*, 11(1): 33–48.

Brennan, D. (2004) Women Work, Men Sponge, and Everyone Gossips: Macho men and Stigmatized/ing Women in a Sex Tourist Town, *Anthropological Quarterly*, 77(4): 705–733.

Cohen, E. (1979) A phenomenology of Tourist Experiences, *Sociology*, 13: 179–201.

Collins-Kreiner, N., & Kliot, N. (2000) Pilgrimage Tourism in the Holy Land: The Behavioural Characteristics of Christian Pilgrims, *GeoJournal*, 50: 55–67.

Daniel, B. (2007) The Life Significance of a Spiritually Oriented, Outward Bound–Type Wilderness Expedition, *Journal of Experiential Education*, 29(3): 386–389.

Doron, A. (2005) Encountering the "Other": Pilgrims, Tourists and Boatmen in the City of Varanasi, *The Australian Journal of Anthropology*, 16(2): 157–178.

Frankl, V. (1994) *Člověk hledá smysl: úvod do logoterapie* [*Human Looping for Meaning: The Introduction into Logotherapy*]. Praha: Psychoanalytické nakladatelství J. Kocourek.

Frankl, V. (1997) *Vůle ke smyslu: vybrané přednášky* [*Will to Meaning: Chosen Lectures*]. Brno: Cesta.

Eliade, M. (2006) *Posvátné a profánní* [*Sacral and Profane*]. Praha: OIKOYMENH.

Greathouse Amador, L.M. (1997) Ethnic, Cultural, and Eco Tourism, *The American Behavioral Scientist*, 40(7): 936–943.

Gupta, V. (1999) Sustainable Tourism: Learning from Indian Religious Traditions, *International Journal of Contemporary Hospitality Management*, 11(2/3): 91. Retrieved June 29, 2007, from http://proquest.umi.com/pqdweb?did=115921216&sid=1&Fmt=3&clientld=45082&RQT=309&VName=PQD

Heintzman, P. (2003) The Wilderness Experience and Spirituality: What Recent Research Tells Us, *JOPERD*, 74(6): 27–32.

Jeffreys, S. (2003) Sex Tourism: Do Women Do It Too? *Leisure Studies*, 22: 223–238.

Laing, J.H., and Crouch, G.I. (2005) Extraordinary Journeys: An Exploratory Cross-Cultural Study of Tourists on the Frontier, *Journal of Vacation Marketing*, 11(3): 209–223.

Moore, A. (1980) Walt Disney World: Bounded Ritual Space and the Playful Pilgrimage Center, *Anthropological Quarterly*, 53(4): 207–218.

Pettman, J.J. (1997) Body Politics: International Sex Tourism, *Third World Quarterly*, 18(1): 93–108.

Rinschede, G. (1992) Forms of religious tourism, *Annals of Tourism Research*, 19(1): 51–67.

Rountree, K. (2002) Goddess Pilgrims as Tourists: Inscribing the Body through Sacred Travel, *Sociology of Religion*, 63(4): 475–496.

Sanchez Taylor, J. (2006) Female Sex Tourism: A Contradiction in Terms? *Feminist Review*, 83: 42–59.

Sawaya, D.B. (2004) Space Tourism: Is It Safe? *The OECD Observer*, 242: 34–36.

Sheldrake, R. (1994) *Tao přírody* [*The Tao of Nature*]. Bratislava: Gardenia Publisher.

Sharpley, R., and Sundaram, P. (2005) Tourism: A Sacred Journey? The Case of Ashram Tourism, India, *International Journal of Tourism Research*, 7: 161–171.

Singh, S. (2005) Secular Pilgrimages and Sacred Tourism in the Indian Himalayas, *GeoJournal*, 64: 215–223.

Stronza, A. (2001) Anthropology of Tourism: Forging New Ground for Ecotourism and Other Alternatives, *Annual Review of Anthropology*, 30: 261–283.

West, P., and Carrier, J.G. (2004) Ecotourism and Authenticity: Getting Away from It All? *Current Anthropology*, 45(4): 483–498.

Yiping Li (2003) Heritage Tourism: The Contradictions between Conservation and Change, *Tourism and Hospitality Research*, 4(3): 247–261.

Zemánek, J. (Ed.) (2005) *Od země přes kopec do nebe . . . : o chůzi, poutnictví a posvátné krajině* [*From the Earth across the Hills to the Heavens . . . : On Walking, Pilgrimages and the Holy Landscape*]. Litoměřice: Argot vitae and the North Bohemian Gallery of the Fine Arts.

# Contributors

**Mark Hamilton** is associate professor of philosophy and NCAA faculty athletics representative at Ashland University in Ashland, Ohio, where he has taught since 1981. Dr. Hamilton has graduate degrees in philosophy, religion and counseling and has published numerous articles and chapters on sports ethics in books such as *Baseball and Philosophy*, *The Image of God in the Human Body*, *Basketball and Philosophy*, *Football and Philosophy*, and his article on the morality of surgical enhancement for athletic performance has been widely circulated. Besides sports ethics, he has taught numerous courses in philosophy of religion, ancient philosophy, ethics, Christian thought, human nature, and on C.S. Lewis. Hamilton is active in the *International Association of Philosophy of Sport*. He has been married 28 years with two adult daughters and sons-in-law and a granddaughter, co-pastors a reformed church and in 2007 he survived a liver transplant. He played and coached collegiate baseball.

**Shirl Hoffmann**, Ed.D., is professor emeritus of kinesiology at the University of North Carolina at Greensboro, North Carolina. He is a former college basketball coach, soccer and basketball official, and for over 30 years has taught and researched various aspects of kinesiology. He is editor of *Introduction to Kinesiology*, now in its third edition. In addition to his broad interest in the field of kinesiology, Hoffman has written and lectured extensively on the topic of sport and Christianity. He is the editor of the first anthology on the topic (*Sport and Religion*, Human Kinetics, 1992) and recently has written *Good Game: Christianity and the Culture of Sports* (Baylor University Press, 2010). He has been featured in a number of documentaries televised on CBS, ESPN and Channel 4 in Britain and on nationally aired radio broadcasts on NPR, BBC and the CBC.

**Ivo Jirásek** is a professor at Faculty of Physical Culture, Palacký University Olomouc in the Czech Republic. He teaches philosophy of physical culture, philosophy of nature, ethics and religion sciences and is interested in philosophical and spiritual aspects of physical culture (game and play, experience, body, movement), in experiential education and its methodology. The author of two monographs (in Czech language: *Experience and Possible Worlds*, 2001, and *Philosophical Kinanthropology: The Meeting Point of Philosophy, Body and Movement*, 2005) and decades of journal papers and book chapters (in both Czech and English), is a member of *International Association for the Philosophy of Sport, British Philosophy of Sport Association*, general secretary of *European Association for the Philosophy of Sport* and vice-president of *International Society for the Social Sciences of Sport*.

**Patrick Kelly, S.J.**, Ph.D., is Assistant Professor of Theology and Religious Studies at the *Center for the Study of Sport and Exercise* at Seattle University. Fr. Kelly played sports throughout his youth and football at Grand Valley State University, Michigan, where he was the captain of a championship team and an all-conference free safety. He has published several articles about sport, human development and the spiritual life and is the coauthor with Jim Yerkovich of the book *WE: A Model for Coaching and Christian Living* (Washington, DC: National Catholic Education Association, 2003). He has lectured about the history of sport and about sport and the spiritual life at conferences in the U.S. and Europe for both academics and practitioners. He is on the editorial board of the *International Journal of Religion and Sport*.

**Scott Kretchmar** is Professor of Exercise and Sport Science at Penn State University. He is a founding member of the *International Association for the Philosophy of Sport* and served as its president. He has been editor of the *Journal of the Philosophy of Sport*, is a fellow in the *American Academy of Kinesiology and Physical Education*, and has authored a popular text in the philosophy of sport. He has written numerous articles on ethics, the nature of sport and the operation of human intelligence in physical activity. He was named Alliance Scholar for AAHPERD in 1996, received the Distinguished Scholar Award from NAPEHE in 1997, and was honored as Distinguished Scholar for the *International Association for the Philosophy of Sport* in 1998 and again in 2006. Kretchmar served as chair of the Department of Kinesiology at Penn State on two occasions, has been president of the University Faculty Senate, and currently served for ten years as the faculty athletics representative to the NCAA. He is the founding editor of the *Journal of Intercollegiate Sport*.

**Ian Lawrence** is currently the Head of Programme for the BA Physical Education and Sports Coaching degree at York St. John University. Before joining the university six years ago, Ian worked as a soccer coach, PE teacher and sports lecturer in both the UK and U.S. As an MA student at the State

University of New York at Stony Brook, Ian pursued research within the theme of professional soccer and its cultural impact. This inspired and ultimately led to his recently completed Ph.D. dissertation entitled *Soccer and the American Dream*. Ian's research has been published in a wide variety of qualitative journals and focuses upon investigating the experiences of individuals within the context of professional soccer.

**Irena Martínková**, Ph.D., is Lecturer in Philosophy of Sport at the Faculty of Physical Education and Sport, Charles University in Prague, Czech Republic. Her principal interests are phenomenology, different conceptions of human being and the human body, and Eastern thinking. Recent publications have concerned the topic of harmony, and different conceptions of the human being in the context of the enrichment of physical education.

**Dr. Mark Nesti** is Reader of Psychology in Sport at Liverpool John Moores University, where he is also head of the M.Sc. in sport psychology. He is the former executive director of the *Centre for the Study of Sport and Spirituality* at York St. John University. Mark is a member of the Catholic 2012 Committee and was invited to attend recent seminars at the Vatican on sport, education and ethics in 2007 and 2009. His applied work draws on the application of existential psychology to sport and current research interests with colleagues at LJM University center on identity, meaning and critical moments in sport. Mark was formerly the counseling sport psychologist to the first team at Bolton Wanderers football club and at Newcastle United FC. During the past two seasons he has been delivering sport psychology for three days a week at Hull City AFC in the Premier League. A BASES accredited sport psychologist and British Psychological Society–chartered psychologist, he has been involved in applied work with many sports during the past 19 years. Formerly course leader for the M.Sc. sport and exercise science at Leeds Metropolitan University, Carnegie College, he has also worked in sport as a development officer and Sport England regional officer.

**Jim Parry** is a visiting Professor, Faculty of Physical Education and Sport, Charles University, Prague. After a first degree in philosophy, he trained and worked as a PE teacher and coach before returning to study. He then worked in teacher training and graduate programs for 12 years before moving to his present position, where he teaches political philosophy and applied ethics. He is Founding Director of he *British Olympic Academy*, and a collaborator with the *International Olympic Academy* in Ancient Olympia for the past 22 years. His publications include the co-edited *Sport and Spirituality: An Introduction, Ethics and Sport and Olympic Games Explained*, all published by Routledge.

**Susan Saint Sing**, Ph.D., was a member of the 1993 U.S. National Rowing Team and has used her 25 years of coaching experience as a coach, freelance writer, author of seven books and many articles, including *Spirituality of Sport: Balancing Body and Soul* (2004, St. Anthony Messenger Press). She received her doctorate in sport history and philosophy from Pennsylvania State University in 2004 and is currently writing a book based her dissertation, to be published in 2008. She has spoken at the University of Seattle in 2007 for the *Inaugural Conference for Youth Sport and Spirituality* and also at Springfield College, Massachusetts, on sport and spirituality.

**Tracy J. Trothen** is Academic Director and Chair of Theological Studies at Queen's School of Religion, Queen's University in Kingston, Ontario. She is Associate Professor of Ethics and a clinical pastoral education supervisor. Her research interests include theological ethics, sport, sexuality and violence. Currently she is completing a book manuscript on child sexual abuse and religious institutions in Canada, and looking forward to spending more time on a book project regarding sport, technology and religion.

**Nick Watson** is a Senior Lecturer in Sport Sociology and Psychology, York St. John University, England. He was the founding director of the *Centre for the Study of Sport and Spirituality* (York St. John University, 2003–2009) and is now a member of the *Centre for Sport, Spirituality and Religion* (University of Gloucestershire, 2009–). Nick is involved researching (and coaching) the theological dimensions of participation in sport for athletes with physical and intellectual disabilities. He coauthored the book *Sport and Spirituality: An Introduction* (2007, Routledge), serves on the editorial board of the *International Journal of Religion and Sport* and was the chair of the *Inaugural International Conference on Sport and Spirituality*, 2007. Bridging the 'theory-practice' gap in the world of sport and faith is also a major focus of his work and this has resulted in recent presentations to trainee clergy, university students and staff and sport mission organizations, such as *YWAM*. Nick has coached soccer in England, Spain and America, was a junior gymnast and footballer and now enjoys golf and hiking with his wife Kate.

# Index